CLOVERNOOK SKETCHES
and Other Stories

THE AMERICAN WOMEN WRITERS SERIES

Joanne Dobson, Judith Fetterley, and Elaine Showalter, series editors

The American Women Writers Series makes available for the first time in decades the work of the most significant, influential, and popular American women writers from the 1820s to the 1920s. Coming during a period of explosive growth in women's studies, this ongoing series challenges many assumptions about our twentieth-century objectivity, the sacred nature of the American literary canon, and nineteenth-century history and culture. Each volume in the series is edited by a major scholar in the field and has been entirely retypeset and redesigned.

ALTERNATIVE ALCOTT
Louisa May Alcott
Elaine Showalter, editor

STORIES FROM THE COUNTRY OF LOST BORDERS
Mary Austin
Marjorie Pryse, editor

CLOVERNOOK SKETCHES AND OTHER STORIES
Alice Cary
Judith Fetterley, editor

QUICKSAND AND *PASSING*
Nella Larsen
Deborah E. McDowell, editor

OLDTOWN FOLKS
Harriet Beecher Stowe
Dorothy Berkson, editor

HOBOMOK AND OTHER WRITINGS ON INDIANS
Lydia Maria Child
Carolyn L. Karcher, editor

"HOW CELIA CHANGED HER MIND" AND SELECTED STORIES
Rose Terry Cooke
Elizabeth Ammons, editor

RUTH HALL AND OTHER WRITINGS
Fanny Fern
Joyce Warren, editor

HOPE LESLIE
Catherine Maria Sedgwick
Mary Kelley, editor

CLOVERNOOK SKETCHES and Other Stories

ALICE CARY

Edited and with an Introduction by

JUDITH FETTERLEY

RUTGERS UNIVERSITY PRESS

New Brunswick and London

Copyright © 1987 by Rutgers, The State University
All rights reserved
Manufactured in the United States of America

Library of Congress Cataloging-in-Publication Data

Cary, Alice, 1820–1871.
Clovernook sketches and other stories.

(American women writers series)
Bibliography: p.
1. Country life—Ohio—Fiction. I. Fetterley, Judith, 1938–
II. Title. III. Title: Clovernook sketches. IV. Series.
PS1264.F47 1987 813′.3 87-4507
ISBN 0-8135-1250-6
ISBN 0-8135-1251-4 (pbk.)

British Cataloging-in-Publication information available

CONTENTS

Contents

ACKNOWLEDGMENTS

I wish to thank Gene Garber and the Department of English at the State University of New York at Albany for providing me with released time during the spring semester of 1986 to do the research necessary for this edition of Alice Cary's short fiction. I also wish to thank the staff of the New York State Library for their invaluable assistance in giving me access to the extensive files of nineteenth-century periodicals located in this library and xeroxing for me materials from these periodicals. Without the library and its staff, I could not have produced this text. I owe my largest debt, however, to Marjorie Pryse, who spent many hours researching periodicals, traveling to archives in search of letters, editing the introduction, and talking with me about Alice Cary.

INTRODUCTION

> Years ago, in an old academy in Massachusetts, its preceptor gave to a young girl a poem to learn for a Wednesday exercise. It began,—
>
> "Of all the beautiful pictures
>   That hang on Memory's wall,
> Is one of a dim old forest,
>   That seemeth best of all."
>
> After the girl had recited the poem to her teacher, he . . . proceeded to tell the story of the one who wrote it—of her life in her Western home, of the fact that she and her sister Phoebe had come to New York to seek their fortune, and to make a place for themselves in literature. It fell like a tale of romance on the girl's heart; and from that hour she saved every utterance that she could find of Alice Cary's, and spent much time thinking about her, till in a dim way she came to seem like a much-loved friend. (Ames 70)

In this recollection of the beginning of her friendship with Alice Cary, Mary Clemmer Ames describes the relationship between Cary and her nineteenth-century audience. As early as 1855, the Cincinnati *Ladies' Repository* could announce that the name Alice Cary "has become like a household word to our eighty thousand readers." On her desk in her room in her New York house, Cary herself had a row of photographs, all of little girls to whom her readers had given the name "Alice Cary" (Ames 82–83). The news of her death in 1871 elicited numerous notices and sketches, many of which share a sense of personal sorrow, as if the writer had lost a friend. To her nineteenth-century audience Alice Cary was a personal friend; today few remember her name. She has disappeared from popular view, she is mentioned in our literary histories briefly or not at all, and for any substantial record of her life we have only the biography of Mary Clemmer Ames.

Ames, ten years younger than Cary and herself a writer of newspaper columns, fiction, and poetry, met Alice and Phoebe Cary in New York in 1859. The sisters befriended her and introduced her to their literary circle; with Alice Cary, Ames formed a particularly close bond. Thus as a biographer Ames is clearly partisan. Nevertheless, her partisanship may be more of a help to us than a hindrance. As the above reminiscence suggests, Cary's life is interesting primarily for its legendary quality. Writing in 1891, W. H. Venable, Cincinnati educator, litterateur, and pioneer regional historian, also articulates the legend: "The world will acknowledge one of these days that a country girl, without a library, without a seminary, without influential friends, without money, without a mother, with younger brothers and sisters to take care of, with irksome drudgery to do, may yet succeed in authorship" (Venable 485). Though Cary herself did not particularly subscribe to the legend, never ceasing to lament her early lack of education and opportunity and rarely seeing herself as successful, nevertheless the story of her life is in many ways remarkable. From a shy, uneducated, verbally awkward and socially inept farm girl, she transformed herself into a woman who occupied the center of an extensive and vital New York literary and social circle and who possessed a library of over a thousand volumes. And from being an unpaid contributor to local journals, she transformed herself into a writer capable of supporting herself by her pen and into a poet whose name was a household word. Such transformations still have the capacity to inspire the lives and work of women.

ALICE CARY WAS BORN April 26, 1820, on a farm in Hamilton County, Ohio, eight miles north of Cincinnati. The village built at the crossroads nearest this farm was called Mount Healthy, and it is this village with its surrounding farms and houses that became the Clovernook of her fiction. The house that Cary was born in still stands, but the house one sees when one goes to visit Clovernook is the "new" one, built when Alice was twelve. To her parents, this new house represented the American dream of material reward for hard work; to Alice Cary, in reconstructing her own life, it signaled the beginning of loss. Before the family moved in, Alice and her parents shared a premonitory vision. Standing in their doorway, they looked across the yard to see Alice's older sister Rhoda at the door of the new house with young Lucy in her arms. Just then "Rhoda herself came downstairs, where she had left Lucy fast asleep," and they all stood and watched "the woman with the child in her arms slowly sink, sink, sink into the ground, until she disappeared from sight" (Ames 18). Alice Cary believed in ghosts; on this particular occasion, the appearance of ghosts foreshadowed the most significant event in her life.

Cary was the fourth child and fourth daughter born to her parents, Elizabeth Jessup and Robert Cary. Five other children followed Alice, among whom was Phoebe (1824–71), who later became Alice's lifelong companion and fellow writer. While a child, however, Cary chose Rhoda, only two years older than herself, as her particular companion. In a letter to the editor of the *Ladies' Repository* (hereafter *LR*) and quoted in an article on Alice Cary published in August 1855, Cary described her relationship to Rhoda: "A beloved sister shared with me in work, and play, and study; we were never separated for a day. . . . Just as she came into womanhood—she was not yet sixteen—death separated us, and that event turned my disposition, naturally melancholy, into almost morbid gloom. To this day she is the first in memory when I wake, and the last when I sleep." The story "The Sisters" (reprinted here) memorializes Cary's relation to Rhoda. To Cary, Rhoda was "the most gifted of all our family," with a genius for narrative (Ames 16). On the way to and from school, Rhoda would tell "wonderful" stories and "when we saw the house in sight, we would often sit down under a tree, that she might have more time to finish the story" (Ames 17). From Rhoda, Cary learned the fascination and art of storytelling. Moreover, Rhoda encouraged Cary's first attempts at poetry. Both mentor and community, she provided a supportive context for Cary's early dreams and ambitions. Her death in November 1833, "foretold" a few months earlier by the ghosts, was an event of tragic proportions for Cary, depriving her at once of her best friend and her primary source of nurturance.

In speaking publicly about her mother, Cary was invariably eulogistic: "My mother was of Irish descent—a woman of superior intellect and of a good, well-ordered life. In my memory she stands apart from all others, wiser and purer, doing more and loving better than any other woman" (*LR,* August 1855). Her fiction, however, tells a different tale; it presents a world without mothering, for mothers offer their children neither physical affection or emotional support. In her fiction, mothers are often overtly hostile to their children; at best they are indifferent. They fail to recognize their child's special nature and they provide no encouragement for her development. In "The Sisters," Cary invokes the term "orphaned" to describe the human condition, and "Orpha" is the name she gives to more than one fictional version of herself. Cary's mother died in 1835, but her sense of being without a mother preceded that event.

Robery Cary had an American ancestry that could be traced back to the Plymouth Colony of 1630. At age fourteen, he had emigrated from New Hampshire to Ohio with his father, a revolutionary war veteran who had been given western land as payment for military service. According to Phoebe, Robert Cary "was fond of reading, especially romance and poetry; but early poverty and the hard exigencies of pioneer life had left him no time for acquiring anything more than the mere rudiments of a common school education" (all comments by Phoebe Cary occur in the same article, listed in the bibliography). Elizabeth Jessup Cary read poetry but cared little for fiction. Her tastes ran instead to history, politics, biography, and moral and religious essays. Though both parents were obviously literate, apparently formal education for their children mattered little to them. In an early letter to Rufus Griswold, prominent editor, critic, and anthologist, Cary comments that her formal education was "limited to the meagre and infrequent advantages of an obscure district school" from which she was "removed altogether at a very early age" (Griswold 239).

Whether from lack of money or lack of interest, books were scarce in the Cary household. Phoebe lists the few resources available; these consisted of "a Bible, hymn-book, The History of the Jews, Lewis and Clarke's Travels, Pope's Essays, and Charlotte Temple, 'a romance, founded on fact.'" Given the frequency with which the theme of seduction appears in

Cary's work, we may assume that *Charlotte Temple,* published in 1791 by Susanna Rowson and subsequently one of the most popular novels in America, played some role in the development of Cary's idea of fiction. A more serious literary model, however, may well have been provided by the *Trumpet,* a Boston based Universalist periodical (both of Cary's parents were Universalists). According to Phoebe, the *Trumpet* was "for many years the only paper seen by Alice, and its poet's corner the food of her fancy and the source of her inspiration."

In 1837, when Alice was seventeen, Robert Cary remarried. Two years later he built another house on the farm and moved into it with his new wife, leaving Alice, now nineteen and the oldest child still at home, in charge of the old house and her four surviving younger siblings (Lucy had died at age three in the same epidemic that killed Rhoda). At the same time that Alice became in effect the head of a household, other changes taking place in the world outside the household were transforming Mount Healthy from a relatively isolated rural village to a Cincinnati suburb. Now farmers found themselves with new neighbors, professional persons interested in literature and capable of recognizing and encouraging literary talent when they saw it. Moreover, by the 1830s, the thriving literary community in Cincinnati aspired to make that city the literary center of the West. Thus, although the Cary legend, as articulated by Ames and Venable, posits a hostile stepmother, who had no interest in literature and who insisted that Alice and Phoebe do housework instead of writing, forcing them to compose at night and hide their manuscripts in a secret closet under the stairs, Cary in fact began her career as a serious writer in a context that provided distinct advantages.

Alice Cary evidently began writing poetry at an early age. Phoebe claims that the death of Rhoda temporarily halted her efforts; nevertheless, five years later she was ready to submit poems for publication. In 1838, the *Sentinel,* Cincinnati's Universalist paper, printed "The Child of Sorrow," her first published poem. For roughly a decade Cary continued to publish in local newspapers and periodicals without payment.

Two events played a central role in transforming Alice Cary from a volunteer poet with a local reputation into a writer capable of establishing a national reputation and earning her living by her pen. In the summer of 1848, Rufus W. Griswold, who had already published two anthologies of

American poetry and prose, wrote Alice and Phoebe Cary requesting material for inclusion in his newest venture, *The Female Poets of America,* which was published the following December. In his introductory sketch, Griswold comments, "It is but two or three years since I first saw the name of either of them, in a western newspaper." For Cary, Griswold served as the channel through which her work reached a national audience. Despite the vicissitudes of their relationship, which may have included a romantic interlude in the early 1850s, Griswold remained until his death in 1857 a staunch supporter of Alice Cary, serving as her sponsor in the eastern literary and publishing world, editing her work for publication, and steadily promoting her interests and career. In 1849, he arranged for the publication of *Poems of Alice and Phoebe Cary.* Indirectly and as a result of his connection with Edgar Allan Poe, Griswold performed another equally important service for Cary. Although Griswold's posthumous treatment of Poe has earned him infamy in American literary history, during Poe's lifetime the relationship was often amicable. During one such period, Poe reviewed *The Female Poets of America* for the *Southern Literary Messenger* (February 1849). No doubt aware of Griswold's positive estimate of the work of Alice Cary, Poe singled her out for special attention, declaring her "Pictures of Memory" to be "*decidedly the noblest poem in the collection,*" and exhorting his readers to "see it and judge for themselves."

Cary's Cincinnati connections also contributed to transforming her into an author with a national audience. William D. Gallagher, a distant cousin and the "Bill Gallagher" of "Dreams and Tokens" (reprinted here), and Lucius A. Hine, both editors of Cincinnati journals to which she had contributed, introduced Cary to Gamaliel Bailey. When Bailey moved from Cincinnati to Washington, D.C., to start the *National Era* (1847–60), the abolitionist paper that serialized *Uncle Tom's Cabin,* another path to a more national audience opened up for Cary. She began publishing fiction in the *Era* in 1847, and from Bailey she received her first regular payment for work. Publication in the *Era* brought with it a further benefit. John G. Whittier, notable for his serious and extensive support of many nineteenth-century American women writers, was a contributing editor for the *Era.* On September 16, 1847, in a review of the *Herald of Truth,* a short-lived Cincinnati monthly edited by Hine, Whittier particularly noted the poetry of Alice Cary, quoting extensively from her contributions to the journal and commenting that she had already "introduced herself favorably to the readers of the Era." On September 22, 1847, Cary wrote to Whittier thanking him for his "kind notice and encouragement" and inviting him to correspond with her, an invitation that he accepted, thus beginning a lifelong friendship.

In the summer of 1850, Alice and Phoebe Cary made a trip east. They went to New York, Boston, and Amesbury, Massachusetts, where Whittier lived. After this trip, Cary determined to make her permanent home in New York. In November 1850, she moved east; in the spring of 1851, Phoebe and Elmina, Cary's youngest sister, joined her in New York. Horace Greeley, whose visit to Alice and Phoebe in the summer of 1849 no doubt diminished for them the distance between Ohio and New York, commented on the significance of Cary's decision, in the obituary he wrote for the *New York Ledger* (March 11, 1871) shortly after Alice's death: "I do not know at whose suggestion they resolved to migrate to this city, and attempt to live here by literary labor; it surely was not mine. If my judgment was ever invoked, I am sure I must have responded that the hazard seemed to me too great, the inducements inadequate." From Cary's point of view, however, the "inducements" may well have seemed considerable. Thirty-one years old at the time of her move and well past the usual age for marriage, she may have surmised that life as a single woman would be far more satisfactory in New York than in Mount Healthy. In addition, New York was the center of the publishing world; residence in New York would enable her to pursue her career more aggressively and manage her literary business more effectively. Ames suggests that a failed love affair drove Alice Cary east. Joy Bayless, biographer of Rufus Griswold, argues that Griswold was the particular attraction. Whether her interest in Griswold was romantic, consolatory, or simply professional, his presence in New York was undoubedly a factor in her decision.

But above all New York offered Cary community. In a letter to Ames, dated September 1866, Cary consoles her friend for being out of the city and comments: "I am afraid you are lonesome. I know how lonesome I used to be in the country and alone. Alone, I mean, so far as the society to which one belongs is concerned. For we all need something outside of ourselves and our immediate family" (Ames 86–87). A number of Cary's contemporaries comment on the anomaly of her refusal to leave the city for the country when in her poetry and fiction the country is presented so positively and the city so negatively. Society, apparently, was essential to Alice Cary, and New York offered society.

The Cary legend tells a success story. The farm girl from Ohio made her reputation in New York. Though Cary returned to Cincinnati for an extensive visit during the spring and summer of 1852 and possibly again in the summer of 1853, when she served as assistant editor of the Cincinnati *Parlor Magazine,* her permanent residence remained New York. By 1855, she was sufficiently established to move into a house on East Twentieth Street, which she eventually purchased and in which she lived until her death. Here she set up a household that included her two younger sisters, Phoebe and Elmina, and two servants who were themselves sisters. Though apparently not her favorite sister (Rhoda, Lucy, and even Elmina, who died in 1862, seem to have been the emotional center of Alice Cary's life), Phoebe was indispensable to Alice and central to the household she established, if for no other reason than the sheer fact of her survival. Ames devotes the final chapter of her biography to a description of the symbiotic nature of the relationship between Alice and Phoebe. At the very least it can be said that Alice needed someone to take care of and Phoebe needed someone to take care of her. Ames's testimony, however, suggests that their temperaments were complementary and that each gave the other a crucial kind of nourishment. The depth of the connection between them can be seen well enough from Phoebe's side: she was literally unable to survive without Alice and lived only five months after Alice's death. Whether Alice could have survived without Phoebe we cannot know. But we do know that she chose to make her life with her sister and to make sisterhood her primary emotional bond.

Alice Cary was both the financial and executive center of her household. She managed the internal arrangements of the house she and Phoebe shared and their social life, organizing, for example, the Sunday evening receptions for which the Carys became famous. To these receptions came such figures as Greeley, Whittier, James T. Fields, Gail Hamilton, Sara Helen Whitman, Anna Dickinson, Robert Dale Owen, William Lloyd Garrison, and Phineas T. Barnum. Cary clearly valued these gatherings for she hosted them every Sunday evening for over fifteen years.

Though Ames presents Cary's life as a success story, she also records the high price Cary paid for her success. Ames portrays Cary as working to live and living to work: "I have never known any other woman so systematically and persistently industrious as Alice Cary. . . . Her pleasure was her labor. Of rest, recreation, amusement, as other women sought these, she knew almost nothing" (Ames 39). Unlike Phoebe, who often took summer vacations and once stopped writing for eight years, Alice always worked, refused to take summer vacations, and remained in New York year after year in spite of her declining health. Indeed Ames attributes Cary's early death to her insistence on constantly working. That Cary herself may have had some doubts about the wisdom and even the morality of her excessive commitment to work can perhaps be seen in the story "Two Sisters," published in the *National Magazine* in April 1856. In this story, the sister who is willing to stop her work and enjoy the world around her receives Cary's implicit and explicit approbation, not the sister who, like herself, lives only to work.

During the last eighteen months of her life Cary was paralyzed and bedridden. By all accounts these months were ones of excruciating pain; according to Phoebe she suffered "in body all that it seemed possible for mortality to suffer and yet survive, and, from the condition of her nerves, such mental torture, such fear of shapeless and nameless terrors as few souls, let us hope, are ever called upon to endure." Alice Cary died on a Sunday morning, February 12, 1871, at her home in New York and was buried two days later in Brooklyn's Greenwood Cemetery. She was fifty years old.

CARY THOUGHT OF HERSELF primarily as a poet and it was as a poet that she achieved her popular success. In addition to the joint volume with Phoebe, Cary published four volumes of poetry during her lifetime: *Lyra and Other Poems* (1852), *Collected Poems* (1855), *Ballads, Lyrics and Hymns* (1866), and *A Lover's Diary* (1868). She also published two collections of material for children: *Clovernook Children* (1854) and *Snowberries* (1867). Three novels appeared in book form: *Hagar, a Story of To-Day* (1852; originally serialized in the *Cincinnati Dollar Weekly Commercial*), *Married, Not Mated* (1856), and *The Bishop's Son* (1867; first serialized in the *Springfield Republican*). A fourth novel, *Holly-Wood,* appeared serially in the *Era* in 1854, and *The Born Thrall,* written for serial publication in the *Revolution,* was left uncompleted at the time of her death. Though she took the form seriously, Cary's novels suffer from incoherence in both plot and character. She could not sustain the kind of plot she felt essential to the genre, and once she left history and fact for her source of lives and moved into the realm of cultural stereotype, her grasp on character disintegrated as well. While contemporary critics frequently condemned her novels, they consistently praised her three volumes of short sketches and stories: *Clovernook; or, Recollections of Our Neighborhood in the West* (1851), *Clovernook, Second Series* (1853), and *Pictures of Country Life* (1859). For her work in this genre Cary deserves a place in our literary history. She saw poetry as compensatory; it belonged to the realm of the imagination and through it one could make up for what was lacking in this world. The sketch, however, belonged to reality, and reality for Cary was grim. Thus the very features that may have led her to value her short fiction less highly than her poetry ensure its continuing interest for the modern reader.

As far as we know, Alice Cary began her career as a published writer of fiction in August 1847, when the first of ten chapters of "Recollections of Country Life" appeared in the *National Era* under the pseudonym Patty Lee. She continued to publish both poetry and prose in the *Era* for over a decade. Publication in the *Era* assured Cary of an audience; it also gave her potential influence on other writers. In 1856, for example, she published a story called "The Young Man Who Went to Town to Live," remarkable for its powerful opening description of urban squalor: "You cannot see all the miserable aspect of the place at this time of night, for the lamps are feeble and few, and the clouds thick and stormy. You cannot see how crooked the streets are, and what small and dark, and ill-ventilated huts, are piled one against another, and one over another. You cannot see all the gutters, where the green water stands from year's end to year's end nor the flat roofs, checked with lines, where the half-washed and squeezed garments of the inhabitants drip and mildew, and at last rot dry." The description reminds the reader of the opening passages from Rebecca Harding Davis's "Life in the Iron Mills" (1861) and may have served as Davis's model.

When Cary left Ohio for New York, she apparently was under contract to furnish material to the Cincinnati *Ladies' Repository,* a Methodist monthly magazine published from 1841 to 1876. Prior to moving she had published a few poems in the journal. Between 1851 and 1855, however, she appeared as a regular contributor, particularly of prose pieces, several of which she later collected into the Clovernook volumes. Among her uncollected fiction, by far the most interesting is a series called "Ghost Stories," one of which is reprinted here. In addition, she first tried her hand at stories for children in this journal, publishing eight of the pieces later collected into *Clovernook Children;* she also contributed a variety of personal essays, many of which describe her experiences traveling between Ohio and New York.

After she moved east, Cary began to write for the *National Magazine,* a Methodist monthly like the *Ladies' Repository* but published in New York. As its name might suggest, this journal, begun in 1852, aspired to compete with such popular nonreligious periodicals as *Harper's New Monthly Magazine* (begun in 1850), and Cary's appearance in it measures her increasing professional success. In the *National Magazine,* Cary published both fiction (three of the stories later collected in *Pictures of Country Life* were first published here) and nonfiction prose, including brief didactic essays and articles on contemporary and historical subjects. Far more interesting, however, are prose works like "Old Christopher" (reprinted here), which cannot be clearly identified as either fiction or autobiography. Such texts indicate the degree to which Cary rooted her fiction in the materials of her life.

In 1856, Cary began to publish in the *New York Ledger,* a weekly newspaper owned and edited by Robert Bonner, famous for his extravagant advertising schemes and his generous payments to writers. For roughly a decade the *Ledger* offered its readers a weekly poem by Alice Cary; for these readers she became the poet in the corner inspiring them as she herself had once been inspired by the poets in the corners of the *Trumpet.* Though Bonner no doubt hired her because of her reputation as a poet, in 1856 and 1857 she also published fiction in the *Ledger,* including "An Old Maid's Story" (July 19, 1856), later collected in *Pictures of Country Life* (reprinted here). A series of pieces entitled "Stories of the Big Red Barn" show her experimenting with writing social satire through the vehicle of the animal fable. The picture of human nature revealed by analogy with life in the barnyard is hardly pleasant. In correspondence with James T. Fields, editor of the *Atlantic Monthly* and partner in the Ticknor and Fields publishing house, Cary frequently refers to these stories and to her desire to expand them into a book-length manuscript.

Nothing ever came of this project, however, and we can only assume that she recognized the material as too bitter to be marketable. From 1858 until her death, Cary also published in the *Atlantic Monthly.* If occupying the poet's corner in the *Ledger* proved her popularity and demonstrated her ability to earn her living by writing, publication in the *Atlantic* testified to the quality of her work. Several poems and two stories appeared in the *Atlantic;* "The Great Doctor" (1866) is reprinted here.

At the end of her career, Cary found a major outlet for her fiction in the pages of *Harper's Monthly.* These stories, which appeared in the 1860s and represent a return to the material of the Clovernook volumes, unfortunately do not demonstrate a new perspective on this material. Many of them are essentially versions of earlier stories rewritten without the subtlety or complexity of vision that informed the original. "Jane Morrison" (1867), for example, is a version of "Eliza Anderson," but in the later fiction the brother is tediously brutal, the sister hopelessly good, and the ending improbably happy. Evidently fiction no longer served Cary as a way to recreate the self or the past. In a number of the later *Harper's* stories, she transposes the sister of the earlier work into a brother whose first name is Hadly, the surname she first gave herself and Rhoda in the autobiographical "Sisters" sequence. Since the sister bond was the primary source of creative energy for Cary, displacing it from the center of her work symbolizes the degree to which she was no longer present in her fiction.

Throughout her career Cary published in a wide variety of newspapers and periodicals, including, for example, *Graham's; Sartain's Union Magazine,* edited briefly by Caroline Kirkland; and the *Overland Monthly,* edited by Bret Harte. In preparing this edition of Alice Cary's short fiction, I was able to examine the files of most of those nineteenth-century periodicals I had reason to believe might have published her work. For the files of nineteenth-century newspapers I can make no similar claim. Despite my interest and commitment, such an investigation would have taken far more than the limited time and energy I had available for this project. More seriously, however, and indicative of the problems facing those who try to recover the work of nineteenth-century American women writers, nineteenth-century periodicals are themselves an endangered species. For example, I have reason to believe that Cary published extensively in a newspaper, begun in 1856, called the *New York Weekly.* Yet I have been unable to locate a complete file of this paper either in the original or on microfilm. In this context, even recovery becomes impossible.

In her lifetime Cary made her own statement against potential obliteration by "signing" her work. In journals from the late 1840s and early 1850s, whose contributors generally went unidentified, the work signed "Alice Cary" stands out. In insisting thus early on a signature that could be used as literal currency, Cary signaled her seriousness as a writer. As a result, her work is more readily recoverable than that of many other nineteenth-century American women writers. Moreover, she indirectly signed her fiction through her titles, which invoke the specific, the particular, the individual, rather than the generic or the general. Catharine Sedgwick could write *A New England Tale,* and an anonymous contributor to the *Ladies' Repository* could write "A German Tale" but Alice Cary would never write "An Ohio Tale." Moreover, Cary's titles reflect the fact that her interest lies in character, not plot, and that, for her, action rarely appears as complete or completed. Thus stories with titles like "The School-Girls' Strategem" or "The Hole in the Carpet" would never appear over the signature "Alice Cary." Not the hole in the carpet but the person who made the hole and then fixed it or didn't fix it and worried about it or didn't mind it would be the subject, focus, and title of an Alice Cary story. The strength of her fiction lies in her insistence on specificity and her resistance to closure; her gift is recollections and sketches, by definition partial, personal, and incomplete, of one particular neighborhood in the West.

IN HER SHORT FICTION, Alice Cary was a writer with a subject. Characters, events, places, and issues appear and reappear, and each piece provides some new information to reconstruct what it meant to grow up in Clovernook. Central to the fiction of Clovernook is the Cary narrator, the eye that is the "I" of her sketches and stories. In much the same way that Emily Dickinson a decade later used poetry, Cary found in short fiction a way to explore her own consciousness. This narrative consciousness constitutes one of the primary unifying features of her work and distinguishes it from that of her contemporaries. For it was an achievement won against the grain of a culture that labeled such privileging of the self in women as negatively egocentric or even pathologically narcissistic. On a personal level Cary was well aware of these strictures; Ames praises that "lack of self-consciousness" that led Cary to burn her letters and to leave among her papers not one line "referring personally to herself" (Ames 85). In one of the few surviving letters, written to her cousin Bill Gallagher in 1852, she asks to be forgiven for her "egotism—I see I have written of nothing but myself" (Venable 493). In her fiction, however, Cary remained self-centered.

Typically Cary's narrator does not directly participate in the lives and events she records, but rather passively observes them. Thus the central action in most of her best fiction derives from the emotional and intellectual effect on the narrator of the events she observes. At the heart of Cary's vision lies a profound sense of mystery; the beginning and the end of human life are essentially unknowable, and what we experience as human life is merely a fragment of some larger, unseen whole. This vision determined Cary's choice of form. In her best work she chose to write in the form of the sketch, a form that permitted her to accept and express the fragmentary and the open-ended in fiction as she perceived it in life. In the sketch, plot is not the primary element; instead character and consciousness move to the center and plot is subordinated to and determined by the fragmentary nature of the reality experienced by her narrative consciousness.

Cary shares with her female contemporaries an interest in realism. Her sketches are filled with minutely recorded details, and we know precisely how the world looks to the narrative eye. Yet her conception of consciousness and event do not so readily agree with our usual use of the term "realistic." For Cary equally shares with her male contemporaries who were writing "romances" an interest in fiction as psychic exploration and dreamwork. Initially these two features of her work may appear oppositional; the coherence of her best fiction, however, proves their deeper connection. If mystery is the ultimate reality of consciousness, then her narrators experience no contradiction between their passion for recording how this world looks to them and their conviction that such precisely recorded details are but a fragment of a larger whole whose meaning cannot be grasped by any conscious effort of the human mind.

For Cary, women represent the human condition and in this sense her fiction is profoundly woman-centered. In her fiction, as in Emily

Dickinson's poetry, extreme psychological and physical deprivation define the human experience. Such deprivation both constitutes a mystery in itself and requires a sense of mystery to comprehend. Parents seem bent on crushing the aspirations of their children. In "About the Tompkinses," for example, "Mrs. Tompkins always talked to her children as if they were greatly to blame for wanting anything, or, in fact, for being in the world at all," and she contemptuously denies her children's most minimal desires. Similarly, in "The Sisters," the mother seems to take pleasure in denying her daughter's long-anticipated trip to town. In this sketch Cary links emotional and physical deprivation, for as a consequence of the mother's cruelty the daughter dies. Literal physical deprivation appears in other works. Adults deny children food and clothing; they force them to live and work in conditions that seem consciously designed to kill them and often, as in "Uncle Christopher's," the children do die. Yet Cary does not present these deaths as spiritually transforming events for either children or parents. The child is simply dead. Those who cared about the child register its death as pure, unredeemed, and unredeemable loss. To those who killed the child, its death confirms their estimate of its weakness and lack of value. Cary's fiction thus provides a harsh antidote to those child-centered fictions by other nineteenth-century American writers, both men and women, in which the child is seen as personally and spiritually crucial to the meaning and value of its world.

In Cary's fiction even apparent nurturance turns out to be a subtle, perverse form of deprivation. Many of her stories present a mother figure who gives herself over completely to a male child (see, for example, "Eliza Anderson"), despite the fact that he may be egocentric, lazy, and incompetent. She encourages him, excuses his faults, makes exceptions of his failures, and, denying herself and her other children, spends precious resources to provide yet another opportunity for him to succeed. The result in "Eliza Anderson" and in other stories is inevitably tragic, for the child as well as the mother. Cary viewed such a woman as complicit in her own oppression and called her a "born thrall," the title she gave to her last and uncompleted novel.

For Cary's narrators there is no escape from deprivation. Her fiction offers no Jamesian theory of compensation in which the discipline of art makes up for the limitations of life. Moreover, though she was a devout and practicing Christian, her fiction is not informed by the possibility of current or future redemption. Art cannot compensate for life, but telling stories can ease the pain of separation, denial, and deprivation. At its best, her fiction contains the double consciousness of the adult remembering and the child remembered. For Alice Cary writing fiction must have been a deeply evocative act, calling up the memory of her storytelling sister and the vision of herself as a listening and fascinated child. In becoming herself a teller of stories, Cary imaginatively recreated both her sister and self and fused them through writing into a bond beyond the reach of death and separation.

CARY'S FIRST FICTION anticipates her later work in both form and content. "Recollections of Country Life," published in the *Era* in 1847 and 1848, is a series of sketches by a single narrator about a particular place. Since each "chapter" is understood to be part of a larger whole, no individual sketch bears the burden of an ending. Thus from the start Cary found the form that would enable her fiction to be open-ended. In these early sketches, her passion for the realism of minute detail is also apparent; "I remember every article of her apparel," she proudly proclaims in her first sketch and proceeds to prove her point. Moreover, the narrator remembers that "conversation" ensued when Aunt Polly, whose appearance she has just described in detail, came to visit and stayed to work, "for the process of spinning two kinds of yarns commenced at once." Perhaps as a result of Cary's singular ability to represent herself in her work, in her fiction most storytellers are women. In the "chapter" reprinted here, "Dreams and Tokens," the two older women are full of stories and the stories they particularly like to tell, like Cary herself, are "ghost" stories. While they may consider Bill Gallagher "no company for anybody" since he "got a fool notion of writing poetry," fiction creates community. In this early sketch Cary distinguishes her narrative voice from the voices of her characters; her characters speak in dialect and her narrator does not. To anyone who has read Harriet Beecher Stowe's *The Pearl of Orr's Island,* "Dreams and Tokens" will seem reminiscent of those first chapters of Stowe's in which Roxy and Ruey discuss the strange circumstances attending Mara's birth and the discovery of Moses. Though Stowe never chose to make her own voice regional, always identifying in her work the regional voice with the dialect character, Cary early located regional consciousness in her narrative voice and after these early sketches rarely created dialect characters.

When Alice Cary published the first volume of Clovernook sketches, she was no longer living in or writing from Mount Healthy. She had left the region and her vision therefore became doubly retrospective. From this distance, she could present herself as historian and interpreter of Clovernook. The most significant technical advance between the early sketches and the first Clovernook volume comes about as Cary develops the role of the narrator and establishes the narrator's consciousness as a central and unifying feature of the material. In this first volume the narrator gives her reader much information about the history of Clovernook. She traces its series of transformations from the appearance of the first white male settler through its existence as a rude crossroads village to its cultivation as a suburb under the direction of eastern men forced to retire to the West because of financial reverses, and she interprets for the reader the meaning of that history for the people who live there.

A profound sense of melancholy pervades the first volume of Clovernook sketches. Each of the first six stories centers around dying and death; moreover many others take place in October or November, a season Cary inevitably associates with mourning. Although many of her stories invoke a contrast between light and shade—"shadows and sunbeams"—the shade predominates. The narrator frequently associates shadows with the death of a sibling for which she feels somehow responsible. Haunted by a sense of guilt, the narrator replays in her mind the scene of abandonment that immediately precedes a sister's death. Yet sometimes she finds herself abandoned to the poverty, provincialism, and drudgery from which her sister has escaped. Though it provided the primary source of love in her life, for Cary the sister bond was considerably vexed.

Like most nineteenth-century American women writers, Alice Cary did not in general theorize about her writing. As a rare instance of commentary on her work, the preface to the first volume of Clovernook sketches is especially interesting. In this preface Cary identifies herself as a writer with both a subject and a form, specifically American and new. She aligns herself implicitly with those among her contemporaries who were busy answering the call for a peculiarly *American* literature. To American literature, she contributes regionalism—that is, "the exhibition of rural life" from the perspective of "participation" in the interest of the "true." A committed realist as well, she offers us her observations as "competent witnesses" to the quality of life in the region. Here Cary begins the work, consummated by later writers, of exposing the regional nature of "universals" and the human significance of "the little histories every day revealed."

Cary specifically wrote "My Grandfather" to open the first volume of *Clovernook; or, Recollections of Our Neighborhood in the West.* Since Cary's own narrative consciousness began with the death of Rhoda, "My Grandfather," a story about the change in consciousness brought about by witnessing death, constitutes the logical beginning for her major fictional work. In this sketch the adult writer recollects herself as a child and seeks to recreate that child at the moment she began to be conscious. This child, literally outside, finds a frightening reflection of herself and her condition in the story of the wild man read aloud by her brother on the inside. Like the wild man, the narrator herself may have reason to fear the approach of human beings. Sitting outside, listening "half afraid," the narrator hears the sound of an approaching horseman and "that night there came upon my soul the shadow of an awful fear," fear perhaps that she too may become wild and hunted. Yet isolation, fear, even wildness have value: "So eagerly I noted every thing, that I remember to this day . . ." Initially blocked in her "irrepressible desire to see" inside, she later, unobserved, makes her way into the room to see her dying grandfather for herself. Though her father may dismiss the story of the wild man as an "improbable fiction," the narrator is determined to make her fiction a probable record of what the wild one sees.

In "The Wildermings" the narrator, though older than in the first sketch, is still too young to make sense of material fully intelligible to the adult writer and reader. Seduction, abandonment, and death precede and produce the events in "The Wildermings," but this material, at the center of many nineteenth-century American women's novels, including Cary's own, here remains in the background because it is beyond the range of the narrator's experience and understanding. Thus "The Wildermings" provides an excellent context for studying precisely how the narrative technique Cary developed for telling the regional tale facilitated her effort to make its form and content different from and other than the form and content of novels. The consciousness of the narrator occupies the center of "The Wildermings," and this narrator experiences life primarily as mystery. Though she herself has never seen any ghosts, others in her neighborhood have. Moreover, the ghost of the dead Mary Wildermings dominates the neighboring cottage, and the living people she encounters there seem more ghostly than real. Strange occurrences and strange, apparently unfathomable, connections fill the story. The "strange child" at the cottage "must die" without closing her eyes because her mother died "watching for one who never came." This "watchful" child, who sits for hours in the woods "without moving her position," bears in turn an uncanny resemblance to the narrator herself, who can sit so quitely that the animals forget her presence and the "brother" passes by without seeing her. Connection, however, comes only indirectly in the form of mystery. The narrator makes an initial visit but no return visit is ever made. Here new neighbors do not bring the blessing of an enlarged community for shared work, talk, and play as they do, for example, in Caroline Kirkland's *A New Home—Who'll Follow?* The isolation between households is doubled by the isolation within households, for at the end of the sketch we suddenly realize that the narrator is as solitary as those she tries to visit.

In "Mrs. Hill and Mrs. Troost," doubling, a frequent feature of Cary's fiction, serves to focus attention on the issue of temperament, for only temperament can explain why two women in the same situation experience the world so differently. Though the story hints that temperament may be controlled by will, Mrs. Troost does not in fact undergo a conversion and become Mrs. Hill. At the end of her visit, she trudges home with the same convictions she had when she left: "Some folks are born to be lucky." Frequently describing herself as "naturally" melancholy, Cary viewed temperament as part of the mystery of human life. Unlike most Cary stories, "Mrs. Hill and Mrs. Troost" relies heavily on dialogue, reminding one of the work of a later writer like Rose Terry Cooke. Equally rare, it contains a portrait of the woman of "faculty." While writers like Stowe, Jewett, and Freeman would develop and transform this figure, most of Cary's characters belong to the class of those who for one reason or another can't or won't make do.

"About the Tompkinses" opens with a request for "something to eat." Susan deprives her brothers because her parents deprive her. Though perfectly clear, like the Michigan "folks" in Kirkland's *A New Home,* as to who is below them, the adult Tompkinses are sure that no one is above them and certainly not those used-to-be city "folks who stuck themselves up with their waiters and their door-bells." To prove her parents' equality, Susan will be kept from the "Haywood fandango." Cary knows how to signify the lives of girls. In "About the Tompkinses," when Susan rips the apron she has so laboriously made over in order to have something nice to wear to the party, we perceive her loss as significant, not trivial, and her response as appropriate, not sentimental. For though she never mistakes appearance for reality, Cary knows that appearance is part of reality. Finding something to wear to a party elicits from Cary's girls an energy, ingenuity, and initiative strikingly different from their usual passivity. With the right dress, they can get out of the house; once out of the house who knows what can happen. Susan, of course, does not get to go out and wonderful things happen to her anyway. But the happy ending to this story seems more fantastic than real. The mysterious stranger arrives out of nowhere and magically decides to remain and marry. Even more magically, he proves to be a nest builder and a feeder, not a sadistic depriver. Given Cary's awareness elsewhere of the connection between men's cruelty to animals and their cruelty to women, we might find a sinister note in the string of dead birds that accompanies his arrival. "About the Tompkinses," however, is not "A White Heron"; Cary's protagonists lack the supportive context that makes it possible for Jewett's Sylvia to choose self over other. The best Cary's girls can hope for is to find an other who will deprive them less than their parents have.

The final selection from the first volume of Clovernook sketches is composed of a slightly abridged version of the first and third "chapters" of a larger sequence, which I have called, for convenience, "The Sisters," after the title given to its first segment. Despite the formula of a narrative "I" who knew the sisters long ago, the sequence is highly autobiographical and as such is of major interest. In its opening chapters, it deals with the relationship between Cary and her older sister Rhoda. In an unpoetic environment, the sisters share a passion for poetry. Together they create an alternate world and ratify each other's deepest sense of reality. But the threat of separation shadows their relationship. Though death is the agent, the source of the shadow lies deeper. Rebecca has already begun to show that interest in courtship that leads to marriage. In story after story Cary shows marriage as destroying the relationship between sisters. Thus Rebecca's death at fifteen years, seven months, and five days old symbolizes the fate of those who love "with a love that was more than love." Indeed, literal death keeps Rebecca more present to Ellie than she would have been had she lived and married. Perhaps such knowledge fuels the guilt the Cary narrator experiences in relation to her dead siblings. In the first paragraph of "The Wildermings," the narrator admits to the desire to see the big tree felled and then to a sense of responsibility for its death.

Cary reveals much about herself in "The Sisters." In particular we note her view of herself as special, different from and better than her surroundings, a "wonderfully gifted" person trapped, as she puts it in a later chapter, in a "husk of awkward rusticity." Feeling awkward because she has no shoes, she presents herself awkwardly to the one person genuinely capable of recognizing her value. Such perversely self-defeating behavior frequently characterizes the Cary narrator and often takes the form, as it does here, of verbal awkwardness. Recognition of the degree to which verbal facility, like clothes, affects one's fate in life permeates Cary's fiction. In *Married, Not Mated,* the narrator puts it succinctly: "Ah me! our success in this world depends greatly on the facility with which we can say Uncle Samuel Peter! Peter, simply, will not do at all . . . I could not say Samuel Peter, half so smoothly as she!"

Though it also contains some of her least significant work, on the whole *Clovernook, Second Series,* represents Cary's most substantial artistic achievement. Unlike the material in the earlier volume, the stories in the second volume possess more readily discernible beginnings, middles, and ends. While the reality presented is still fragmentary and open-ended, Cary renders her vision more effectively by virtue of her greater mastery of form. In this second series, the narrator figures in almost every story and she scrupulously establishes her connection with, point of view on, and authority over the material she records. This later volume, however, contains no equivalent for "My Grandfather," "The Wildermings," or "The Sisters"; only indirectly, through the implicit identification of the narrator with the person whose history she tells, do we learn the effect of the material on her. Here the narrator more explicitly assumes the role of artist and defines her task as shaping the history of others into effective and moving stories.

"Uncle Christopher's," one of Cary's best stories, combines her passion for realistic details and her fascination for fiction as psychic exploration and dreamwork. In this story minutely detailed descriptions of the contents of Uncle Christopher's attic coexist with the portrait of seven women, exactly alike, knitting the same stocking in the same way at the same time. Indeed, "Uncle Christopher's" contains much that we usually associate with fairy tale and myth. The "visit" itself resembles a trip to the underworld and Uncle Christopher, whom the narrator visits on a brutally cold winter's night, like an underworld god, blights everything he touches. To himself, Uncle Christopher is a god; to the narrator, however, he is all too ordinarily crude, boring, sadistic, and fat. He maintains a virtual monopoly over resources and feeds himself while starving others. Subjecting those around him to interminable monologues about himself, he controls both how much anyone else can talk and what they can talk about. While the narrator is at Uncle Christopher's, she too is silent. In the story she tells after she leaves, however, she takes her revenge on fathers.

Uncle Christopher thrives on power and on the use of power to compel others to his will. He takes pleasure in being cruel and he uses his power over others only to deprive, steal, and kill. He enjoys making Mark throw the kitten down the well; he enjoys stealing Mark's money; he enjoys readying a switch to use on Mark and enjoys the discovery that the boy has done something to allow and justify his violence. Why, then, are fathers so willing to place their children in the hands of Uncle Christopher? Uncle Christopher and the narrator's father are related, however distantly, and the similarities between them are clear. This father, from the region where winters "keep their empire nearly half the year," loves the cold and dark as much as his daughter loves the fire, the light, and home. Though more subtle in his use of power than Uncle Christopher, he takes his daughter away from her fire and leads her into darkness. At the end of a trip that nearly freezes her, he abandons her to Uncle Christopher, a fate she is powerless to resist and can only hope to survive. Cary paints a chilling picture of the virtually unlimited power of fathers. Nothing stands between Uncle Christopher and his grandson Mark and the father is literally free to kill the child. Is "Uncle Christopher's" simply a bad dream from which the narrator can awaken? Unfortunately, all the fathers in this story, in giving their children over to him, become versions of Uncle Christopher. When the narrator wakes up, she will still be in her father's house.

In "Why Molly Root Got Married" Molly Root, female, single, poor, and older than she used to be, leads the most miserable of lives. Yet despite the humiliation of her position as a poor relation in Mrs. Trowbridge's house, she has until the time of this story retained a degree of identity sufficient to allow her to stay unmarried. Molly's identity resides in her attic "museum." Her ritual retirement to this museum, where she recollects herself by sorting through her things, keeps alive in a hostile environment her self-respect. Molly's museum represents her better, happier past and symbolizes as well her own niche, however small, in a world that measures value in terms of possessions. Molly is forced into marriage by a discovery that shatters her sense of reality and as a result shatters the identity she has so carefully preserved for so many years. For many nineteenth-century American women writers, the rigid distinctions between men and women presented serious problems for women's sense of reality. Because men and women occupied separate spheres and led separate lives, and because the experience of women was far more limited than that of men, women often accorded major significance to events that were trivial and inconsequential to men. Molly, rooted in her sense of a significant past, would never have become Molly Pell had she not discovered the insubstantiality of these roots. A lover faithful, though dead, is one thing; a lover alive and faithless is quite another. Having to exchange the former for the latter entails a radical revision of reality. In the light of her new perspective, the silliness of Mr. Pell must seem minor compared to her own much larger foolishness, for most certainly she has been silly, silly, silly.

Unlike those in the previous two stories, the narrator is not an eyewitness to the experience recorded in "Charlotte Ryan," though she carefully establishes here, as always, her relation to her subject and thus her authority for the story she tells. Perhaps this technical difference makes it easier for us to see in Charlotte Ryan a self-portrait. Charlotte's story is, after all, a version of the story Cary tells about herself as well as others. It is the story of the "wonderfully talented" rustic girl encountering the world. Significantly, in this story Cary connects class and gender issues. In Ames's account of Cary's life, the lover who never returned was a man superior to her "in years, culture, and fortune. . . . A proud and prosperous family brought all their pride and power to bear on a son, to prevent his marrying a girl to them uneducated, rustic, and poor" (Ames 29). Here Sully Dinsmore merely trifles with Charlotte; his interest in her terminates with the arrival of the more suitable, upper-class Miss Herbert.

Men who claim to be poets generally do not fare well in Cary's fiction. In nineteenth-century America, poetry served, among other things, as a special women's language. Cary clearly recognized that men often adopted the pose of poet in order, like Mr. Dinsmore, to gain access to women for sympathy or sex. This seductive and seducing male frequently gets his comeuppance in Cary's fiction, but a bond between women rarely proves the agency of his justly deserved humiliation. "Charlotte Ryan" provides a rare instance of female bonding. Miss Herbert actually prefers Charlotte to the "poet" and sets out consciously to win her affection in order to provide for her. Though I doubt that Cary intended to cast a sinister light on the relationship between Charlotte and Miss Herbert by quoting from Coleridge's "Christabel," nevertheless the end of her story presents the "rescue" as problematic. Charlotte has every apparent reason to be happy, yet she isn't. The situation from which she longed to escape now appears supremely desirable to her. At the end of his adventures Huckleberry Finn wants to light out for a territory that no longer exists except in his imagination and his story. Waiting for Sully Dinsmore, Charlotte spends an entire day alone on a hill while the daily life of others transpires below her. At the end of his day the farmer she has watched turns homeward; Charlotte herself has no place to go. Her final tears are inexplicable save as testimony to the fact that home does not now and never did exist.

Despite their differences, the two volumes of Clovernook sketches have a unity and integrity that join them together and distinguish them as a whole from the later collection, *Pictures of Country Life.* Cary signals the completion of her Clovernook project by ending the second series with a "Conclusion." In it, she again identifies herself as an American writer, seeking to produce a literature appropriate to "our nationality." And once again she identifies the regional perspective and the regional subject as the truly American. Defending herself against contemporary critics who have called her work too melancholy, she asserts her right to paint life as she sees it. Aware perhaps of the pressure on women to write of and from the "sunny side," she carefully distinguishes herself from those writers of her own sex who, she implicitly suggests, have falsified their experience and vision by writing only of "wealth and splendor . . . luxury and art." In this context, her somber tone becomes a suitable form of defying both critics and conventions. Though Death may be a mother, when one's mother wears the masque of death, the child has a right to be terrified by such play and to say so.

In *Clovernook Children,* published in December of 1854, Cary creates, as she did in the first volume of Clovernook sketches, an authentic child-self from whose perspective most of the stories in the collection are written. *Clovernook Children* does not present a nostalgic view of childhood as a happy time in a safe place. Rather, Cary's child inhabits a world of danger in which children are constantly at risk and little care is taken of or given to them. In the opening scene of "Having Our Way," a story centered on the conundrum of "female development," the mother bird lures the little bird out of the nest with a false assurance of competence; as a result the cat gets a live treat. The human mother, in an effort to pacify her little ones, sends them to the fields with water for the "hands." Here they encounter men who are vaguely threatening. One of these men offers to tell them where they can find berries. As they rush off to pick and taste this new experience, Peter calls out a warning. The danger that surrounds their way soon materializes. They emerge from the briars discussing what they will make of their fruit. Peter calls, "Look here," and runs at them waving a snake. Should their mother have kept them at home? Has this mother consciously betrayed her children, or is mothering simply impossible, given the world that girls must inevitably enter? Because once out in the world of Peters, the girls are in over their heads. Peter has little trouble making the girls complicit in his abuse of them. He gets them to cover up his initial betrayal by offering them the possibility of another new experience—a trip to town. Yet the trip to town proves as fraught with danger as the trip to the fields. Like the mother bird, Peter deludes the girls with false assurances about the value of their berries and then abandons them to the consequences of believing him. Their hope of new dresses in which to make further explorations vanishes with the discovery that, in this world, beer and cakes take all they earn. They have had their way and are sorry for it, but would not having had their way have been any better? From this experience they may learn to distrust their own desire, but it is not at all clear whose wish they are to trust. Indeed, "Having Our Way" implies that there is in fact no way for girls to have.

Published in the *Ladies' Repository* in February 1855, "Ghost Story, Number II," though filled with material that usually makes for melancholy in Cary's fiction, provides a relatively positive view of human beings and their affairs. Like most nineteenth-century American women regionalists, Cary refuses to glorify or worship the American boy. Instead she sees this boy as dangerous, and she perceives his refusal to grow up as simply an excuse for cruelty, a pose that enables him to spend his life as a practical joker. In the figure of Amos Hill, Cary offers us a revision of Rip van Winkle, and while the story opens with a description of a trick Amos once played on the children, he is now finally dead. Cary's community gathers not to celebrate the miraculous return and apparently perpetual life of their boy-man, but rather to celebrate their being rid of him.

At the center of "Ghost Story, Number II," Cary sets not Amos Hill but Jenny Baxter, the woman of faculty whose visits people look forward to and welcome because of her wonderful sympathy and her talent for telling stories. A rare instance in Cary's fiction of a woman who likes herself, Jenny by liking herself also nurtures others. And a knitter of more than just stockings, Jenny keeps her community from unraveling. Responding to the tension developing between Mr. Claverel and Nattie, Jenny tells a story that satisfies both of them and reunites the community in recalling, not how a man got rid of his wife and thus lived forever, but rather how a man found new life through love and marriage. Though one of the ghosts in this story can be easily explained to the satisfaction of Mr. Claverel, this explanation leaves untouched the far greater mystery of human love and its power to revitalize. And the other ghost, the ghost that can't be explained, equally testifies to that mystery, presenting the possibility that feeling has a life of its own and can survive the death of the body.

In "Old Christopher," published in the July 1855 issue of the *National Magazine,* Cary explores her relation with a figure who appears frequently in her work, haunting both the woods of Clovernook and her own imagination. A homegrown version of the wild man encountered in "My Grandfather," Christopher is isolated, cut off from the human community, and perceived as queer, different, and dangerous. And like the wild man, Christopher reflects the narrator's condition and embodies her fears. But in this story, the narrator "tames" the wild man, discovers his secrets, and without severing her connection to him, learns from her experience how to avoid his fate. In order to get to Christopher, the narrator must first learn to disentangle myth from reality. Clovernook considers Christopher dangerous, but when the narrator treats him kindly, he responds in kind and out of the trust thus established he reveals to her the source of his "madness." Long ago Christopher married an image. But the image turned into a person who didn't behave the way the image was supposed to, and now Christopher can no longer distinguish reality from fantasy. Christopher has been betrayed not just by his wife and children, not even by Woman, but by a culture defined by the disparity between ideology and reality and the craziness that results from it.

Cary, in trying to tell the story of motherlessness to a culture obsessed by the ideology of motherhood, ran the risk of being seen as and going crazy, but the lessons she learns from and through Christopher help keep her sane. For, like the narrator, Christopher is also an artist to whom isolation and craziness have brought insight, vision, and prophecy. Though Clovernook views these powers negatively, the narrator wants access to them, and though her reasons for seeking out Christopher are complex, prime among them is the fact that "he often promised to bestow his prophetic powers on me when he died." In relating to Christopher, the narrator accepts the artist in herself—the self that believes in visions and history, the self that wants to tell people's stories and sees in them a great mystery, the self that others may well call crazy. "Old Christopher" provides an alternative to the experience presented in "Having Our Way." Against the advice and warnings of parents and peers, and in the face of accusations of "tampering with the devil," the narrator has her own way on the subject of Christopher and her own way is right.

As a collection, *Pictures of Country Life* (1859) represents diminished formal and thematic possibilities. Unlike the Clovernook volumes, the stories here are not interconnected. Nothing replaces the concept of Clovernook or compensates for its loss. Without the Clovernook framework there is no context for the narrator, who no longer figures as a major character with a clearly defined and aesthetically functional role. Yet someone insists on talking frequently with and to the reader. Since no intelligible context for these intrusions exists, they affect us as annoying interruptions. Moreover, since this someone is not a character who has a clearly defined role to play in the story she tells, her voice is reduced to the function of moralizing and generalizing. Indeed, on occasion it seems as if the story exists simply to allow this disembodied voice the opportunity to point out a particular moral.

Thematically, *Pictures of Country Life* manifests an acceptance of convention remarkably absent from Cary's earlier work. In "Lem Lyon," for example, the initial story in *Pictures of Country Life,* a man who begins by wishing there was a separate world for women and children is transformed by the death of a baby girl into a loving husband and father. Reminiscent here of Stowe in her handling of little Eva, in yet another story on the theme of female influence, Cary even echoes Stowe's language: "Perhaps those little fingers, in their workings, were gathering strength for such a blow." Most of the stories in this collection rely heavily on the "miraculous" ending, which is also the happy ending and the neat ending, to solve all problems of form and content. Obviously the three stories from *Pictures of Country Life* chosen for inclusion here—"Passages from the Married Life of Eleanor Homes," "Eliza Anderson," and "An Old Maid's Story"—represent triumphant exceptions to this general pattern. In each of them Cary executes brilliant solutions to her formal and thematic difficulties.

Though many of Cary's stories are dreamlike in their associative patterns, as far as I know only in "Passages from the Married Life of Eleanor Homes" does she explicitly use the dream as a way to tell and frame a story. However, since we do not discover that the story is a dream until the end and since the story doesn't read like a dream before that point, we can perhaps assume that Cary chose the dream frame because it offered her certain otherwise unavailable freedoms, in particular the freedom to explore the possibilities of exclusive subjectivity and interiority. In this story the narrator's consciousness, experience, feelings, and perceptions form the sole subject of the text. Cary justifies such textual "narcissism," so counter to the conventions governing women and fiction in nineteenth-century America, by calling her story a dream.

Cary's narrator in "Passages" is distinctly unconventional. Consumed by rage, spite, and jealousy, she is first murderous and then suicidal; she openly engages in a struggle for power and she hates those she fights and she hates losing. The narrator's rage, which permeates the entire story, is triggered by her discovery of the radical disparity between courtship and marriage. Though Cary wrote many stories portraying bad marriages, in "Passages" she engages marriage as an institution, no doubt because the story is, after all, "only a dream." During courtship women are led to believe that in the intimate relation between men and women equality and mutual consideration predominate, and that within this relationship women's needs will be taken as seriously as those of men. Here Cary dramatically and decisively demonstrates the distinction between courtship and marriage. The relationship between Eleanor and Harry changes the moment the wedding is over. Married, tender Harry becomes a vicious and tyrannical master. With a flick of his whip, he signals his possession of his wife's body and mind. He injures her eye so that she can no longer see clearly and then requires her to accept the subsequent distortion as reality. He blames her for the injury and labels her reaction hysteric. Within minutes, marriage reduces the narrator to a child and renders her powerless to regain adult status. Disabused of her dream of an equality based on mutual consideration, the narrator cannot even achieve an equality based on mutual aggravation. Her efforts to annoy her husband have no power when set against his ability to leave when he wants to, return when he wants to, live where he wishes and with whom he wishes. In "Passages" Cousin Jane plays a key role in Cary's analysis of marriage, just as Sister Jane would function some fifty years later in Charlotte Perkins Gilman's "The Yellow Wallpaper." Eleanor Homes hates Jenny as a rival for her husband's attention, but she hates her far more because she represents a living, live-in lesson, daily telling her that a wife should be a good-natured, simple-minded, totally subservient child with the body of a woman. Though nature may say one thing to women, men in marriage say the opposite: I will take this woman and of her make a child of my own.

In "Passages from the Married Life of Eleanor Homes" the dream frame doesn't literally work. It has freed Cary to write a chillingly realistic story, but this very realism ensures that we will not read the story as simply a bad dream. When we are finally told that "such things could not have really happened," we simply don't believe it and we don't believe Cary intends us to believe it. Instead we feel invited to read the ending as Cary's way of dramatizing women's desperate need to believe in illusion. The narrator falls asleep holding a picture and wakes up when it falls to the floor. Yet against all sense she needs to believe in the picture. What other choice does she have?

"Passages" contains traces of a narrative presence. In the opening and closing sections of the story, someone other than Eleanor herself speaks, a vestige of the Clovernook technique of narrator as character. In "Eliza Anderson," however, Cary keeps herself personally out of the story, choosing instead the role of third person omniscient narrator and letting the material speak for itself. She avoids all opportunities to soften her material: she does not let us see the mother's death; George never reforms; and Caspar remains resolutely cold. As a result, "Eliza Anderson" is stark, bitter, and uncompromising. Filled with scenes of eating and with images and metaphors based on food, it tells the story of how men feed off women and how women willingly give themselves to men as food. George Anderson, another Rip van Winkle, wants only to escape his wife, his house, and the role of provider. When his wife dies, however, we discover the social reality that Irving has inverted. George literally lives off his wife and he cannot survive without her. Before he dies, however, he provides for his son. He instructs his daughter, Eliza, already prepared for her role by a mother who willingly deprives her daughter to feed her son, to allow her brother, George, to live off her. Though Eliza has been told directly and indirectly that she is "very much blest in having a little brother," the story suggests that she would be infinitely better off without her brother, just as her mother would have been better off without her father. Indeed, "Eliza Anderson" radically challenges the wisdom and morality of those conventional hierarchies that place men, no matter how selfish, weak, and lazy, over women no matter how competent, energetic, and strong.

Caspar, the schoolmaster who boards with the Andersons, longs to have the handling of George, and to some degree the reader is invited to participate in this wish. Yet Caspar is no hero. Though superficially he seems more nurturant, tender, and responsible than either of the Georges, his desire to have power over George junior has a hint of brutality in it realized in the final scene between himself and Eliza when he remains cruelly insistent on dominance. If married to Eliza, Caspar would no doubt stay home, but he would probably find as many ways to starve Eliza by his presence as her father found to starve her mother by his absence. In this story at least all men live off women and women's reality boils down to a choice of whom they will feed.

On the surface, "An Old Maid's Story" looks rather conventional, making its point the revelation that old maids have secret loves. Yet at the heart of this story lies a far more serious issue, namely the narrator's struggle to negotiate a viable relation with her community, one that will enable her to transcend her village, yet still live in it. In the opening paragraphs we sense the narrator's isolation. Though surrounded by images of community and openness—Jane on the porch, the mowers in the field, people going by on the road—she herself is alone and shadowed. Outwardly idle but inwardly active, she sits in the shade of an entangled grapevine and cherry tree and her thoughts are similarly tangled. Unlike the simple girl on the porch who tangles neither her thread nor her thoughts and who thus can spin and smile and smile and spin all day, the narrator confronts a world of whys. When a visitor arrives, she hastens to conceal her book and pick up her needle because "to be found reading or idle would have been considered alike disgraceful in the estimation of our neighbors." At this point the narrator, though aware of her own difference, wishes to appear "normal" in order to have access to community; she is prepared to try to enter village life on its own terms. The shock of recognition that ensues when she realizes there will be no invitation forces her back into herself, where she must confront the question of how to relate to a community that has already foreclosed on her possibility of participating in it.

In "An Old Maid's Story," Cary purposely leaves vague the nature of the contact established between the narrator and the minister during the long night of watching with the dead. What happens within the narrator, however, is clear enough. The experience she has enables her to shift her point of view and change her frame of reference so that she no longer takes her definition of self from Emeline and Jane, from those who see her as an old maid. Though she will no doubt continue to figure in the stories of others, she now has a story of her own to make and tell. The element of fantasy in the narrator's solution to her situation may seem excessive, but in the context set by the rest of Cary's work the fact that she has learned how to nurture herself is far more significant than the specific form that nurturance takes. Successful here, she can now be herself, however different, and at the end of her story triumphantly say, "Nothing now would tempt me away from the hills I was born among."

"The Great Doctor," one of two stories Cary published in the *Atlantic Monthly* (July and August 1866), though seriously flawed, has the imaginative power that characterizes her best work. Cary herself may have died of cancer. Perhaps "The Great Doctor" derives its power from recording a deeply personal terror. The image of a tree strangled by mistletoe is rather ordinary, but Cary evokes from this image a most extraordinary feeling. Looking at the tree, Hobert sees himself, doomed like the tree by an illness systemic, not superficial. Though he recognizes the folly of his impulse to save the tree by cutting away the mistletoe, his terror overwhelms his reason and makes him determined to be cured at any cost. Doctors feed on this terror, exploiting the refusal of their patients to be patient. Indeed, Cary presents the medical profession as itself a cancer with its roots deep in the body of the human community. In Cary's view there are far more Killmanys than Shephards. But finally the great doctor can only kill many if many willingly subject themselves to his knife.

In "The Great Doctor" the knife of self-recognition strikes deep. The editorial knife, however, did not strike deep enough, for the story would be much improved if the first part were cut. The second part, not the first part, contains the story Cary has to tell. Moreover, in the first part she attempts a belated, and unsuccessful, return to the use of dialect. Because Cary understood character primarily as an interior creation revealed through the way a person talks to herself and not as a product of interaction with others revealed through conversation, her regionalism, unlike that of a writer like Rose Terry Cooke, does not depend on dialect and dialogue. For Cary, regionalism, located in her narrative consciousness, served as a way to explore interior, psychic territory. Exceptional among nineteenth-century American women for her exploration of female subjectivity and for the formal experiments that accompanied and made possible that exploration, Alice Cary at once reminds us of the limitations of our current map of nineteenth-century American literature and requires that we revise it.

SELECTED BIBLIOGRAPHY

Ames, Mary Clemmer. *A Memorial of Alice and Phoebe Cary, with Some of Their Later Poems.* New York: Hurd and Houghton, 1873.

Armstrong, M. F. "Alice and Phoebe Cary—a Remembrance." *Woman's Journal,* September 9, 1871.

Bayless, Joy. *Rufus Wilmot Griswold.* Nashville, Tenn.: Vanderbilt University Press, 1943.

Carnahan, Ada. "Phoebe Cary." *Ladies' Repository* 48 (July 1872): 1–11.

Cary, Phoebe. "Alice Cary." *Woman's Journal,* August 5, 1871.

Derby, James C. *Fifty Years among Authors, Books, and Publishers.* New York: G. W. Carleton, 1884.

Griswold, William McCrillis, ed. *Passages from the Correspondence of Rufus W. Griswold and Other Papers.* Cambridge, Mass.: Griswold, 1898.

Kolodny, Annette. *The Land Before Her.* Chapel Hill: University of North Carolina Press, 1984.

Mott, Frank Luther. *A History of American Magazines, 1850–1865.* Cambridge, Mass.: Harvard University Press, 1939.

Pulsifer, Janice G. "Alice and Phoebe Cary, Whittier's Sweet Singers of the West." *Essex Institute Historical Collections* 109 (January 1973): 9–59.

Venable, W. H. *Beginnings of Literary Culture in the Ohio Valley.* Cincinnati, Ohio: Robert Clarke, 1891.

A NOTE ON THE TEXT

In preparing this edition of the work of Alice Cary, I have used wherever applicable texts from the collected volumes of short fiction. Cary made few textual changes between periodical and book publication, but those changes she did make result in greater economy and directness. Thus the later texts seem preferable. The stories are reprinted in the order in which they were published, an order that in Cary's case reflects with relative accuracy the chronology of composition. The stories reprinted from the two volumes of Clovernook sketches and from *Pictures of Country Life,* however, are presented here in the order Cary gave them when she collected them into book form, not in the order of their publication in periodicals. I have been able to discover periodical publication for the following stories from the three volumes of collected fiction: "Mrs. Hill and Mrs. Troost," signed Patty Lee, appeared in the *Era,* April 24, 1851; "The Wildermings," published under the title "A Reminiscence" and also signed Patty Lee, first appeared in the *National Era,* June 5, 1851; "Passages from the Married Life of Eleanor Homes" appeared in *The Home: A Fireside Monthly Companion and Guide for the Wife, the Mother, the Sister, and the Daughter,* January 1859; "Eliza Anderson" appeared in *Peterson's,* October and November 1856; "An Old Maid's Story" appeared in the *New York Ledger,* July 19, 1856. I have made no textual changes except to correct obvious typographical errors. In the case of "The Sisters," I have omitted the second chapter and most of the opening paragraphs of the third.

Like many nineteenth-century American writers, Alice Cary frequently quoted poetry in her fiction. In striking contrast to our current situation, nineteenth-century writers could assume that their readers shared and indeed had memorized a common body of poetry from which they could quote without reference. Cary was more fond of this practice than many of her contemporaries, perhaps because it allowed her to demonstrate that, despite the lack of a formal education, she was highly literate. In a brief letter to R. W. Griswold dated October 10, 1851, discussing the forthcoming publication of the first volume of Clovernook sketches, J. G. Whittier writes, "I think if I were Alice I would leave out all poetical quotations—as a general thing they injure and weaken the effect of her admirable prose." Though Cary did not immediately follow Whittier's advice, if indeed she ever received it, over the course of her career one can observe a steady decrease in her use of poetry in fiction. I have been able to make the following identifications for the fiction reprinted here: in "Dreams and Tokens" the quotation in the first paragraph is a version of the final lines from Thomas Moore's "Believe me, if all those endearing young charms"; the Rogers referred to is no doubt Samuel Rogers (1763–1855), who published a collection of verse tales entitled "Italy" between 1822 and 1828. In "The Wildermings" the first and third quotations come from Gray's "Elegy Written in a Country Churchyard"; the second comes from *Paradise Lost,* Book IV. Both the first quotation from Gray's "Elegy" and the lines from *Paradise Lost* are slightly incorrect, no doubt as a result of Cary's quoting from memory. In "About the Tompkinses," "native and to the manner born" is a version of the line from *Hamlet,* Act I, Scene iv. "Why Molly Root Got Married" contains a quotation from Coleridge's "Love," and in "Charlotte Ryan" Cary quotes from Coleridge's "Christabel." In the "Conclusion" to the second volume of Clovernook sketches, Cary quotes from Psalm 127 ("He giveth his beloved sleep"), Gray's "Elegy" ("simple annals of the poor"), and Coleridge's "Love" ("All thoughts, all passions, all delights"). In "Passages from the Married Life of Eleanor Homes," the lines are from the fourth of Wordsworth's "Lucy" poems.

CLOVERNOOK SKETCHES

and Other Stories

DREAMS AND TOKENS

The dull cold rain of autumn had given place to the long sunshiny days of the Indian summer. The squirrels were busy gathering in nuts for the coming winter—the rabbits made themselves beds in the long white grass, and slept—and now and then a bee came forth and hummed, but not with the blithe hum of summer time, for a brief season, and retired again to its sweet, sweet home. In garden and forest the flowers were dead, unless it were that here and there a dry seedy sunflower might be seen, that no longer "turned to her god when he set, the same look that she gave when he rose." And if I might venture an opinion, I should say the human heart is inclined to turn something less fondly toward its vanishing loves, notwithstanding the poet's assertion to the contrary.

We had two beautiful oxen, at the time of which I write—not such mouse-colored ones as Rogers saw, "plowing up and down" in the fair fields of Italy, but equally handsome, I am sure. Well, this has nothing to do with what I am about to tell, only I remember they were bowing their patient necks beneath the heavy yoke, and Millie and I feeding them with the "bruised and wounded rind" of a pumpkin, and talking of the merriment we should have in the corn field—for we had secretly determined to be Ruths for that day, and glean. But all our pleasant plans vanished like raindrops from the sand, before the—Patty and Millie! come in, both of you—that we presently heard. We neither said—what do you want? nor,

I'll come! but, marvelling as to the portent of the summons, went immediately.

Our toilet required brief delay, and with a small parcel, which I, being the older, carried, we set off towards Mrs. Starks's, the tailoress of Summerville. Now, Mrs. Starks must have possessed wonderful intuitive perceptions, for she not only knew everybody, but everything which came within the range of her observation, which, by the way, was bounded by the suburbs of Summerville. She was very tall, and very lean, with coarse, black hair, streaked with gray, and very prominent cheek bones. Though not above forty at the time I write of, the loss of most of her teeth, and three deep wrinkles, that lay in parallel lines across her forehead, gave her the appearance of being much older. Her dress was always of sable, for one of her husbands, I presume; but, as she had had five, it is difficult to say for which. However, as she often asserted positively that she was a *drotted* sight better off without any of them, it may be that she mourned for things in general. She used to pass a day at our house every now and again, and I was as much afraid of her as I would have been of the spirit from beneath, for one of my juvenile misdemeanors was to steal her shears, when she was professionally engaged; whereupon, she never failed to threaten me with cutting off my ears; and as hers were shears that are shears, as Charles Lamb would say, I was awfully afraid she might put her threat into execution. Her house was of hewn logs, containing only one room, and standing at the western extremity of our village. In the rear was a cabbage garden, and in front some "rosy bushes" and lilacs, or lalces, as she called them. The windows were shaded with green papers and white muslin, and her furniture consisted of a bedstead, the posts of which stood on bricks, I know not, and I never knew, for what purpose—but the custom prevailed to a considerable extent formerly—a small looking-glass in a poplar frame, deeply stained, evidently the object of peculiar pride, as the wall where it hung was garnished with some two yards of paper of the gaudiest colors, and beneath it were suspended needle cushions of all sorts and sizes, some sprigs of asparagus, dry and faded, half a dozen skeins of thread, a huge silver watch, a memento of one of her deceased lords, and a pair of very small and very bright scissors. A few old chairs and a small table completed the furniture.

"Come in!" was the loud, clear response to our timid rap, and we entered accordingly. "Help yourselves to cheers, and sit down," she continued, without rising from the corner where she sat, with the "press board" on her knees, and a hot smoothing-iron in her hand. In the opposite corner, sat Mrs. Rony, the intimate friend of Mrs. Starks, and our entrance interrupted a very interesting colloquy, as appeared by the sequel.

"Take off your bonnets, young 'uns," said our hostess, looking at us so sternly that we almost trembled, and as she examined the parcel I presented, added, "a wescut for the old man Lee! I'll block it out when I get ready, and not before! None of your sass!" she exclaimed, seeing we had not removed our bonnets; "off with them, and let's see how slick your wigs are! Now, just be as aisy as you can for the matter of two hours, for I've got these overalls to finish for John Harvy by three o'clock, to go to the raising—so keep still-mouthed, mind, I tell you!"

"Yes," said Mrs. Rony, looking up from her knitting, "you musn't disapint John, he's so dreadful tender-hearted. Why, don't you think the other day he went out to the barn, and cried like everything, because they laughed at him amongst 'em, something about a new pair of pegged boots*—I don't mind just what?"

"No!" (said Mrs. Starks,) apparently resuming a conversation in which our entrance had made an episode; "they needn't try to make me believe there ain't no such things; I know what I've seen with my own eyes. Didn't half a dozen women of us, the night Aunt Liddy died, see the shades of a black dog walk along right finents** her high post bedstead?"

"Do tell!" exclaimed Mrs. Rony; "here, Patty, honey, just turn the seam for me—my eyes blur so! Some things are always bad signs with me," and she resumed her knitting.

"I reckon," said the first speaker, "you've heard Abby Hill tell about the ugly dream she had, the night before her father went crazy? It was a dreadful bad sign with her always to dream of a woman's bare feet. Well,

*Pegged boots are boots whose soles are fastened to the uppers by means of wooden pegs.

**I have been unable to find "finents" in any dictionary, historical, regional or standard. From the context, I assume that it is a version of "anents," which means "beside, in a line with, side by side with," or "in front of, before, opposite, over against."

she dreamed of a woman's bare feet that night, and waked up all in a trimor, and she heard her father whisper and whuss to himself then, she said; and the next day he was clean crazy—delirious, as some calls it. They had all the Doctors in the world, a'most, to him, but they never done him any good—and Abby said she never could get over that dream and how her father whispered and whussed, and she laid awake and heard him; and she said it seemed to her then as if something was going to happen; and she said the moon ris about midnight, and shined just as bright!"

Verily, if the incident of the moonlight were true, Abby Hill had sufficient data from which to anticipate some event fatal to her happiness.

"But," interposed Mrs. Rony, "I shouldn't think the whispering such a bad sign—some folks do that, that aint crazy. Why, it was only the other day I heard Mrs. Jameson tell about 'Bill Gallagher's' doing a'most as bad as the old man Hill. Bill used to be right good company, Mrs. Jameson says, before he got a fool notion of writing poetry, and now he's no company for anybody—he just walks the floor of his chamber, and mutters to himself, she says, half a day to a time."

I must here be permitted to remark, that the complacent exterior of William D. Gallagher affords no index to this frightful imputation above recorded. However, my first impression of the poet was in part neutralized by hearing Mrs. Jameson herself say that "Bill" was *turtle** fond of flowers; but words cannot express the horror I felt at the time I received my first impression of a poet.

> "She spoke, and the stranger's guise fell off,
> And a phantom form stood there."

"I shall never forget a dream I had oncet," resumed Mrs. Starks, "the night before my third old man left me. I remember everything that happened the day before he set off, just as if it was yesterday. He came in—I'd just got up—for I'd been busy all day making overalls a good deal like these of John's; and I'd got up, I know, to red my dresser, and he came in; he was a cupper, you know, but he didn't make barls often, he made mostly half barls; well, he came in, and he stood up before the fire; it had been raining a little, and was dampish like, and his coat I know was buttoned up

* "Turtle" no doubt is a corruption of "turrible," that is, "terribly."

close—he had a fashion of wearing the blue one he got when we was married that way—he thought it set better. Well, he had that blue coat on, and it was buttoned up just as he always wore it, and he stood up before the fire—I'd got through with my dresser, and gone to make my bed, and he looked at me mournful as could be for a good while, but I was busy with my work, and didn't mind; and then, says he—and he turned right around and looked in the fire—says he, Eunice—he always called me Euny—it was a fashion he got into about the time we were married, for if you mind he wasn't hash like most men, but had regard always for a woman's feelings—but then he said, Eunice; and I looked up, for I wondered why he didn't say Euny, and he didn't say anything more for a'most a minute; and then, says he, 'I'm going to leave you in the morning!' If a thunderbolt had struck me, I couldn't have been worse skeert, for I just felt right away that he was going to an Ingen settlement."

"Do tell!" exclaimed Mrs. Rony; "well, it's strange what curious feelings a body will have sometimes. I remember that summer my Emeline was a baby, I was dreadful skeery. One night I know I got skeered at a speckled fowl in a cherry tree. Lord help us, but I was wild a'most when I got in—and 'he' did laugh at me! But the dream, Mrs. Starks; what did you dream?"

"O yes," said that lady, "but just see how this thread knots; I guess John Harvy will wear those to a wedding instead of a raising! Here, Patty, sit up here and wax my thread, you've nothing else to do!" It is needless to say that I obeyed, for very confident was I, that a refusal would bring my head to the block. Besides, I always found it pleasant to sit by the fire with good old folks, and let them tell me tales, and my curiosity was now wrought up to the highest pitch about the dream.

Some folks count it bad to dream of one thing, and some of another," continued the oracle. "Now, with some it's an ugly dream to dream of oats in the sheaf; but with me, that is always a sign I'll hear good news from some of my relations. But, as I was going to say, the night before he went away, I dreamed all night long the queerest things. I'd been up pretty late, mending up things for *him,* and after I got through I sat down by the fire, for I felt that bad it seemed as if I couldn't sleep no way at all. We'd had batter-cakes for supper, and the little crock I'd mixed them in stood in the corner, with my press-board laid over it, and there was a mackerel against the other jamb, ready to brile for breakfast—I can see how it all looked, just as well! His things were hanging all about the fire-place, and it looked *so lonesome,* I tried my best to persuade him to put off his journey for a day or two, because the next day was Friday; but he wouldn't hear to me, and to get rid of my teazing, went off to bed. So I sat there alone, and he kep snorin' so loud, it seem'd lonesome and bad to me; and I noticed, too, that the shadder of the mackerel on the jamb looked a'most like a coffin, and that made me have ugly thoughts. At last, as the roosters began to crow for midnight, I thought, may be, I was borrowing trouble, and so I went to bed. I was determined he should have a good night's rest, and so I crep in carefully, but I hardly touched the pillow till I was asleep—though I felt flighty, and jumped two or three times, and thought I was falling, before I was quite asleep. It seemed to me as if I was with Betsey Rose—we used to be together when we was girls a great deal, and always told each other all our secrets, and she was my waiter when I was married the first time. Well, I thought she was with me, and it seemed as if she had all her hair cut off; and it seemed as if we were walking up a great long hill, and Betsey, I thought, was telling me about a white heifer her father had given her the day she was eighteen; and just as we got a'most to the top of the hill, it seemed as if we saw a queer-looking old man with a big club in his hand; and he started to chase us, I thought, and it seemed as if we couldn't run; and just as the old man got nearly up with us, I waked up, and I can tell you the daylight looked good."

"I'll dare say!" exclaimed Mrs. Rony; "and your old man never got back again, sure enough."

Sorry enough was I, when Mrs. Starks, giving the finishing touch to John Harvy's trousers, said she would block out that wescut in the twinkling of a sheep's eye.

> "Say not 'tis vain'! I tell thee some
> Are warned by a meteor light,
> Or a pale bird flitting calls them home,
> Or a voice on the winds by night!"

Provides a context of dream interpretation, women's community, and story-telling.

PREFACE TO

CLOVERNOOK; OR, RECOLLECTIONS OF OUR NEIGHBORHOOD IN THE WEST

THE PASTORAL LIFE of our country has not been a favorite subject of illustration by painters, poets, or writers of romance. Perhaps it has been regarded as wanting in the elements of beauty; perhaps it has been thought too passionless and even; or it may have been deemed too immediate and familiar. I have had little opportunity for its observation in the eastern and northern states, and in the south there is no such life, and in the far west where pioneers are still busy with felling the opposing trees, it is not yet time for the reed's music; but in the interior of my native state, which was a wilderness when first my father went to it, and is now crowned with a dense and prosperous population, there is surely as much in the simple manners, and the little histories every day revealed, to interest us in humanity, as there *can* be in those old empires where the press of tyrannous laws and the deadening influence of hereditary acquiescence necessarily destroy the best life of society.

Without a thought of making a book, I began to recall some shadows and sunbeams that fell about me as I came up to womanhood, incidents for the most part of so little apparent moment or significance that they who live in what is called the world would scarcely have marked them had they been detained with me while they were passing, and before I was aware, the record of my memories grew to all I now have printed.

Looking over the proof sheets, as from day to day they have come from my publisher, the thought has frequently been suggested that such experiences as I have endeavored to describe will fail to interest the inhabitants of cities, where, however much there may be of pity there is surely little of sympathy for the poor and humble, and perhaps still less of faith in their capacity for those finer feelings which are too often deemed the blossoms of a high and fashionable culture. The masters of literature who at any time have attempted the exhibition of rural life, have, with few exceptions, known scarcely anything of it from participation, and however brilliant may have been their pictures, therefore, they have seldom been true. Perhaps in their extravagance has been their greatest charm. For myself, I confess I have no invention, and I am altogether too poor an artist to dream of any success which may not be won by the simplest fidelity. I believe that for these sketches I may challenge of competent witnesses at least this testimony, that the circumstances have a natural and probable air which should induce their reception as honest relations unless there is conclusive evidence against them. Having this merit, they may perhaps interest if they do not instruct readers who have regarded the farming class as essentially different and inferior, and entitled only to that peculiar praise they are accustomed to receive in the resolutions of political conventions.

MY GRANDFATHER

CHANGE IS THE order of nature; the old makes way for the new; over the perished growth of the last year brighten the blossoms of this. What changes are to be counted, even in a little noiseless life like mine! How many graves have grown green; how many locks have grown gray; how many, lately young, and strong in hope and courage, are faltering and fainting; how many hands that reached eagerly for the roses are drawn back bleeding and full of thorns; and, saddest of all, how many hearts are broken! I remember when I had no sad memory, when I first made room in my bosom for the consciousness of death. How—like striking out from a wilderness of dew-wet blossoms where the shimmer of the light is lovely as the wings of a thousand bees, into an open plain where the clear day strips things to their natural truth—we go from young visions to the realities of life!

I remember the twilight, as though it were yesterday—gray, and dim, and cold, for it was late in October, when the shadow first came over my heart, that no subsequent sunshine has ever swept entirely away. From the window of our cottage home streamed a column of light, in which I sat stringing the red berries of the brier-rose.

I had heard of death, but regarded it only with that vague apprehension which I felt for the demons and witches that gather poison herbs under the new moon, in fairy forests, or strangle harmless travellers with wands of the willow, or with vines of the wild grape or ivy. I did not much like to think about them, and yet I felt safe from their influence.

There might be people, somewhere, that would die some time; I didn't know, but it would not be myself, or any one I knew. They were so well and so strong, so full of joyous hopes, how could their feet falter, and their eyes grow dim, and their fainting hands lay away their work, and fold themselves together! No, no—it was not a thing to be believed.

Drifts of sunshine from that season of blissful ignorance often come back, as lightly

> As the winds of the May-time flow,
> And lift up the shadows brightly
> As the daffodil lifts the snow—

the shadows that have gathered with the years! It is pleasant to have them thus swept off—to find myself a child again—the crown of pale pain and sorrow that presses heavily now, unfelt, and the graves that lie lonesomely along my way, covered up with flowers—to feel my mother's dark locks falling on my cheek, as she teaches me the lesson or the prayer—to see my father, now a sorrowful old man whose hair has thinned and whitened almost to the limit of three score years and ten, fresh and vigorous, strong for the race—and to see myself a little child, happy with a new hat and a pink ribbon, or even with the string of brier-buds that I called coral. Now I tie it about my neck, and now around my forehead, and now twist it among my hair, as I have somewhere read great ladies do their pearls. The winds are blowing the last yellow leaves from the cherry tree—I know not why, but it makes me sad. I draw closer to the light of the window, and slyly peep within: all is quiet and cheerful; the logs on the hearth are ablaze; my father is mending a bridle-rein, which "Traveller," the favorite riding horse, snapt in two yesterday, when frightened at the elephant that (covered with a great white cloth) went by to be exhibited at the coming show,—my mother is hemming a ruffle, perhaps for me to wear to school next quarter—my brother is reading in a newspaper, I know not what, but I see, on one side, the picture of a bear: let me listen—and flattening my cheek against the pane, I catch his words distinctly, for he reads loud and very clearly—it is an improbable story of a wild man who has recently been discovered in the woods of some far-away island—he seems to have been there a long time, for his nails are grown like claws, and his hair, in rough and matted strings, hangs to his knees; he makes a noise like something between the howl of a beast and a human cry, and, when pursued, runs with a nimbleness and swiftness that baffle the pursuers, though mounted on the fleetest of steeds, urged through brake and bush to their utmost speed. When first seen, he was sitting on the ground and cracking nuts with his teeth; his arms are corded with sinews that make it probable his strength is sufficient to strangle a dozen men; and yet on seeing human beings, he runs into the thick woods, lifting such a hideous scream, the while, as make his discoverers clasp their hands to their ears. It is suggested that this is not a solitary individual, become wild by isolation, but that a race exists, many of which are perhaps larger and of more terrible aspects; but whether they have any intelligible language, and whether they live in caverns of rocks or in trunks of hollow trees, remains for discovery by some future and more daring explorers.

My brother puts down the paper and looks at the picture of the bear. "I would not read such foolish stories," says my father, as he holds the bridle up to the light, to see that it is neatly mended; my mother breaks the thread which gathers the ruffle; she is gentle and loving, and does not like to hear even implied reproof, but she says nothing; little Harry, who is playing on the floor, upsets his block-house, and my father, clapping his hands together, exclaims, "This is the house that Jack built!" and adds, patting Harry on the head, "Where is my little boy? this is not he, this is a little carpenter; you must make your houses stronger, little carpenter!" But Harry insists that he is the veritable little Harry, and no carpenter, and hides his tearful eyes in the lap of my mother, who assures him that he is her own little boy, and soothes his childish grief by buttoning on his neck the ruffle she has just completed; and off he scampers again, building a new house, the roof of which he makes very steep, and calls it grandfather's house, at which all laugh heartily.

While listening to the story of the wild man I am half afraid, but now, as the joyous laughter rings out, I am ashamed of my fears, and skipping forth, I sit down on a green ridge which cuts the door-yard diagonally, and where, I am told, there was once a fence. Did the rose-bushes and lilacs and flags that are in the garden, ever grow here? I think so—no, it must have been a long while ago, if indeed the fence were ever here, for I can't conceive the possibility of such change, and then I fall to arranging my string of brier-buds into letters that will spell some name, now my own, and now that of some one I love. A dull strip of cloud, from which the hues of pink and red and gold have but lately faded out, hangs low in the west; below is a long reach of withering woods—the gray sprays of the beech clinging thickly still, and the gorgeous maples shooting up here and there like sparks of fire among the darkly magnificent oaks and silvery columned sycamores—the gray and murmurous twilight gives way to darker shadows and a deeper hush.

I hear, far away, the beating of quick hoof-strokes on the pavement; the horseman, I think to myself, is just coming down the hill through the thick woods beyond the bridges. I listen close, and presently a hollow rumbling sound indicates that I was right; and now I hear the strokes more faintly—he is climbing the hill that slopes directly away from me; but now again I hear distinctly—he has almost reached the hollow below me—the hollow that in summer is starry with dandelions and now is full of brown nettles and withered weeds—he will presently have passed—where can he be going, and what is his errand? I will rise up and watch. The cloud passes from the face of the moon, and the light streams full and broad on the horseman—he tightens his rein, and looks eagerly toward the house—surely I know him, the long red curls, streaming down his neck, and the straw hat, are not to be mistaken—it is Oliver Hillhouse, the miller, whom my grandfather, who lives in the steep-roofed house, has employed three years—longer than I can remember! He calls to me, and I laughingly bound forward, with an exclamation of delight, and put my arms about the slender neck of his horse, that is champing the bit and pawing the pavement, and I say, "Why do you not come in?"

He smiles, but there is something ominous in his smile, as he hands me a folded paper, saying "Give this to your mother," and, gathering up his reins, he rides hurriedly forward. In a moment I am in the house, for my errand, "Here, mother, is a paper which Oliver Hillhouse gave me for you." Her hand trembles as she receives it, and waiting timidly near, I watch her as she reads; the tears come, and without speaking a word she hands it to my father.

That night there came upon my soul the shadow of an awful fear; sorrowful moans and plaints disturbed my dreams that have never since been wholly forgot. How cold and spectral-like the moonlight streamed across my pillow; how dismal the chirping of the cricket in the hearth; and how more than dismal the winds among the naked boughs that creaked against my window. For the first time in my life I could not sleep, and I longed for the light of the morning. At last it came, whitening up the East, and the stars faded away, and there came a flush of crimson and purple fire, which was presently pushed aside by the golden disk of the sun. Daylight without, but within there was thick darkness still.

I kept close about my mother, for in her presence I felt a shelter and protection that I found no where else.

"Be a good girl till I come back," she said, stooping and kissing my forehead; "mother is going away to-day, your poor grandfather is very sick."

"Let me go too," I said, clinging close to her hand. We were soon ready; little Harry pouted his lips and reached out his hands, and my father gave him his pocket-knife to play with; and the wind blowing the yellow curls over his eyes and forehead, he stood on the porch looking eagerly while my mother turned to see him again and again. We had before us a walk of perhaps two miles—northwardly along the turnpike nearly a mile, next, striking into a grass-grown road that crossed it, in an easternly direction nearly another mile, and then turning northwardly again, a narrow lane bordered on each side by old and decaying cherry-trees, led us to the house, ancient fashioned, with high steep gables, narrow windows, and low, heavy chimneys of stone. In the rear was an old mill, with a plank sloping from the door-sill to the ground, by way of step, and a square open window in the gable, through which, with ropes and pulleys, the grain was drawn up.

This mill was an especial object of terror to me, and it was only when my aunt Carry led me by the hand, and the cheerful smile of Oliver Hillhouse lighted up the dusky interior, that I could be persuaded to enter it. In truth it was a lonesome sort of place, with dark lofts and curious binns, and ladders leading from place to place; and there were cats creeping stealthily along the beams in wait for mice or swallows, if, as sometimes happened, the clay nest should be loosened from the rafter, and the whole tumble ruinously down. I used to wonder that aunt Carry was not afraid in the old place, with its eternal rumble, and its great dusty wheel moving slowly round and round, beneath the steady tread of the two sober horses that never gained a hair's breadth for their pains; but on the contrary, she seemed to like the mill, and never failed to show me through all its intricacies, on my visits. I have unravelled the mystery now, or rather, from the recollections I still retain, have apprehended what must have been clear to older eyes at the time.

A forest of oak and walnut stretched along this extremity of the farm, and on either side of the improvements (as the house and barn and mill were called) shot out two dark forks, completely cutting off the view, save toward the unfrequented road to the south, which was traversed mostly by persons coming to the mill, for my grandfather made the flour for all the neighborhood round about, besides making corn-meal for Johnny-cakes, and "chops" for the cows.

He was an old man now, with a tall, athletic frame, slightly bent, thin locks white as the snow, and deep blue eyes full of fire and intelligence, and after long years of uninterrupted health and useful labor, he was suddenly stricken down, with no prospect of recovery.

"I hope he is better," said my mother, hearing the rumbling of the mill-wheel. She might have known my grandfather would permit no interruption of the usual business on account of his illness—the neighbors, he said, could not do without bread because he was sick, nor need they all be idle, waiting for him to die. When the time drew near, he would call them to take his farewell and his blessing, but till then let them sew and spin, and do all things just as usual, so they would please him best. He was a stern man—even his kindness was uncompromising and unbending, and I remember of his making toward me no manifestation of fondness, such as grandchildren usually receive, save one, when he gave me a bright red apple, without speaking a word till my timid thanks brought out his "Save your thanks for something better." The apple gave me no pleasure, and I even slipt into the mill to escape from his cold forbidding presence.

Nevertheless, he was a good man, strictly honest, and upright in all his dealings, and respected, almost reverenced, by everybody. I remember once, when young Winters, the tenant of Deacon Granger's farm, who paid a great deal too much for his ground, as I have heard my father say, came to mill with some withered wheat, my grandfather filled up the sacks out of his own flour, while Tommy was in the house at dinner. That was a good deed, but Tommy Winters never suspected how his wheat happened to turn out so well.

As we drew near the house, it seemed to me more lonesome and desolate than it ever looked before. I wished I had staid at home with little Harry. So eagerly I noted every thing, that I remember to this day, that near a trough of water, in the lane, stood a little surly looking cow, of a red color, and with a white line running along her back. I had gone with aunt Carry often when she went to milk her, but to-day she seemed not to have been milked. Near her was a black and white heifer, with sharp short horns, and a square board tied over her eyes; two horses, one of them gray, and the other sorrel, with a short tail, were reaching their long necks into the garden, and browsing from the currant bushes. As we approached they trotted forward a little, and one of them, half playfully, half angrily, bit the other on the shoulder, after which they returned quietly to their cropping of the bushes, heedless of the voice that from across the field was calling to them.

A flock of turkeys were sunning themselves about the door, for no one came to scare them away; some were black, and some speckled, some with heads erect and tails spread, and some nibbling the grass; and with a gabbling noise, and a staid and dignified march, they made way for us. The smoke arose from the chimney in blue, graceful curls, and drifted away to the woods; the dead morning-glory vines had partly fallen from the windows, but the hands that tended them were grown careless, and they were suffered to remain blackened and void of beauty, as they were. Under these, the white curtain was partly put aside, and my grandmother, with the speckled handkerchief pinned across her bosom, and her pale face, a shade paler than usual, was looking out, and seeing us she came forth, and in answer to my mother's look of inquiry, shook her head, and silently led the way in. The room we entered had some home-made carpet, about the size of a large table-cloth, spread in the middle of the floor, the remainder of which was scoured very white; the ceiling was of walnut wood, and the side walls were white-washed—a table, an old-fashioned desk, and some wooden chairs, comprised the furniture. On one of the chairs was a leather cushion; this was set to one side, my grandmother neither offering it to my mother, nor sitting in it herself, while, by way of composing herself, I suppose, she took off the black ribbon with which her cap was trimmed.

This was a more simple process than the reader may fancy, the trimming, consisting merely of a ribbon, always black, which she tied around her head after the cap was on, forming a bow and two ends just above the forehead. Aunt Cary, who was of what is termed an even disposition, received us with her usual cheerful demeanor, and then, re-seating herself comfortably near the fire, resumed her work, the netting of some white fringe.

I liked aunt Carry, for that she always took especial pains to entertain me, showing me her patchwork, taking me with her to the cow-yard and dairy, as also to the mill, though in this last I fear she was a little selfish; however, that made no difference to me at the time, and I have always been sincerely grateful to her: children know more, and want more, and feel more, than people are apt to imagine.

On this occasion she called me to her, and tried to teach me the mysteries of her netting, telling me I must get my father to buy me a little bureau, and then I could net fringe and make a nice cover for it. For a little time I thought I could, and arranged in my mind where it should be placed, and what should be put into it, and even went so far as to inquire how much fringe she thought would be necessary. I never attained to much proficiency in the netting of fringe, nor did I ever get the little bureau, and now it is quite reasonable to suppose I never shall.

Presently my father and mother were shown into an adjoining room, the interior of which I felt an irrepressible desire to see, and by stealth I obtained a glimpse of it before the door closed behind them. There was a dull brown and yellow carpet on the floor, and near the bed, on which was a blue and white coverlid, stood a high-backed wooden chair, over which hung a towel, and on the bottom of which stood a pitcher, of an unique pattern. I know not how I saw this, but I did, and perfectly remember it, notwithstanding my attention was in a moment completely absorbed by the sick man's face, which was turned towards the opening door, pale, livid, and ghastly. I trembled and was transfixed; the rings beneath the eyes, which had always been deeply marked, were now almost black, and the blue eyes within looked glassy and cold, and terrible. The expression of agony on the lips (for his disease was one of a most painful nature) gave place to a sort of smile, and the hand, twisted among the gray locks, was withdrawn and extended to welcome my parents, as the door closed. That was a fearful moment; I was near the dark steep edges of the grave; I felt, for the first time, that I was mortal too, and I was afraid.

Aunt Carry put away her work, and taking from a nail in the window-frame a brown muslin sun-bonnet, which seemed to me of half a yard in depth, she tied it on my head, and then clapt her hands as she looked into my face, saying, "bo-peep!" at which I half laughed and half cried, and making provision for herself in grandmother's bonnet, which hung on the opposite side of the window, and was similar to mine, except that it was perhaps a little larger, she took my hand and we proceeded to the mill. Oliver, who was very busy on our entrance, came forward, as aunt Carry said, by way of introduction, "A little visiter I've brought you," and arranged a seat on a bag of meal for us, and taking off his straw hat, pushed the red curls from his low white forehead, and looked bewildered and anxious.

"It's quite warm for the season," said aunt Carry, by way of breaking silence, I suppose. The young man said "yes," abstractedly, and then asked if the rumble of the mill were not a disturbance to the sick room, to which aunt Carry answered, "No, my father says it is his music."

"A good old man," said Oliver, "he will not hear it much longer," and then, even more sadly, "every thing will be changed." Aunt Carry was silent, and he added, "I have been here a long time, and it will make me very sorry to go away, especially when such trouble is about you all."

"Oh, Oliver," said aunt Carry, "you don't mean to go away?" "I see no alternative," he replied; "I shall have nothing to do; if I had gone a year ago it would have been better." "Why?" asked aunt Carry; but I think she understood why, and Oliver did not answer directly, but said, "Almost the last thing your father said to me was, that you should never marry any man who had not a house and twenty acres of land; if he has not, he will exact that promise of you, and I cannot ask you not to make it, nor would you refuse him if I did; I might have owned that long ago, but for my sister (she had lost her reason) and my lame brother, whom I must educate to be a schoolmaster, because he never can work, and my blind mother; but God forgive me! I must not and do not complain; you will forget me, before long, Carry, and some body who is richer and better, will be to you all I once hoped to be, and perhaps more."

I did not understand the meaning of the conversation at the time, but

I felt out of place some way, and so, going to another part of the mill, I watched the sifting of the flour through the snowy bolter, listening to the rumbling of the wheel. When I looked around I perceived that Oliver had taken my place on the meal-bag, and that he had put his arm around the waist of aunt Carry in a way I did not much like.

Great sorrow, like a storm, sweeps us aside from ordinary feelings, and we give our hearts into kindly hands—so cold and hollow and meaningless seem the formulae of the world. They had probably never spoken of love before, and now talked of it as calmly as they would have talked of any thing else; but they felt that hope was hopeless; at best, any union was deferred, perhaps, for long years; the future was full of uncertainties. At last their tones became very low, so low I could not hear what they said; but I saw that they looked very sorrowful, and that aunt Carry's hand lay in that of Oliver as though he were her brother.

"Why don't the flour come through?" I said, for the sifting had become thinner and lighter, and at length quite ceased. Oliver smiled, faintly, as he arose, and saying, "This will never buy the child a frock," poured a sack of wheat into the hopper, so that it nearly run over. Seeing no child but myself, I supposed he meant to buy me a new frock, and at once resolved to put it in my little bureau, if he did.

"We have bothered Mr. Hillhouse long enough," said aunt Carry, taking my hand, "and will go to the house, shall we not?"

I wondered why she said "Mr. Hillhouse," for I had never heard her say so before; and Oliver seemed to wonder, too, for he said reproachfully, laying particular stress on his own name, "You don't bother Mr. Hillhouse, I am sure, but I must not insist on your remaining if you wish to go."

"I don't want you to insist on my staying," said aunt Carry, "if you don't want to, and I see you don't" and lifting me out to the sloping plank, that bent beneath us, we descended.

"Carry," called a voice behind us; but she neither answered nor looked back, but seemed to feel a sudden and expressive fondness for me, took me up in her arms, though I was almost too heavy for her to lift, and kissing me over and over, said I was light as a feather, at which she laughed as though neither sorrowful nor lacking for employment.

This little passage I could never precisely explain, aside from the ground that "the course of true love never did run smooth." Half an hour after we returned to the house, Oliver presented himself at the door, saying, "Miss Caroline, shall I trouble you for a cup, to get a drink of water?" Carry accompanied him to the well, where they lingered some time, and when she returned her face was sunshiny and cheerful as usual.

The day went slowly by, dinner was prepared, and removed, scarcely tasted; aunt Carry wrought at her fringe, and grandmother moved softly about, preparing teas and cordials.

Towards sunset the sick man became easy, and expressed a wish that the door of his chamber might be opened, that he might watch our occupations and hear our talk. It was done accordingly, and he was left alone. My mother smiled, saying she hoped he might yet get well, but my father shook his head mournfully, and answered, "He wishes to go without our knowledge." He made amplest provision for his family always, and I believe had a kind nature, but he manifested no little fondnesses, nor did he wish caresses for himself. Contrary to the general tenor of his character, was a love of quiet jests, that remained to the last. Once, as Carry gave him some drink, he said, "You know my wishes about your future, I expect you to be mindful."

I stole to the door of his room in the hope that he would say something to me, but he did not, and I went nearer, close to the bed, and timidly took his hand in mine; how damp and cold it felt! yet he spoke not, and climbing upon the chair, I put back his thin locks, and kissed his forehead. "Child, you trouble me," he said, and these were the last words he ever spoke to me.

The sun sunk lower and lower, throwing a beam of light through the little window, quite across the carpet, and now it reached the sick man's room, climbed over the bed and up the wall; he turned his face away, and seemed to watch its glimmer upon the ceiling. The atmosphere grew dense and dusky, but without clouds, and the orange light changed to a dull lurid red, and the dying and dead leaves dropt silently to the ground, for there was no wind, and the fowls flew into the trees, and the gray moths came from beneath the bushes and fluttered in the waning light. From the hollow tree by the mill came the bat, wheeling and flitting blindly about, and once or twice its wings struck the window of the sick man's chamber. The last sunlight faded off at length, and the rumbling of the mill-wheel was still: he had fallen asleep in listening to its music.

The next day came the funeral. What a desolate time it was! All down the lane were wagons and carriages and horses, for every body that knew my grandfather would pay him the last honors he could receive in the world. "We can do him no further good," they said, "but it seemed right that we should come." Close by the gate waited the little brown wagon to bear the coffin to the grave, the wagon in which he was used to ride while living. The heads of the horses were drooping, and I thought they looked consciously sad.

The day was mild, and the doors and windows of the old house stood all open, so that the people without could hear the the words of the preacher. I remember nothing he said: I remember of hearing my mother sob, and of seeing my grandmother with her face buried in her hands, and of seeing aunt Carry sitting erect, her face pale but tearless, and Oliver near her, with his hands folded across his breast save once or twice, when he lifted them to brush away tears.

I did not cry, save from a frightened and strange feeling, but kept wishing that we were not so near the dead, and that it were another day. I tried to push the reality away with thoughts of pleasant things—in vain. I remember the hymn, and the very air in which it was sung.

"Ye fearful souls fresh courage take
The clouds ye so much dread,
Are big with mercy, and shall break
In blessings on your head.
Blind unbelief is sure to err,
And scan his works in vain;
God is his own interpreter,
And he will make it plain."

Near the door blue flagstones were laid, bordered with a row of shrubberies and trees, with lilacs, and roses, and pears, and peach-trees, which my grandfather had planted long ago, and here, in the open air, the coffin was placed, and the white cloth removed, and folded over the lid. I remember how it shook and trembled as the gust came moaning from the woods, and died off over the next hill, and that two or three withered leaves fell on the face of the dead, which Oliver gently removed, and brushed aside a yellow-winged butterfly that hovered near.

The friends hung over the unsmiling corpse till they were led weeping and one by one away; the hand of some one rested for a moment on the forehead, and then the white cloth was replaced, and the lid screwed down. The coffin was placed in the brown wagon, with a sheet folded about it, and the long train moved slowly to the burial-ground woods, where the words "dust to dust" were followed by the rattling of the earth, and the sunset light fell there a moment, and the dead leaves blew across the smoothly shapen mound.

When the will was read, Oliver found himself heir to a fortune—the mill and the homestead and half the farm—provided he married Carry, which he must have done, for though I do not remember the wedding, I have had an aunt Caroline Hillhouse almost as long as I can remember. The lunatic sister was sent to an asylum, where she sung songs about a faithless lover till death took her up and opened her eyes in heaven. The mother was brought home, and she and my grandmother lived at their ease, and sat in the corner, and told stories of ghosts, and witches, and marriages, and deaths, for long years. Peace to their memories! for they have both gone home; and the lame brother is teaching school, in his leisure playing the flute, and reading Shakespeare—all the book he reads.

Years have come and swept me away from my childhood, from its innocence and blessed unconsciousness of the dark, but often comes back the memory of its first sorrow!

Death is less terrible to me now.

The death of her grandfather.
Is this autobiography or fiction?

THE WILDERMINGS

THERE CAME TO reside in the neighborhood a family consisting of three persons—an old lady, a young man, and a child some fourteen years of age. The place they took was divided by a little strip of woods from Clovernook, and I well remember how rejoiced I was on first seeing the blue smoke curling up from the high red chimneys; for the cottage had been a long time vacant, and the prospect of having people so near us, gave me delight. Perhaps, too, I was not the less pleased that they were to be new acquaintances. We are likely to underestimate persons and things we have continually about us; but let separation come, and we learn what they were to us. *Apropos* of this—in the little grove I have spoken of I remember there was an oak tree, taller by a great deal than its fellows; and a thousand times I have felt as though its mates must be oppressed with a painful sense of inferiority, and really wished the axe laid at its root. At last, one day, I heard the ringing strokes of that destroyer—and, on inquiry, was told that the woodman had orders no longer to spare the great oak. Eagerly I listened at first—every stroke was like the song of victory; then the gladness subsided, and I began to marvel how the woods would look with the monarch fallen; then I thought, their glory will have departed, and began to reflect on myself as having sealed the warrant of its death, so that when the crash, telling that it was fallen, woke the sleeping echoes from the hills, I cannot tell how sad a feeling it induced in my heart. If I could see it standing once more, just once more! but I could not, and till this day I feel a regretful pang when I think of that grand old tree.

But the new neighbors. Some curiosity mingled with my pleasure, and so, as soon as I thought they were settled, and feeling at home, I made my toilet with unusual care for a first call.

The cottage was a little way from the main road, and access to it was by a narrow grass-grown lane, bordered on one side by a green belt of meadow land, and on the other by the grove, sloping upward and backward to a clayey hill, where, with children and children's children about them,

"The rude forefathers of the hamlet slept."

A little farther on, but in full view of its stunted cypresses and white headstones, was the cottage. Of burial grounds generally I have no dread, but from this particular one I was accustomed, from childhood, to turn away with something of superstitious horror. I could never forget how Laura Hastings saw a light burning there all one winter night, after the death of John Hine, a wild, roving fellow, who never did any real harm in his life to any one but himself, hastening his own death by foolish excesses. Nevertheless, his ghost had been seen more than once, sitting on the cold mound beneath which the soul's expression was fading and crumbling: so, at least, said some of the oldest and most pious inhabitants of our neighborhood. There, too, Mary Wildermings, a fair young girl who died, more sinned against than sinning, had been heard to sing sad lullabies under the waning moon sometimes, and at other times had been seen sitting by her sunken grave, and braiding roses in her hair, as for a bridal. *I* never saw any of these wonderful things; but a spot more likely to be haunted by the unresting spirits of the bad could not readily be imagined. The woods, thick and full of birds, along the roadside, thinned away toward the desolate ridge, where briers grew over the mounds, and about and through the fallen fences, as they would, with here and there a little clearing among weeds and thistles and high matted grass, for the making of a new grave.

It was the twilight of a beautiful summer day, as I walked down the grassy lane and past the lonesome cemetery, to make this first call at the cottage, feeling, I scarcely knew why, strangely sad. By an old broken bridge in the hollow, between the cottage and the field of death I remember that I sat down, and for a long time listened to the trickling of the water over the pebbles, and watched golden spots of sunlight till they quite faded out, and "came still evening on, and twilight gray, that in her sober livery all things clad."

So quietly I sat, that the mole, beginning its blind work at sunset, loosened and stirred the ground beneath my feet, and the white, thick-winged moths, coming from beneath the dusty weeds, fluttered about me, and lightened in my lap, and the dull beating of the bat came almost in my face.

The first complaint of the owl sounded along the hollow and died over the next hill, warning me to proceed, when I heard,—as it were the echo of my own thought, repeated in a low, melancholy voice—the conclusion of that beautiful stanza of the elegy in reference to that moping bird. I distinctly caught the lines—

"Of such as wandering near her sacred bower,
Molest her ancient, solitary reign."

Looking up, I saw approaching slowly, with arms folded and eyes on the ground, a young and seemingly handsome man. He passed without noticing me at all, and I think without seeing me. But I had the better opportunity of observing him, though I would have foregone that privilege to win one glance. He interested me, and I felt humiliated that he should pass me with his unkind indifference. His face was pale and very sad, and his forehead shaded with a heavy mass of black hair, pushed away from one temple, and falling neglectedly over the other.

"Well!" said I, as I watched him ascending the opposite hill, feeling very much as though he had wantonly disregarded some claim I had on him, though I could not possibly have had the slightest; and, turning ill-humoredly away, I walked with a quick step toward the cottage.

A golden-haired young girl sat in the window reading, and on my approach arose and received me with easy gracefulness and well-bred courtesy, but during my stay her manner did not once border on cordiality. She was very beautiful, but her beauty was like that of statuary. The mother I did not see. She was, I was told, indisposed, and, on begging that she might not be disturbed, the daughter readily acquiesced. Every thing about the place indicated refinement and elegant habits, but whence the family came, how long they proposed to remain, and what relation the young man sustained to the rest, I would gladly have known.

Seeing a flute on the table, I spoke of music, for I suspected it to belong to the absent gentleman. I received no information, however; and as the twilight was already falling deeply, I felt a necessity to take leave, without obtaining even a glimpse of the person whom I had pictured in my fancy as so young and fair, and, of course so agreeable.

The sun had been set some time, but the moon had risen full and bright, so that I had no fear even in passing the graveyard, but walked more slowly than I had done before, till, reaching the gate, I paused to think of the awful mysteries of life and death.

This is not a very desolate spot after all, I thought, as, leaning over the gate, something of the quiet of the place infused itself into my spirits. Here, I felt, the wicked cease from troubling, and the weary are at rest; the long train of evils that attach to the best phases of humanity, is quite forgotten; the thorn-crown is loosened from the brow of sorrow by the white hand of peace, and the hearts that were all their lifetime under the shadows of great and haply unpitied afflictions never ache any more. And here, best of all! the frailties of the unresisting tempted, are folded away beneath the shroud, from the humiliating glances of pity, and the cold eyes of pride. We have need to be thankful that when man brought on the primal glory of his nature the mildew of sin, God did not cast us utterly from him, but in the unsearchable riches of his mercy struck open the refuge of the grave. If there were no fountain where our sins of scarlet might be washed white as wool, if the black night of death were not bordered by the golden shadows of the morning of immortality, if deep in the darkness were not sunken the foundations of the white bastions of peace, it were yet an inestimable privilege to lay aside the burden of life, for life becomes, sooner or later, a burden, and an echo among ruins.

In the corner of the burial ground, where the trees are thickest, a little apart from the rest, was the grave of Mary Wildermings, and year after year, the blue thistles bloomed and faded in its sunken sod.

The train of my reflections naturally suggested her, and, turning my eyes in the direction of her resting place, I saw, or thought I saw, the outline of a human figure. I remembered the story of her unresting ghost, and at first little doubted that I beheld it, and felt a tumult of strange emotions on finding myself thus alone near so questionable a shape.

Then, I said, this is some delusion of the senses; and I passed my hand over my eyes, for an uncertain glimmer had followed the intensity of my gaze. I looked towards the cottage to reassure myself by the light of a human habitation, but all there was dark; a cloud had passed over the moon, and, without venturing to look towards the haunted grave, I withdrew from the gate, very lightly, though it creaked as I did so. Any sound save the beating of my own heart gave me courage; and when I had walked a little way, I turned and looked again, but the dense shadow would have prevented my seeing any thing, if any thing had been there. Certain it is, I saw nothing.

On reaching home, I asked the housekeeper, a garrulous person usually, if she remembered Mary Wildermings, and what she could tell me of her burial, in the graveyard across the wood.

"Yes, I remember her, and she is buried in the corner of the ground, on the hill. They came to my house, I know, to get a cup, or something of the sort, with which to dip the water from her grave, for it rained terribly all the day of her funeral. She added, "But what do you want to talk of the dead and gone for, when there are living folks enough to talk about?"

Truth is, she wanted me to say something of our new neighbors, and was vexed that I did not, though I probably should have done so had they not been quite driven from my mind by the more absorbing event of the evening; so, as much vexed and disappointed as herself, I retired. The night was haunted with some troublous dreams, but a day of sunshine succeeded, and my thoughts flowed back to a more pleasing channel.

Days and weeks went by, and we neither saw nor heard anything of our new neighbors, for my call was not returned, nor did I make any further overtures towards an acquaintance. But often, as I sat under the apple tree by the door, in the twilight, I heard the mellow music of the distant flute.

"Is that at the cottage?" said the housekeeper to me, one night: "it sounds to me as though it were in the corner of the graveyard."

I smiled as she turned her head a little to one side, and encircling the right ear with her hand, listened some minutes eagerly, and then proceeded to express her conviction that the music was the result of no mortal agency.

"Did you ever hear of a ghost playing the flute?" I said.

"A flute!" she answered, indignantly, "it's a flute, just as much as you are a flute; and for the sake of enlightening your blind understanding, I'll go to the graveyard, night as it is, if you will go with me."

"Very well," I said; "let us go."

So, under the faint light of the crescent moon, we took our way together. Gradually the notes became lower and sadder, and at length quite died away. I urged my trembling companion to walk faster, lest the ghost should vanish too; and she acceded to my wish with a silent alacrity, that convinced me at once of the sincerity of her expressed belief. Just as we began to ascend the hill, she stopped suddenly, saying, "There! did you hear that?"

I answered, that I heard a noise, but that it was no unusual thing to hear such sounds in an inhabited neighborhood, at so early an hour. "It was the latching of the gate at the graveyard," she answered solemnly. "As you value your immortal soul, go no further."

In vain I argued, that a ghost would have no need to unlatch the gate. She positively refused to go farther, and with a courage not very habitual to me, I walked on alone.

"Do you think I don't know that sound?" she called after me. "I would know if I had forgotten everything else. Oh, stop, till I tell you! The night Mary Wildermings died," I heard her say; but I knew the sound of the gate as well as she, and would not wait even for a ghost story. I have since wished I had, for I could never afterwards persuade her to proceed with it.

Gaining the summit of the hill, I saw, a little way before me, a dark figure, receding slowly; but so intent was I on the superhuman, that I paid little heed to the human; though afterward, in recalling the circumstance, the individual previously seen while I sat on the bridge became in some way associated with this one.

How hushed and solemn the graveyard seemed! I was half afraid, as I looked in—quite startled, in fact, when, latching and unlatching the gate, to determine whether the sound I had heard were that or not, a rabbit, roused from its light sleep, under the fallen grass, sped fleetly across the still mounds to the safer shelter of the woods. I saw nothing else, save that the grass was trampled to a narrow path all the way leading toward Mary's grave.

During the summer, I sometimes saw the young girl in the woods, and I noticed that she neither gathered flowers nor sang with the birds; but would sit for hours in some deep shadow, without moving her position in the least, not even to push away the light curls which the wind blew over her cheeks and forehead, as they would. She seemed neither to love nor seek human companionship. Once only I noticed, and it was the last time she ever walked in the woods, that he whom I supposed to be her brother was with her. She did not sit in the shade, as usual, but walked languidly, and leaning heavily on the arm of her attendant, who several times swept off the curls from her forehead, and bent down, as if kissing her.

A few days afterwards, being slightly indisposed, I called in the village doctor. Our conversation, naturally, was of who was sick and who was dead.

"Among my patients," he said, "there is none that interests me so deeply as a little girl at the cottage—indeed, I have scarcely thought of anything else, since I knew that she must die. A strange child," he continued; "she seems to feel neither love of life nor fear of death, nor does she either weep or smile; and though I have been with her much of late, I have never seen her sleep. She suffers no pain—her face wears the same calm expression, but her melancholy eyes are wide open all the time."

The second evening after this, though not quite recovered myself, I called at the cottage, in the hope of being of some service to the sick girl. The snowy curtain was dropped over the window of her chamber, the sash partly raised, and all within still—very still. The door was a little way open, and, pausing, I heard from within a low, stifled moan, which I could not misunderstand, and pushing the door aside, I entered, without rapping.

In the white sheet, drawn straight over the head and the feet, I recognised at once the fearful truth—the little girl was dead. By the head of the bed, and still as one stricken into stone, sat the person I so often wished to see. The room was nearly dark, and his face was buried in his hands—nevertheless, I knew him—it was he who had passed me on the bridge.

Presently the housekeeper, or one that I took to be her, entered, and whispering to him, he arose and went out, so that I saw him but imperfectly. When he was gone, the woman folded the covering away from the face, and to my horror I saw that the eyes were still unclosed. Seeing my surprise, she said, as she folded a napkin, and pinned it close over the lids—

"It is strange, but the child would never in life close her eyes—her mother, they say, died in watching for one who never came, and the baby was watchful and sleepless from the first."

The next day, and the next, it was dull and rainy—excitement and premature exposure had induced a return of my first indisposition, so that I was not at the funeral. I saw, however, from my window, preparations for the burial—to my surprise, in the lonesome little graveyard by the woods.

In the course of a fortnight, I prepared for a visit of condolence to the cottage, but on reaching it, found the inhabitants gone—the place still and empty.

Returning, I stopped at the haunted ground: close by the grave of Mary Wildermings was that of the stranger child. The briers and thistles had been carefully cut away, there was no slab and no name over either, but the blue and white violets were planted thickly about both. That they slept well, was all I knew.

An unsolved mystery about the family in the next cottage over – who they are, their relations to one another and to Mary Wildermings, buried in graveyard. the girl of the family dies and is buried next to Mary W.

MRS. HILL AND MRS. TROOST

IT WAS JUST two o'clock of one of the warmest of the July afternoons. Mrs. Hill had her dinner all over, had put on her clean cap and apron, and was sitting on the north porch, making an unbleached cotton shirt for Mr. Peter Hill, who always wore unbleached shirts at harvest time. Mrs. Hill was a thrifty housewife. She had been pursuing this economical avocation for some little time, interrupting herself only at times to *"shu!"* away the flocks of half-grown chickens that came noisily about the door for the crumbs from the table-cloth, when the sudden shutting down of a great blue cotton umbrella caused her to drop her work, and exclaim—

"Well, now, Mrs. Troost! who would have thought you ever *would* come to see me!"

"Why, I have thought a great many times I would come," said the visitor, stamping her little feet—for she was a little woman—briskly on the blue flag stones, and then dusting them nicely with her white cambric handkerchief, before venturing on the snowy floor of Mrs. Hill. And, shaking hands, she added, "It *has* been a good while, for I remember when I was here last I had my Jane with me—quite a baby then, if you mind—and she is three years old now."

"Is it possible?" said Mrs. Hill, untying the bonnet strings of her neighbor, who sighed, as she continued, "Yes, she was three along in February," and she sighed again, more heavily than before, though there was no earthly reason that I know of why she should sigh, unless perhaps the flight of time, thus brought to mind, suggested the transitory nature of human things.

Mrs. Hill laid the bonnet of Mrs. Troost on her "spare bed," and covered it with a little, pale-blue crape shawl, kept especially for like occasions; and, taking from the drawer of the bureau a large fan of turkey feathers, she presented it to her guest, saying, "A very warm day, isn't it?"

"Oh, dreadful, dreadful; it seems as hot as a bake oven; and I suffer with the heat all summer, more or less. But it's a world of suffering;" and Mrs. Troost half closed her eyes, as if to shut out the terrible reality.

"Hay-making requires sunshiny weather, you know; so we must put up with it," said Mrs. Hill; "besides, I can mostly find some cool place about the house; I keep my sewing here on the porch, and, as I bake my bread or cook my dinner, manage to catch it up sometimes, and so keep from getting over heated; and then, too, I get a good many stitches taken in the course of the day."

"This *is* a nice, cool place—completely curtained with vines," said Mrs. Troost; and she sighed again; "they must have cost you a great deal of pains."

"Oh, no—no trouble at all; morning-glories grow themselves; they only require to be planted. I will save seed for you this fall, and next summer you can have your porch as shady as mine."

"And if I do, it would not signify," said Mrs. Troost; "I never get time to sit down from one week's end to another; besides, I never had any luck with vines; some folks have'nt, you know."

Mrs. Hill was a woman of a short, plethoric habit; one that might be supposed to move about with little agility, and to find excessive warmth rather inconvenient; but she was of a happy, cheerful temperament; and when it rained she tucked up her skirts, put on thick shoes, and waddled about the same as ever, saying to herself, "This will make the grass grow," or "it will bring on the radishes," or something else equally consolatory.

Mrs. Troost, on the contrary, was a little thin woman, who looked as though she might move about nimbly at any season; but, as she herself often said, she was a poor unfortunate creature, and pitied herself a great deal, as she was in justice bound to do, for nobody else cared, she said, how much she had to bear.

They were near neighbors—these good women—but their social

interchanges of tea-drinking were not of very frequent occurrence, for sometimes Mrs. Troost had nothing to wear like other folks; sometimes it was too hot, and sometimes it was too cold; and then again, nobody wanted to see her, and she was sure she didn't want to go where she wasn't wanted. Moreover, she had such a great barn of a house as no other woman ever had to take care of. But in all the neighborhood it was called the big house, so Mrs. Troost was in some measure compensated for the pains it cost her. It was, however, as she said, a barn of a place, with half the rooms unfurnished, partly because they had no use for them, and partly because they were unable to get furniture. So it stood right in the sun, with no shutters, and no trees about it, and Mrs. Troost said she didn't suppose it ever would have. She was always opposed to building it, but she never had her way about anything. Nevertheless, some people said Mr. Troost had taken the dimensions of his house with his wife's apron strings—but that may have been slander.

While Mrs. Troost sat sighing over things in general, Mrs. Hill sewed on the last button, and shaking the loose threads from the completed garment, held it up a moment to take a satisfactory view, as it were, and folded it way.

"Well, did you ever!" said Mrs. Troost; "you have made half a shirt, and I have got nothing at all done. My hands sweat so I can't use the needle, and it's no use to try."

"Lay down your work for a little while, and we will walk in the garden."

So Mrs. Hill threw a towel over her head, and taking a little tin basin in her hand, the two went to the garden—Mrs. Troost under the shelter of the blue umbrella, which she said was so heavy that it was worse than nothing. Beans, radishes, raspberries, and currants, besides many other things, were there in profusion, and Mrs. Troost said everything flourished for Mrs. Hill, while her garden was all choked up with weeds. "And you have bees, too—don't they sting the children, and give you a great deal of trouble? Along in May, I guess it was, Troost (Mrs. Troost always called her husband so) bought a hive, or rather he traded a calf for one—a nice, likely calf, too, it was—and they never did us one bit of good"—and the unhappy woman sighed.

"They *do* say," said Mrs. Hill, sympathizingly, "that bees won't work for some folks; in case their king dies they are very likely to quarrel, and not do well; but we have never had any any ill luck with ours; and we last year sold forty dollars worth of honey, besides having all we wanted for our own use. Did yours die off, or what, Mrs. Troost?"

"Why," said the ill-natured visitor, "my oldest boy got stung one day, and, being angry, upset the hive, and I never found it out for two or three days; and sending Troost to put it up in its place, there was not a bee to be found, high or low."

"You don't tell! the obstinate little creatures! but they must be treated kindly, and I have heard of their going off for less things."

The basin was by this time filled with currants, and they returned to the house. Mrs. Hill, seating herself on the sill of the kitchen door, began to prepare her fruit for tea, while Mrs. Troost drew her chair near, saying, "Did you ever hear about William McMicken's bees?"

Mrs. Hill had never heard, and expressing an anxiety to do so, was told the following story:

"His wife, you know, was she that was Sally May, and it's an old saying—

'To change the name, and not the letter,
You marry for worse, and not for better.'

"Sally was a dressy, extravagant girl; she had her bonnet 'done up' twice a year always, and there was no end to her frocks and ribbons and fine things. Her mother indulged her in everything; she used to say Sally deserved all she got; that she was worth her weight in gold. She used to go everywhere, Sally did. There was no big meeting that she was not at, and no quilting that she didn't help to get up. All the girls went to her for the fashions, for she was a good deal in town at her Aunt Hanner's, and always brought out the new patterns. She used to have her sleeves a little bigger than anybody else, you remember, and then she wore great stiffners in them—la, me! there was no end to her extravagance.

"She had a changeable silk, yellow and blue, made with a surplus front; and when she wore that, the ground wasn't good enough for her to walk on, so some folks used to say; but I never thought Sally was a bit proud or lifted up; and if anybody was sick, there was no better-hearted creature than she; and then, she was always good-natured as the day was long, and would sing all the time at her work. I remember, along before she was married, she used to sing one song a great deal, beginning

'I've got a sweetheart with bright black eyes;'

and they said she meant William McMicken by that, and that she might not get him after all—for a good many thought they would never make a match, their dispositions were so contrary. William was of a dreadful quiet turn, and a great home body; and as for being rich, he had nothing to brag of, though he was high larnt, and followed the river as clark* sometimes."

Mrs. Hill had by this time prepared her currants, and Mrs. Troost paused from her story while she filled the kettle, and attached the towel to the end of the well-sweep, where it waved as a signal for Peter to come to supper.

"Now, just move your chair a leetle nearer the kitchen door, if you please," said Mrs. Hill, "and I can make up my biscuit, and hear you, too."

Meantime, coming to the door with some bread-crumbs in her hand, she began scattering them on the ground, and calling, "Biddy, biddy, biddy—chicky, chicky, chicky"—hearing which, a whole flock of poultry was about her in a minute; and stooping down, she secured one of the fattest, which, an hour afterwards, was broiled for supper.

"Dear me, how easily you get along!" said Mrs. Troost.

And it was some time before she could compose herself sufficiently to take up the thread of her story. At length, however, she began with—

"Well, as I was saying, nobody thought William McMicken would marry Sally May. Poor man, they say he is not like himself any more. He may get a dozen wives, but he'll never get another Sally. A good wife she made him, for all she was such a wild girl.

"The old man May was opposed to the marriage, and threatened to turn Sally, his own daughter, out of house and home; but she was

*"Followed the river as clark" means "worked on a steamboat as a clerk," but with the sense of going from boat to boat, thus earning one's living by following the river.

headstrong, and would marry whom she pleased; and so she did, though she never got a stitch of new clothes, nor one thing to keep house with. No; not one single thing did her father give her, when she went away, but a hive of bees. He was right down ugly, and called her Mrs. McMicken whenever he spoke to her after she was married; but Sally didn't seem to mind it, and took just as good care of the bees as though they were worth a thousand dollars. Every day in winter she used to feed them—maple-sugar, if she had it; and if not, a little Muscovade* in a saucer or some old broken dish.

"But it happened one day that a bee stung her on the hand—the right one, I think it was,—and Sally said right away that it was a bad sign; and that very night she dreamed that she went out to feed her bees, and a piece of black crape was tied on the hive. She felt that it was a token of death, and told her husband so, and she told me and Mrs. Hanks. No, I won't be sure she told Mrs. Hanks, but Mrs. Hanks got to hear it some way."

"Well," said Mrs. Hill, wiping the tears away with her apron, "I really didn't know, till now, that poor Mrs. McMicken was dead."

"Oh, she is not dead," answered Mrs. Troost, "but as well as she ever was, only she feels that she is not long for this world." The painful interest of her story, however, had kept her from work, so the afternoon passed without her having accomplished much—she never could work when she went visiting.

Meantime Mrs. Hill had prepared a delightful supper, without seeming to give herself the least trouble. Peter came precisely at the right moment, and, as he drew a pail of water, removed the towel, from the well-sweep, easily and naturally, thus saving his wife the trouble.

"Troost would never have thought of it," said his wife; and she finished with an "Ah, well!" as though all her tribulations would be over before long.

As she partook of the delicious honey, she was reminded of her own upset hive, and the crisp-red radishes brought thoughts of the weedy garden at home; so that, on the whole, her visit, she said, made her perfectly wretched, and she should have no heart for a week; nor did the

*Muscovade is unrefined cane sugar.

little basket of extra nice fruit, which Mrs. Hill presented her as she was about to take leave, brighten her spirits in the least. Her great heavy umbrella, she said, was burden enough for her.

"But Peter will take you in the carriage," insisted Mrs. Hill.

"No," said Mrs. Troost, as though charity were offered her; "it will be more trouble to get in and out than to walk"—and so she trudged home, saying, "Some folks are born to be lucky."

Opposite female personalities:
Mrs. Hill is efficient and productive
Mrs. Troost is a lazy gossip

doubling
temperment
Sketch vs. Story - no change

ABOUT THE TOMPKINSES

NOT UNLIKE THE Whitfields, were a family in another direction from Clovernook, named Tompkins. The Tompkinses were not quite so respectable as the deacon's folks; they were not so well-to-do in the world, and were by no means regular in their attendance at meeting; and their relations, generally, were of a lower level. Nevertheless the two families were in many respects very much alike, and, as this chapter will show, liable to similar experiences.

It was dark and chilly out of doors, as it well might be, for the sun had been set an hour, and the snow was falling in great heavy flakes. The little branches of the sweet-brier that grew close under the window, were bending lower and lower, and the cherry-trees, beside the house, looked like pyramids, so much snow had lodged in their limbs. On the sill, the great watch dog lay crouched from the cold, and whined sometimes as he heard the merry laughter of the children within, who, in the warm sunshiny days, were often his play-fellows. These children were three, the eldest, a girl of above fifteen, silently knitting by the firelight, for the hickory logs blazed brightly on the great stone hearth, making the silver spoons, fancifully set up in a kind of paling along the open dresser, and before the carefully outspread china, to glow and glitter in the warm cheerful light. The other children were boys of nine and eleven, as like as two peas, with the exception of a slight difference in size. Their hair was a sandy-yellow, cut in a straight line over the forehead, and an inch or so above their big gray eyes; and never was it perceptibly longer or shorter, for once a month, at the time of the new moon, their good mother, combing it very smoothly, tied it down with a string, and trimmed it off with mathematical precision. Their faces were round, and completely gray with freckles; their cheeks standing out with fatness, and shining as if just washed; and their hands of the chubby sort, red, and checked off, just now, with the cold. When they were tired of play—for they had been for an hour boisterously chasing each other about the room, tearing up the carpet in every direction, and tumbling and jostling against their sister, who, knitting quietly, did not seem to heed them—they lay down before the fire, and commenced a kind of whining cry, which as one ceased, from exhaustion, the other took up.

"I say, Susan, give me something to eat; give me something, I say; I'm hungry, I am; Susan, give me some cake—I'll tell mammy—see if I don't."

"You had better be still," said Susan, at last, quite worn out; "I hear your father coming." Susan never said "father," when speaking to her brothers, but "your father," as though she were a great deal older, and a great deal wiser than they—quite out of the reach of paternal authority, in fact, which was by no means the case, she being yet considered a mere child by her parents, though she had attained the stature and full development of womanhood and in every way her privileges were much more circumscribed than were those of her saucy brothers; and it cannot be denied that she sometimes exercised the power she found herself possessed of, in something such sort as she was accustomed to feel, and if her brothers had continued their sniveling all night, they would not have obtained the cake with her permission; and though she threatened them with the approach of their father, it was on her own account, and not theirs, for she well knew they would not have to repeat the request in his hearing.

In a moment there was a muffled stamping on the snowy door-steps, and Mr. Tompkins, with a very red face, and an unusually surly expression, presented himself. Now, Mr. Tompkins was of the most bland and genial manner imaginable, when he went visiting, or to mill, or to meeting, but at home, he maintained the most uncompromising austerity, only relaxing a little when some neighbor chanced to drop in. He evidently thought the least talk with his children, on terms of equality, an abatement of proper dignity, and so he seldom talked, and never smiled, for that might seem to imply a willingness to talk. To Mrs. Tompkins, he sometimes yielded a little, because she would talk whether he responded or not.

Drawing off his great coat, he shook out the snow, some of which fell on the upturned faces of the two boys, and some in the lap of Susan, making her needles grate under their yarn stitches. This accomplished, he hung it on the back of a chair before the fire to dry, and taking off his hat, shook it roughly over his hand, by way of loosening the snow from the little fur that remained on it. Mr. Tompkins never got a new hat, at least not since I remember, though his wife wore fine shawls and dresses.

William and John, meantime, kept up their cry for the cake, but not till Mr. Tompkins had been sometime seated before the fire, and quite a little puddle of water had thawed from his boots, and soiled the bluestone hearth, did he sanction their appeal—not by words, but by slowly and gravely turning his head toward Susan, and slightly elevating his eyebrows, perceiving which, she at once put down her work, lighted a tallow candle, and went to the cellar, to do which, she was obliged to go out of doors, and half-way round the house, whence she presently returned with her light blown out by the wind, and a great rent in her apron, caused by its catching, in the dark, on the loose hoop of the vinegar-barrel. The tears came to her eyes, partly from anger, partly from sorrow, for the apron was of silk, and made with special reference to a gathering of friends, which was to take place the next evening at Dr. Haywood's. It was made of old material to be sure, being composed of two breadths of her mother's brown wedding dress; but she had done her best for it, dipping it in water, and ironing it, while wet, and setting it off with knots of ribbon, which, by the way, it would have looked much better without, as they were of an unsuitable color, in some places of very deep dye, and in others pale, from having been worn one summer on the bonnet of Mrs. Tompkins, and two on that of Susan. But how should she know, poor child! She had seen Mary Haywood wear an apron similarly adorned, and naturally wished to be in the fashion. She was by no means in the habit of wearing a silk apron at home, but she had completed this in her mother's absence, and under pretence of showing its effect—a harmless stratagem—as a quiet reminder of the approaching party, she had ventured to wear it for one evening.

In every neighborhood there must be one family more fashionable, more aristocratic, than the rest. This family, in Clovernook, was the Haywoods. Owing more to fallen fortunes, than for the sake of free air and exercise for the children—the ostensible motive—they had but lately removed from the city, where they had previously resided, to the farm adjoining that of Mr. Tompkins. The dilapidated homestead, with the addition of new wings, piazzas, shutters, and some green and white paint, was speedily made to assume a cottage-like and comfortable appearance. The main entrance was adorned with a silver plate, on which was engraved, the name of Dr. Haywood, and this, with the bell-handle, completed the effect: no other house in the neighborhood boasting such superfluous ornaments.

Dr. Haywood, naturally of a social and democratic manner, and a little influenced, it may be, by the hope of professional success, was not long in making himself a very popular man. He even condescended to accept the office of trustee of the district school—attending on set occasions, and inspecting copybooks and geographies, and listening to the children's rhetorical readings from Peter Parley's First Book of History, with an easy dignity, as though

"Native and to the manner born."

He also interested himself in the improvement of stock, and was a frequent visitor to the barnyards of his neighbors, talking of his own wheat and potato crops, and now and then asking advice relative to the rules of planting and harvesting.

Still there were some malcontents, who persisted in calling the family "big-bugs," for that Mrs. Haywood wore flowers in her cap every day, kept a negro woman in the kitchen, and had visitors from town. Moreover, the Doctor, though he had been seen in his shirt-sleeves among the hay-makers, very rarely, it must be owned, wrought with his own hands. But the prejudice almost ended, when he made a great raising for his new barn, to which he invited all the men and boys, in person, very often repeating the jest, that a farmer must have a barn whether he had any house or not. At the conclusion of the raising, a very excellent supper was provided—Mrs. Haywood doing the honors of the coffee-urn, and inviting all the men to come and bring their wives, regretting her own poor efforts to make the neighborhood social.

This dissolved much of the unkind feeling, but any innovation on established custom, is likely to meet opposition among much wiser people than those of whom I write, and Mr. and Mr. Tompkins could or would not be reconciled to folks who stuck themselves up with their waiters and door-bells. Mrs. Haywood, waiving ceremony, had herself made the first call, and the Doctor had made informal visits to Mr. Tompkins, in the barn, repeatedly, with no effect.

Susan, however, had none of the obstinancy of her parents, and consequently when she received a written invitation, to honor, with her presence, Mary Haywood's birth-day, she was on tip-toe with the desire to go. To her great discomfort, she had as yet received but little encouragement, her father treating the whole thing as preposterous, and her mother, though there was sometimes a yielding in her look, seeming to feel that her dignity required her to present an unshaken front against all temptations. So the probabilities of the gratification of Susan's darling wish were exceedingly dubious, up to the time referred to in the beginning of this chapter, which was the evening preceding the "Haywood fandango," as Mrs. Tompkins was pleased to describe it.

Stealthily, time and again, had Susan examined her scanty wardrobe, trying on all her old summer dresses to see which would look the best; but as they were all faded calicoes, it was difficult to make a choice. In her own mind, at last, she decided on a pink, and bringing it from its winter quarters to press it off, and make it look as smart as possible, her mother, as if without the remotest conception of its intended use, dampened, and almost prostrated all her hopes, by inquiring what she intended to do with that thin gewgaw, this time of year. The poor child could not summon the courage to say what she felt her mother already knew, and so, simply remarking that she wanted to see how it looked, carried it away, and hung it in its accustomed place. In a day or two her hopes revived, and she made up the brown apron, with which she felt pretty well satisfied, picturing to herself how it would look with the pink dress, until the fatal hour it received that "envious rent."

There was one hope left: if her mother would only let her wear her

Sunday silk! True, it might not fit precisely, but no body would notice that; she would ask, as soon as her mother came home; at any rate, there was a bare possibility of success. Stimulated with this hope, and revolving in her mind in what way she should approach the subject, she again took up her knitting, and tried to forget her ruined apron, but her courage sadly misgave her, when, towards eight o'clock, looking as blustery as the storm through which she had been plodding, her mother returned. She had been to the village—for Tompkins's house was nearly a mile from Clover-nook—to look at a corpse.

"Well, mother, doesn't it snow pretty hard?" said Mr. Tompkins, breaking silence for the first time during the evening. "Why, no," said the good woman; "there's now and then a flake, but I think it's quite too warm to snow." She thought the remark implied a reproof to her for being out.

"I hope it will stop before to-morrow night," said Susan, and her fingers flew faster than before; and receiving no notice, she continued, after a moment, "because I can't go to the party if it snows."

"I guess you can't if it don't snow," said Mrs. Tompkins, and Susan felt it almost a relief, when one of the children, rising from his recumbent posture on the carpet, said, "Mammy, Susan tore her new silk apron, she did." "I'll dare say, Susan is always doing mischief—how did it happen, child?" she continued, querulously, taking the torn apron in her hand, and fitting it together. Susan explained how it chanced, but her mother said, "if she had not had it on, as she had no business to have it, this would not have happened."

There is no telling how long she would have gone on, but for the boy's asking her why she didn't get him something pretty, to which she replied, "Something pretty costs money: do you think it grows on bushes? Your father and me have to get you shoes, and coats, and something to eat, and to pay your schooling, and I don't know what all, before we get pretty things." Mrs. Tompkins always talked to her children as if they were greatly to blame for wanting anything, or, in fact, for being in the world at all; and it did not soften her present mood when the child continued, that Walter Haywood had a knife, and he wanted one.

"Walter Haywood," she replied, "has a great many things that you can't have; and if you had everything he has, you couldn't be Walter Haywood: they are rich folks."

Mr. and Mrs. Tompkins embraced every opportunity of impressing their children with the consciousness of their humility and unworthiness; and, in keeping with this, she on the present occasion told her little boy that *he* could not be Walter Haywood—as though he belonged to quite a different order of beings.

The little fellow sat down and hung his head, feeling very uncomfortable. At length he asked his mother when he should grow big—thinking, childishly, perhaps, of some great thing he might then do. "La, child," she said, "I don't know any more than the man in the moon: here, Susan, take him to bed—it's time little boys were asleep."

So he was reluctantly dragged away, without any sort of idea when he should become a man, and feeling that most likely he could not be like Walter Haywood, if he were one.

When Susan returned, she found her parents engaged in an unusually lively conversation about the recent death, and the time of the funeral, and who would preach, and Mrs. Tompkins concluded by saying "it was a very pretty corpse, and looked just as natural."

Mrs. Tompkins went to look at every body who died within four or five miles—a peculiar taste, that of hers—and Susan thought her mother's heart must be softened, and was about to ask if she might go to the party, when she suddenly turned the conversation in a different channel by exclaiming in a very earnest tone—"Have you heard, father, of the great robbery last night?"

"No, mother, I can't say that I have; *I've* been busy in the barn, winnowing up a few bushels of oats." There was another evident reproof, and Mrs. Tompkins was silent, perceiving which, he asked where the robbery was, and what its nature.

"At Mr. Miller's;" and the offended was again silent.

"What was lost?"

"Some hams, I believe, and other things."

"How many hams, and what other things?"

"I didn't ask how many; a fine shirt was taken, too."

"Do they suspect anybody in particular?"

"Yes."

"Who is it? somebody about here?"

"Not very far off."

"Ah, indeed!" and Mr. Tompkins seemed to feel no further curiosity. Whereupon, Mrs. Tompkins put the embers together and related all she knew of the matter.

"I expect," she said, "I have the story pretty straight: Mrs. Miller told me herself about it. She says she thinks she was awake at the very time. She had some toothache, along the fore part of the night, and didn't get to sleep till almost midnight, and then she got into a kind of a doze, and dreamed, she said, that all the cattle had broke into the door-yard, and the dog was trying to drive them out; and then, she said, she thought one of the cows hooked open the smokehouse-door, and she was scared, for she thought she would eat up a bag of buckwheat that had been put in there that day; and she woke up with a kind of start, she said, and the dog was barking and making a dreadful racket, and she thought at first she would get up, and then she thought it was foolish—it was just some of the neighbor's dogs or something or other, and so she lay still and went to sleep. When she got up in the morning, she said, she saw the smokehouse-door open, but she though the wind had blown it open, likely, and didn't think anything till she went out to cut the ham for breakfast, and found them all gone, and the bag of buckwheat into the bargain. It seems likely it was somebody that had some spite against them, she says, for Mr. Troost had his hams there being smoked, and not one of them was touched."

"That *is* strange," said Mr. Tompkins; "we must get a pad lock; they'll be after us next. Mr. Miller is pretty spunky; I shouldn't wonder, mother, if he got out a search-warrant."

"There has a family lately moved into Mr. Hill's old house, that people think are no better than they should be," said Mrs. Tompkins. "They don't work, they say, and no body knows how they live; but we all know they must eat, and some think they get it between two days. Did you bring the towels off the line, Susan?"

Mr. Tompkins put on his great-coat, and taking the hammer from the mantel where it always lay, went out and nailed up the door of the smokehouse, and chained the dog to the cellar door—making him a kennel of an old barrel, which he turned down for the purpose, and partly filled with straw, for he was merciful to his beasts. This done, he wound up his watch, hung it under the looking-glass, after first holding it to his ear a moment, and retired. Mrs. Tompkins stirred up a little jar of batter-cakes for breakfast, covering it with a clean towel, and placing it on the hearth to rise; and, telling Susan it was time for little girls to be sleepy, went to bed.

After thinking over the chances for the next evening—whether she should be able to go, and if so, whether her mother would let her have the dress, and in that case how it would look—that young lady betook herself to her chamber.

In the morning she arose bright and early, and had the breakfast nearly prepared when her mother came down, for she hoped in that way to merit a little extra indulgence. Cheerfully she flew about the house, doing everything, and more than everything, that was required of her—singing snatches of songs, and running after the children, who were always ready with, "Susan, give me something."

Dinner came and passed just as usual, and Mrs. Tompkins prepared to go to the funeral without speaking of the evening. While she was gone, Susan put all her best things where she could readily get them, combed and arranged her hair in the most tasteful manner imaginable, and made ready the tea, so that nothing could detain her. She could not eat any supper, and finding longer suspense intolerable, said abruptly, "Mother may I go?"

"Go where, child?"

"To Mary Haywood's party: all the girls are going, and I want to go."

"It's a pretty story, if you are to be running about to parties of nights, child as you are! What do you think Mary Haywood wants of you? besides, I have use for you at home."

Poor Susan; it would be in vain to attempt a description of her feelings, but they availed nothing, and with a terrible headache she sat down to her knitting—her brothers saying every now and then, "Eh, Susan, I knew you wouldn't get to go, if you did comb your hair so nice!"

The crickets chirped under the hearth—the boughs of the cherry-trees creaked against the panes, as the rough wind went and came: to Susan it had never seemed so lonesome, and she scarcely could help the wish she were out of the world. Suddenly the dog rattling his chain, barked furiously, then was still for a moment, and then barked louder than before. There was a stamping at the door, and a loud quick knock. "Come in," said Mr. Tompkins.

"And presently the latch was raised,
And the door flew open wide,
And a stranger stood within the hall."

He was a dark handsome fellow, of perhaps twenty—in one hand holding a small knapsack, and in the other a fine rifle, highly polished and profusely plated with silver, together with a string of dead birds. He bowed gracefully to the old people, and something more than gracefully to Susan; and then asked Mr. Tompkins if he were the proprietor of the farm—and whether he would like to hire an assistant. Mr. Tompkins said he "believed not; he had not much to do in the winter; was not very well able to hire," &c. But Mrs. Tompkins was generally opposed to her husband in every thing, and said she "thought for her part there was plenty do do; all the fences were out of repair, which would be work enough for one man for six months—then it would soon be sugar-making, and what could one man do without help?"

"I don't know but you are right, mother," said the husband; "what may be your terms, young man?"

This the young man scarcely knew; he was not a farmer, but was willing to do his best, and receive whatever should be right. So it was agreed that he should remain for a month, and putting by knapsack and gun, he drew up to the fire, and was soon quite at home—relating odd adventures of travel, and talking of different countries, and, also, saying something of himself. He was, as the conversation developed, a Frenchman, who coming to this country to seek his fortune, had exhausted his means, and finding himself slightly out of health, had resolved to spend some months in the country for the benefit of both.

In listening to his stories of sea and land—for he talked well, Susan forgot Mary Haywood and her party; and when he bid her goodnight, he called her Miss Tompkins, producing a new and altogether charming sensation, for every one had called her Susan, or Miss Susan, till then.

The next day Mr. Maurice Doherty, for that was his name, accompanied Mr. Tompkins to mill, taking his rifle to bring down any game that might chance to put itself in his way. During the day, Susan found time to mend her apron, and also to press with extra care her black flannel frock, in which, having prepared tea, she arrayed herself, and sat down with her knitting, as usual, but listened very eagerly for the rumbling of the mill wagon. At last it came, and when the horses were duly stabled, and the bags deposited in the barn, Maurice presented himself, with three birds in his hand, their wings dropping loose and sprinkled with blood. These he presented to Susan, giving her directions as to the best method of dressing them, which she engaged to undertake, for his breakfast.

She was not handsome, being short and chubby, but she was sprightly, intelligent, of an exceedingly fair complexion—which, especially when talking to Maurice, became roseate—and she really looked pretty.

At breakfast the birds were forthcoming, and Mr. Doherty said he had never before eaten any that were so deliciously seasoned. He understood much better than Dr. Haywood, how to ingratiate himself with the old people and was not long in becoming a great favorite with them; so that when the month of his engagement was expired, he was re-engaged for three months longer.

Time wore on—the fences were propt and mended, stumps uprooted, apple-trees trimmed, and many other things done, making Mr. Tompkins feel how much better than one, two persons could attend to his farm.

He should never try to get along alone again, and now that he had assistance, he proposed building a little cabin in the edge of the sugar-camp, which would be an admirable convenience during the sugar making, and could afterwards when Maurice was gone, be let to a tenant. The young man entered heartily into the merits of the plan, and the work immediately began. But Maurice insisted on its being well done; "it was," he said, "the first house he had ever built, and it must be worthily executed: a carpenter must be had to make the door and windows, to lay the floor and put in a closet or two, and a mason to build the chimney and lay down the hearth. Mr. Tompkins contended stoutly that it was all a useless expense; it was only for a tenant; but Maurice urged the propriety of its being comfortable and durable, and finally carried the point; and when it was completed, it was really a convenient and habitable looking cottage, especially when the fire was made on the hearth for the sugar-making.

During the season, Susan was often sent down to tend the kettles, while Maurice went to the house, to attend the evening chores. But the cottage was all bright with fire-light, and Maurice entertained his guest so pleasantly, that she sometimes chanced to stay after he returned. One twilight, toward the close of the sugaring, Susan tied on her bonnet, and taking a little basket of apples and cakes with which Maurice might regale himself and wile away the time, went to the "camp."

Al the way she was thinking, The sugar-making will soon be over, and Maurice will go away; and she felt very sad; she did not ask herself why, she only knew she had never been so happy as while he was there, and she would be very lonesome when he was gone.

"Why, what is the matter with my little wood-nymph?" said Maurice, as she presented the basket and was sorrowfully turning away; "you must sit down and tell me."

She did sit down, and half turning away her face, said simply, "I was thinking that we might, perhaps, never boil sugar here any more."

"Perhaps not," said Maurice, putting his arm about her neck and turning her cheek to his lips, "but couldn't we live here without boiling sugar?"

The following morning after breakfast, he told Mr. Tompkins if he was still disposed to let the cottage, he and Susan would take it.

The story of Susan Tompkins who has a tough rural life and no pleasures of a young woman. Maurice comes by looking for work, stays, and marries her, moving in to the cabin they built.
Story of smokehouse robbers is left unresolved.

THE SISTERS

YEARS AGONE, there lived in a humble dwelling, a little way from Clovernook, two little girls, neither beautiful nor yet inordinately plain. They were sisters, loving each other with a love that was more than love; but they were not, as might be supposed, the only children of their parents. Not precisely alike in their disposition, though perhaps the better mated on that very account, they were never from their first years separated for a single day. In the woods and the orchards, on the hills, out in the meadows, and at school, they were still together. The name of the younger was Ellie, that of the elder, Rebecca. Ellie was gentle and sad, sad even in childhood, but years, and the weight of sorrow that fell from them, weighed down her heart, so that a calm but constant melancholy veiled the sunshine of her life. The calmness arose not so much from a clear perception of the great purposes God has about our wo,* as from that worst round which humanity ever fills,—apathy, indifference to the chill and the warmth, the flower and the frost. But let me not anticipate. Rebecca had a less dreamy and poetic temperament, more firmness and strength of character, more cheerfulness and elasticity of disposition, so that the younger wound herself about her as a vine winds round a young and vigorous bole, or rested by her side as a daisy rests in the shadow of a broad tree.

A thousand times have I seen them, long ago, their arms about each

* "Wo" is a variant spelling of "woe."

other, and their dark, heavy locks blown together by the wind. I remember a hill, half-covered with maples, where often in the summer times they sat, one with knitting or sewing—and this one was usually Ellie—and the other with a book, from which she read aloud, for she was fond of reading, and as soon as she could read at all, read well. Sometimes, indeed, she put aside her book and related long stories to her admiring and wondering sister, who as yet had learned to give no utterance to her mused thought. Sometimes her dark eyes filled with tears, as she heard these, to her, beautiful relations; and she would say, mournfully, but half reproachfully, "I shall never do any thing half so well as you." Then the elder would move away the tresses from the forehead of the younger, and, kissing her many times, say, "Dear Ellie, you will be a poet;" and so would coax her to read the verses she had written yester eve, or the last Sabbath. Creditable they were, no doubt, but love and an unschooled judgment exaggerated their merits; still, pleased, each with herself and the other, they toward sunset crossed the homeward meadows, as if they came in inspiration from the holiest mount of song. The home in which they lived was a little brown cottage, with no poetic surroundings, save the apple tree, that in winter-time creaked against the wall, and in summer blossomed and bore fruit against the windows, with some rose bushes that grew by the garden fence, and climbed through it and over it as they would. The chamber in which the sisters slept was low, and there was no ceiling beneath the roof, so, often they lay awake listening to the fall of the rain—that beautiful music—they built castles in the clouds, and peopled them with the airy beings of their imagination. Stately chambers they built with pictured walls and elaborate ceilings, through which the patter of rain, the unknown inspiration of their dreams, could not be heard. The days came soon enough, at least for one, when the light of setting suns was all the light she knew.

They were strange children, unlike any others I ever met, wonderfully gifted, sensitive exceedingly, but of rustic parentage, and almost totally uneducated. They began very early to be dissatisfied, and to think that beyond their little world there was one full of sunshine and pleasure. They read eagerly all the books, of whatever nature they could seize upon; went apart from the others in the family, for there were children older and younger; and talked and dreamed.

True, they were required to work when they were not at the school; but when the tasks of the morning were done, with sewing or knitting they went to the meadows or the orchard. Often have I seen them in a field of sweet clover sitting in the shade of a beautiful maple, just on the slope of a hill, washed at the base by a runnel of silvery water, along which grew a thick hedge of willows that hung their long, green branches almost to the stream's surface. All the valley was full of dandelions, now brightening out of slender stems, and now falling and drifting lightly away, as the grass perished, and the flowers of the grass. There were also many other flowers, little delicate wild flowers, some of them beautiful, and some of them very plain, as are children; but their names I do not even know, for I learned not the science, but only the beautiful worship of Flora, and pure worship has never much to do with names. Cattle grazed here and there, or lay in the cool umbrage of other trees; and sheep and lambs skipped over the hills, all making a quiet and lovely picture.

This favorite haunt looked, on one side, toward the willow valley; beyond which, dark and thick, stretched a long line of woods; and on the other, toward the road, on the opposite side of which, under clusters of locust and cedar, gleamed the white stones of the graveyard I have mentioned sometimes, and the cottage where died Mary Wildermings.

"If you live longer than I, dear Ellie," said Rebecca, one day, after they had been a long time silent, "don't let them bury me there."

Tears came to the eyes of the young girl, and putting her arms around the neck of her sister, she said, "What makes you talk so? You will never die."

"Why not I?"

"Because I love you," said Ellie, "and no one I ever loved is dead."

It was a sad smile which came over the face of Rebecca and lighted up her dark eyes, as she answered, "You will part away the thick boughs in yonder burial ground before long, Ellie, for I am sure they will lay me there, and you will read on a plain little headstone,—*Rebecca Hadly, fifteen years*—and a few months and days, I don't know precisely how many; but I shall die before I am sixteen. It will not be long," she continued, as if thinking aloud, "I shall be fifteen in a few months."

"Do not talk so any more," said Ellie, half crying, "let us go home, and I will give you my new apron that mother made for me." Rebecca did not rise, but with her hands folded together in her lap, and her eyes cast down, continued to sit on the grass in silence; while Ellie, picking the wild flowers around her, made wreaths which she hung about her neck, and twined among her hair, prattling of a thousand things in order to make her sister forget that there was such a thing in the world as death. But the effort to forget kept the evil in remembrance, and like a dark cloud, it lay before her whichever way she turned.

That day passed, and another, and another, and though the sisters never talked of death any more, there lay thereafter on the hearts of both an oppression—the consciousness of thinking often of what the lips must not speak.

In going to and returning from school, they always passed the little graveyard, when Ellie never failed to hurry by her sister, and to talk with more life and energy than was her custom. The cheek of Rebecca was the fullest and reddest, her step the most elastic, and her spirit the most buoyant generally, yet, at times, there came over her an impenetrable gloom—haply the prophetic assurance of ultimate destiny. Under the subdued and more habitually melancholy temperament of Ellie, lay a substratum of energy that no one ever suspected—that, for years, she never suspected herself.

One evening as they were returning from school—their long shadows stretching clear across the road—returning slowly, and talking of the schoolmaster, they were unexpectedly interrupted.

Troop after troop of noisy little urchins passed them by, tossing dinner baskets in the air, shuffling up the dust and getting each other's "tag," for they were in high glee—school had been dismissed an hour later than usual, and each one felt himself the bearer of a most important dispatch. Flushed and excited were they as they hurried past each other, eager to communicate at home what they supposed would tell awfully against the master.

"A pretty teacher," said Bill Martin, a rough, bullying boy, "I'd just like to have him keep us in this late again, and I'd show him!" With this exclamation he shook his stout fist in the air, as though in the face of a mortal enemy, and on bringing it down, turned it suddenly at a sharp angle, knocking off the hat of a quiet little boy of half his years—which feat being performed, he ran forward, raising, as he did so, a cloud of dust that prevented the frightened child from seeing in what direction the hat was gone. He began to cry, on which Bill stopped and called out, "That's a good fellow! cry on, and go home without your hat if you are a mind to, and when you get there your father will whip you for losing it, and then you will have something to cry for." This speech failing to produce the soothing effect he seemed to have expected, he ran to one side of the road, and climbing to the topmost rail of the fence, raised himself on tip-toe, and appearing to look far across the fields, said, "Yes, I told you so, your father has heard you already, and I see him cutting a switch from the peach tree; now he is looking to see if it's a strong one; now he has put up his jackknife, and now he is coming this way as fast as he can come—you had better be still, cry-baby, or he will beat you to death." Having finished this salutary admonition, he jumped from the fence completely over the head of a little girl, who stood listening near, and called out, "Boys, it's pitch dark in the woods! who is with me to go back and give the old master a fight: I wish he would just dare to keep us in this way again!"

Now the schoolmaster was not an old one by any means, but, on the contrary, quite young—certainly not more than five and twenty. Poor fellow! the children of his charge were, though sensible enough, rude and undisciplined, scarce half civilized, as it were, and little inclined to be studious. Their slow advances were all, by them, and too often by their parents, attributed to the inefficiency of the master. The general feeling against him had, on the evening referred to, broken out with uncommon vehemence, and promised, as most of the pupils hoped, his speedy ejectment.

"Let us walk slow," said one. "and make it late as we can, for it's as late as it can be any how."

"I had cyphered away beyond where I am now long ago," said another; "I don't believe he knows how to cypher himself, and that's the reason he puts me back all the time."

Thus the majority talked—outraged that the school had been dismissed a little later than usual—a result, in part, of their own neglected lessons—but they expected wisdom to flow into their understandings without any effort of their own, and if it did not, the teacher was of course a blockhead.

Far behind the rest walked Rebecca and Ellie, talking of the master, too, but in a different vein. They seemed to loiter, for they had gone aside to recover the little boy's hat, blown by the wind into the middle of a stubble field. Then, too, they were conversing more earnestly than usual, and so quite forgot that it was late.

"I am sure he is sick," said Ellie, "and not to blame for keeping us a little late; he could not attend to the lessons, I know, he looked so pale, and kept coughing all the time."

"The first day I came, I thought he was so ugly," she continued; "didn't you, Rebecca?"

"Ugly! no, to my thinking, he was always handsome, and his voice is music."

Ellie laughed outright, and Rebecca, blushing at her own enthusiasm, said, half angrily, "what do you laugh at? because I don't think the school-master as ugly as you do?"

"Oh, don't be vexed; I didn't laugh at anything, and sometimes in afternoons, when his cheeks grow red, I think him almost beautiful. To-day when he was reading in the Bible before dismissing school, he looked so, and, Rebecca, he thinks you pretty, too."

"No, Ellie, you are mistaken; no one thinks me pretty, nor am I."

Mournfully as this was said, a smile came over her face which *did* make her really beautiful, as Ellie continued, "I saw him writing poetry to-day, and under pretence of asking some question, I went close to the desk to see what it was, and though I could not see that, I *did* see written over it, *'To Rebecca.'*"

"There are a great many Rebeccas in the world," said the elder sister, "and his poem, if he were really writing a poem, was probably to some friend."

"Probably it was, for you are his friend."

"Well, Ellie, if you will have it so, I shall make him the hero of a story, such as I tell you, and read it on the last day, but what did he say to you after he spoke of putting you in French, to-day?"

"Nothing, I guess; let me see—Oh, he asked me how old I was, and then he said, 'Rebecca is two years older, yes, you must study French'—that was all he said."

"I wish, Ellie," said Rebecca, after they had walked a little way in silence, "I wish we had shoes to wear to school."

"Oh, what a beautiful dog!" exclaimed Ellie, as one of the finest of his tribe passed her; "I wish he were mine."

"Do you really think him beautiful?" asked a voice close at hand—not rudely, but with singular affability and sweetness. It was one of those voices which one instinctively recognises as belonging to a person of cultivated mind and manner; for in the voice there is, to my thinking, as much indication of character as in the countenance.

The face of the young girl blushed crimson—she had never before found herself in such immediate contact with one so evidently her superior, in position and education, and it was not without hesitation and almost painful embarrassment that she replied, "Yes, sir, I think him very pretty."

Probably seeing her confusion, the gentleman did his best to make amends, continuing to converse in an easy way of such things as he naturally supposed her to be most familiar with—the neighborhood, the characters of the people, the productive qualities of the land, and so on. Poor Ellie, she felt that she stammered—appeared awkward—and this consciousness only heightened her native rusticity. She could not say what she knew half so well as to any one in whose eyes the effect she produced was indifferent to her. She wished, much as she wanted to perceive that she knew more than she seemed to know, that he would walk on, talk to Rebecca, do anything, in short, but walk slowly and talk to her.

The elder sister had taken no part in the conversation; no question had been especially addressed to her, and her thoughts not being such as she could give expression to, she did not care to talk at all.

When, however, the stranger said, "Your teacher—what is his name? for you have been to school, as I guess," she looked up with interest, and as Ellie hestitated, as though that were a question demanding a reply from her, she did reply, and the stranger continued interrogatively,

> "And still the wonder grew,
> That one small head could carry all he knew!"

Rebecca made no answer. The gentleman had made no favorable impression on her mind, and it was all in vain that he added, "I shall be happy to make his acquaintance."

There was perhaps a little sarcasm in the tone, as Rebecca said, "And *he* cannot be otherwise than happy." Whether there was or not, the stranger evidently thought so, for he turned to Ellie, and reverting to their previous conversation said, "I am glad, my little friend, to hear so good an account of the people and the country hereabout, inasmuch as I think of pitching my tent under some of these hills, and an acquaintance so informally begun, on my part, will, I hope, result in our friendship. *We* shall be amiable neighbors, I am sure," he added, rather to Ellie, who, unaccustomed to such civilities, could think of nothing to say in reply, but looking across the field, as though suddenly absorbed in the beauties of the landscape, she scarcely saw the polite inclination, or heard the "Good evening, young ladies," with which, the gentleman, mending his pace, was soon too far away to hear them.

"I wonder," said Rebecca, at last, for neither of the sisters spoke for some time, "I wonder if tea will be ready?"

"I don't know," answered Ellie, adding presently, "how much I wish we had shoes."[. . .]*

THE WINTER, with its chill winds and leafless trees, shining icicles and capricious sunshine, was gone; the blue birds were building, and the lilacs budding through; here and there, along the northern sides of the hills, and close under the shelter of the fence, there was a ridge of snow, hard and sleety; and the young lambs, their fleeces just twisting into curl, skipped about their dams, and nibbled the tender grasses. The daffodils were all bright by the doors of the cottages, and the flags had sent up from the long dead grass their broad green blades; while the housewives, their aprons full of seeds, made plans for the new beds in the garden. [. . .]

Rebecca and Ellie had gathered their laps full of flowers, and, by a mossy brookside, where the clear cold water trickled over the blue flagstones, sat down together—one braiding her flowers into wreaths, enraptured with their beauty, and light of heart—the other suffering hers to wither on the ground at her side, while, locking her hands over her knees, she gazed mutely and steadfastly into the stream; the little birds flitted among the boughs, only as yet fringed with verdure, filling all the

*Ellipses within brackets indicates the omission of part of the text.

woods with song and chirp and twitter; the oxen ploughed up and down the hills; and the bees flew hummingly out from their hives. All day long they sat together there amid the sweet music of nature. Gradually the sad smile brightened on the lip of Rebecca, for Ellie did not cease her efforts to turn her thoughts into sunny and hopeful ways. The next week they were going to the city, where they had never been but once in their lives, so that it was of course regarded by them as a most important and interesting event. New dresses they were to have, and bonnets, besides some other things which I have forgotten, and they talked a great deal as to what styles and colors would be pretty and becoming, and then they talked of where they should go and what they should do in the new costume. The sun was burning among the western tree-tops, when they arose, and crossing a meadow where their way might be trailed through the green undulations of the grass, struck into the main road about the distance of half a mile from their home, and directly opposite the lonesome graveyard. Attracted by some sort of noise within it, they drew near, but their voices silenced the movements of the person, so that they began to think they had misapprehended what was perhaps after all but the stirring of the leaves, and were about turning away, when, leaning on his spade, and parting the thick briers through which he cautiously peered, they beheld the black eyes and pale face of Billy Martin. He was filling up the schoolmaster's grave. Ere they reached home, a carriage passed them, the same that had taken Billy to school in the morning, whence a gentleman, smiling recognition, gave the salutation of the evening. Ellie, almost trembling with confusion, dropt half her flowers, but Rebecca said calmly, "That is the same person that we saw coming from school," but her thoughts flowed back to the old time; but from the first moment of seeing him a deep interest had been created in the mind of the younger sister, and she continued musing as to who he was, and whether he lived in the neighborhood, until they reached the gate.

"Come, girls," said Mrs. Hadly, who was just coming from the smoke-house, with a plate of fresh-cut ham, "I want you to help me a little about supper." "Who is at our house?" inquired Ellie, in an eager tone, and coming close to her mother—for to have a visitor at tea was a great event.

Mrs. Hadly said it was Mrs. Grey, and added, "What will she think of you great girls, almost women, if she sees you with your hands full of playthings? Throw away your flowers, and go in and set the table." At this moment, the vision of a white muslin cap, profusely trimmed with black ribbon, appeared at the window, together with a little brown withered hand, checked with blue knotty veins, which flew briskly and vigorously up and down—for Mrs. Grey was an industrious woman, and never thought of sitting down, at home or abroad without some sort of work. She never forgot that "Satan finds some mischief still for idle hands to do," and often repeated it, though her temperament was not at all poetical.

Mrs. Hadly, having got her supper "under way," left it to the care of the girls, and taking a pair of woollen socks, one of many that garnished a frame attached to the ceiling, she sat down close beside her neighbor, whose work, previously to commencing her own, she examined. It was a child's apron, made of bird's-eye diaper,* and in a style which Mrs. Hadly had never seen, and holding it up admiringly, she said, "Now do tell me where you got this pretty pattern."

"Do you like it? I thought it would look pretty for a change, and the way I came by the pattern was this: The new folks that have moved into the old Graham place send over to our house a good deal for things. The very first night they got there they sent for a number of things. Mr. Hampsted didn't come himself, I suppose may be he was too proud, but I don't know as I ought to say that either—likely he had something to do at home—moving makes busy times, you know—at any rate, he sent a black man, with good sized basket, and I couldn't tell you what all he got! Let me see—in the first place he wanted to buy a loaf of bread—I *did* think that was queer, but I couldn't think of making any charge for that—then he got two pounds of butter, and a ham and a dozen eggs, and a quart of milk, and a few potaters he got of Grey, I don't know just how many, but the strangest was, he put them right into a white Irish linen piller-case." And Mrs. Grey continued to say that they must be very extravagant people, for that the black man never asked the price of any thing till he got the passel in his basket, and that he then took out his puss, and paid her just what she

*A bird's-eye diaper is a white cotton or linen fabric, patterned with small, duplicative, diamond-shaped figures, each having a dot in the center.

asked, adding that for such trifling things as bread and milk she had no heart to charge any thing.

"I didn't know," said Mrs. Hadly, for both parties had quite forgotten the apron pattern, "that there were new folks in the Graham place."

"Is it possible? They have been there for four or five days, and you not heard of it? Why, I saw Mr. Hampsted go along here not five minutes ago—you must have seen him, gals."

"The gentleman who just passed in the carriage, driving the black horse?" said Ellie, "I saw him—and he lives near by, it seems;" and though she scarcely knew why, Ellie was glad he did live near by.

"I expect, from all accounts," continued Mrs. Grey, "they won't have much to do with plain farmer folks like us, for Mrs. Hamstid, they say, keeps dressed up all the time reading books, and don't even nuss her own baby. As I was coming here to-day I saw her in the garden, with a bonnet on nice enough to wear to meeting, and I noticed that her hands looked just like snow." And Mrs. Grey finished with an "Ah, well! every one to their notion!" or seemed to finish so, but she presently added, "It looks strange to me to see three gals in one house—a chambermaid and nuss and cook, and they say they call them all sarvents; dear me, what will the world come to? I tell my man we shall have to make a vandue* like Mr. Smith, and go off to a new country, there are so many town folks coming about with their man sarvents and maid sarvents, and fine carpets and furniture."

Poor Mrs. Grey! she was an old-fashioned woman, and her preconceived notions would not readily yield to modern innovations. She sighed, and by way of diverting her mind, Mrs. Hadly said, "What did you say the name was?"

"I don't know as I can make sartain," said Mrs. Grey, "I understood the black man to call him Hampstead, and some call him Hampton, but for my part I guess the name is Hamstid."

Rebecca went out and in, and up and down the stairs, busy about the table, and paying little attention to this conversation. She was thinking about the schoolmaster and of Billy Martin, who, stealthily hidden among the briers, was filling up his grave. But Ellie managed to hear all that was

* "Vandue" is a variant of "vendue," a public sale or auction.

said in reference to the strange gentleman, secretly hoping to herself that when she should have her new dress and bonnet, she would meet him again; "for," she thought, "if I look better I shall act better, and I do not want him to think me a simple rustic, as he does now; and how can he think any thing else?"

Meanwhile, Mrs. Grey finished her apron and folded it away, quite forgetful of how she got the pattern; and clapping her hands playfully together in the face of little Lucy Hadly—who having come in from her playhouse in the weeds, where she had been all day alone, paused a little way from the visitor, and crossing her hands meekly behind her, regarded her attentively, but not rudely—said, "Is this my little girl?" Lucy, not much accustomed to strangers, made no reply; but with the long lashes dropping over her eyes, and a faint crimson breaking through her pale cheeks, stood silent.

"Can't you speak," said her mother, "and tell Mrs. Grey what your name is?"

"No," said Mrs. Grey, "she can't speak—the cat has got her tongue! Poor little girl, she hasn't got any name."

"I am quite ashamed of you, my child," said Mrs. Hadly, smoothing away the golden locks which the wind had blown into tangles. Wiping the tears with her little brown hand, the child turned away; her lips trembled, for she was sensitively alive to blame; and Mrs. Grey kindly drew her towards her, patted her cheek, and said, "I told a story, didn't I? for you have got a pretty name; and the cat hasn't got your tongue either." Lucy said "No;" and in proof showed her tongue to Mrs. Grey, who answered delightedly, "That's a little lady: I knew it!" She then unrolled the apron, and exhibited it to Lucy, and then she tried it on by way of pleasing her, and the large melancholy eyes of the child sparkled with pleasure, as nestling against the bosom of the kindly woman, she regarded herself admiringly.

I called Mrs. Grey a kindly woman—such she was, though not always prudent; and leaning toward Mrs. Hadly, she said, "Is Re——," she called the rest of the name so low that Lucy could not hear it, and added, "still moping and melancholy about the——." Here she called a name again, but so low, that Lucy could not hear it any more than before.

Mrs. Hadly smiled as she answered that a child's grief was not likely to be very durable; and though both the girls had loved their teacher very much, she believed, it was scarcely in the nature of things, that they should always mourn for him. Mrs. Hadly spoke sincerely, and according to the best of her knowledge; so her talkative friend continued—"Then you didn't know how somebody went to see somebody after he was dead!"

"Yes, she had liberty to do so."

"And did you know, too, how somebody left a present for somebody, and in that present a letter that nobody ever saw?"

"Do you allude to the Bible—of which each of the pupils received a copy?"

"Yes, I believe it was; but each of the pupils didn't have a letter, did they?" said Mrs. Grey.

"A few words of admonition, and farewell—nothing more. I am sorry a different impression has gone abroad: it would grieve Rebecca to know it."

"Hush, hush!" said Mrs. Grey, "little folks have big ears, sometimes;" and addressing herself to Lucy, she said, "Run out, and show the girls what a pretty new apron you have got."

She then told Mrs. Hadly, that it was currently reported, that Rebecca and the schoolmaster were engaged to be married; that they were in the habit of meeting each other in the woods, by the school-house; and that Rebecca went to see him after he was dead, and wept and moaned at such a rate, that they heard her all over the house. Now, if all this had been true, there would have been no actual wrong in it; but not so thought Mrs. Hadly, viewing things, as she did, through the most severe and restricting media. Besides, the harmless liking of the young persons had, in the mouths of village gossips, been made to assume an exaggerated and distorted form. It is a fault which many old, and some middle aged persons fall into, to regard all innocent amusements in the young as indiscreet, and all approach toward love between the sexes as absolutely sinful, forgetful that they themselves were ever young and giddy, as they term it, forgetful that they ever loved and married, in all probability, whom they chose. Into this error Mrs. Hadly had fallen; and she resolved, that so flagrant a violation of what she considered propriety should not go unpunished. She was a woman of energy and decision, of severe and strict morality, regarding the dreamy and poetic dispositions of her children as great misfortunes; something worse in fact—something to be ashamed of. Little aid by encouragement did they receive from her in their juvenile efforts; indeed, she was scarcely aware of their existence. An uneducated, plain, practical woman, she had no idea of genius or its uses. More discreet than her neighbor, she said nothing of her convictions or determination, but for a week thereafter pondered them in her heart.

And now the elder portion of the family were at tea; the sun was gone down, the chickens to their roost, and Ellie and Rebecca to the cow yard, where, while filling their pails, they talked much more gaily than usual: a little of the new neighbors, a little of Mrs. Grey and her gossip, and a little of going to town, and their new dresses and bonnets. While thus engaged, Lucy, in her new apron, came timidly near, half proud, and half ashamed. "Whose little girl is this?" said Rebecca, pretending not to know her; "it's Mr. Johnson's little girl, I guess; yes it is. How do you do, little Sally Johnson?" Lucy laughed, saying that her name was not Sally, but Lucy. "Oh yes; I see now," said Rebecca, reaching one arm toward her, "it's nobody but our Lucy with a new apron on."

"Won't you get me an apron like this when you go to town?" and she smoothed it with her hand, regarding it with unspeakable admiration.

Poor little girl! she never before had seen such an apron; never possessed one in her life; but she was pleased with a happy delusion, for Rebecca said she would get one, if mother would let her. Sorry enough was the child when it was time for Mrs. Grey to go home, and she must part with the apron.

A week went by, and not one word said Mrs. Hadly in reference to the information she had received, or of the odious light in which she regarded it. Her manner toward her children was always reserved and chilling; there were no little confidences; no playful words or actions ever between them; and though the children loved her, they stood in too much awe of her to communicate any of their hopes or fears, or joys or sorrows.

It was Saturday morning; a light green wagon, before which two plump and sleek sorrel horses were harnessed, stood by the door of Mr. Hadly. Ellie and Rebecca were arrayed in their best calico gowns, and though they had no gloves, and could scarcely keep their feet in their outgrown and rundown shoes, they left their low chamber filled with echoes of laughter, as they descended and climbed into their places, nestling down in the clean fresh straw, with which it was partly filled. Half-sunken in clover, a little way off, and wet with dew, glistened the little white feet of Lucy, her eyes half full of sunshine and half of tears. Her brown little hands locked together behind her, a faint smile on her slightly parted lips, and her yellow hair, partially curled, falling and drifting about her neck and shoulders, she had just found courage to say, "Don't forget the apron, will you?" as Mr. Hadly, his benevolent countenance shadowed by his broad-rimmed hat, untied the reins from the bough of the cherry tree.

"Stop," said Mrs. Hadly, appearing at the door; "Rebecca is not going to town to-day." This she said in a calm low tone, and as though pronouncing a sentence from which there was no appeal. Rebecca felt it to be so, and without question or hesitancy, obeyed, getting out of the wagon.

"I will stay, too, mother," said Ellie, in a trembling voice.

"No, my child; go to town and get you a new dress and bonnet: Rebecca don't deserve any."

This was said in a tone of self-commiseration, and as though she acted under the force of some terrible duty, and not in accordance with her will. Mr. Hadly looked puzzled a moment, pushed his hand through his iron-gray hair, stepped into his place, and drove away, saying to Ellie, in a tone half sad, half peevish, "I wonder what made your mother take such a notion? what has your sister done that is so bad?" Lucy sank down in the grass where she was standing, and, plucking the long blades, plaited them listlessly together, the tears dropping silently into her lap. But Rebecca, calm and unquestioning, resumed her work-day dress and her accustomed labors. All the day her thoughts were colored with saddest memories. She had little appetite for dinner, and less for supper, but forebore to speak of the headache with which she suffered, performing every task which usually fell to herself and Ellie, alone.

Toward night, while she milked, she listened eagerly to the sound of every wagon, but one after another passed by, and it was not until the lilac by the door was full of twilight birds, that the sorrell horses were seen coming over the hill.

Scarcely had she and Ellie been parted for a day, but the time had seemed very long, and now that she so much felt the need of the words and the endearments of sympathy, it is no wonder she ran to the gate eagerly as she did. But Ellie was not there. Aunt Jane, who lived in three rooms, and did plain sewing, had prevailed on her to stay and have her new dress made and her bonnet trimmed a little in the fashion, and so return home when her father should come to market the next week.

The moon rose round and full, filling the little chamber with a flood of trembling golden light, checkered with the windowsash and dotted with the leaves of the cherry tree without. Lucy had sobbed herself to sleep in the arms of Rebecca, and every now and then a long stifled breath disturbed the silence that else closed round her.

Sometimes the sleepless girl pressed one hand against her head; sometimes she turned, restlessly; and at last, wearied out, adjusting her pillow to support her, she sat upright. Very calmly fell the moonlight in the chamber—very still was the world without; but neither her heart nor her head would be lulled. She thought of Ellie, alone, and far away as the distance that separated them seemed to her; she thought of the schoolmaster and his solitary grave; she thought of herself; and thought, and thought, and thought, till at last the birds fluttered twittering from the lilac, and the pink and crimson streaks went blushing up the whitening East, without her having slept.

The world is full of bruised and crushed hearts and desolate spirits; moans of sorrow creep vein-like through the sunshine, and underlie the laughter, however gay and loud; pillows of pain, and chambers where the soft step of sleep will not tread, are all over the world; since the serpent folds were among the flowers, there is no perpetual bloom; and since sin furrowed the world with grave-mounds, and the white wings of the angels darkened away from the curse, there is no rest and no solace for us any more.

Orphaned as we are, we have need to be kind to each other—ready, with loving and helping hands and encouraging words, for the darkness and the silence are hard by where no sweet care can do us any good. We have constantly before us the beautiful example of Him who went about doing good, yet how blindly, how perversely we err! A few bitter drops may poison the fountain of life, and the current flow sluggish and heavy forever.

The week of Ellie's visit was over: her new bonnet was trimmed and her dress made in pretty style, and she was glad when she saw the sorrel horses and the green wagon with its straw cushion before her aunt's tidy chamber. Delightedly she ran to meet her father, and ask if all were well, but the smile with which he met her was sad, and his voice full of melancholy forebodings. Rebecca was very sick.

"Oh, father! is she very *sick?*" Ellie asked, in a tumult of fear.

Mr. Hadly tried to assume a more cheerful tone, and, turning away his face, said, "I hope she will be better to-night. Get ready, Ellie, and we will drive home as fast as we can, for she wants to see you, poor girl!" Tying on her new bonnet, but with no pleasure now, and with her dress folded to a neat parcel, she was soon in her place in the wagon. But Rebecca had no new dress or bonnet, and her own long-coveted treasures were now worthless. All the way she tormented herself with reproaches. If she had staid at home, or if she had gone back!—true, she was blameless, but for that her sufferings were not the less acute. She was impatient to be at home, yet she dreaded to arrive there.

She saw some laborers cutting trees in the woods, and whistling as they did so, and felt wronged almost that they neither knew nor cared about her sorrow. Carriages of gaily dressed people, driving toward the city, passed them, and she looked on them reproachfully. It was noon when they reached the school-house. The shutters and the door were open, the new teacher in the old one's place, and the children playing and shouting in the woods, the same as though none were sick and none were dead. Lucy was waiting at the gate. There were no tears in her large melancholy eyes, for she knew not what death was; but she was oppressed with a vague fear, and kept out of the house all the time. The horse and carriage of Mr. Harmsted stood in the yard, but all within seemed hushed—only Mrs. Grey was seen at the window sewing something that was very white.

Both Ellie and her father forbore to ask about Rebecca of Lucy, who, crossing her hands behind her, looked wonderingly at the new bonnet. Mr. Hadly began to unharness his horses, that, tired with the fast drive, neighed impatiently to be in the stable; and Ellie stood hesitating, her new dress in one hand, and her old bonnet in the other, when Mr. Harmsted, coming from the house silently, touched the hands of each, and then taking the reins from Mr. Hadly, told them, in a low sad voice to go in. The father, brushing the tears away with the back of his hand, but in silence, and the young girl weeping out aloud, obeyed. Mrs. Grey, putting down her sewing—a thin muslin cap—came forward to meet them, and relieving

Ellie of the new dress and bonnet, said "Will you go up and see her now?" and softly opening the door, they followed to her chamber. The light was partly darkened away, and on the narrow bed where she had dreamed so many bright dreams, lay Rebecca, dreaming now no more. Ellie kissed her white lips, but their calm smile brightened not for the pressure; folded her hands lovingly, but they fell back heavily and cold. Through the white gates of the morning her spirit had gone where the night never falleth. In the graveyard opposite the old playground, is a simple head-stone, on which is graven—

REBECCA HADLY,

AGED FIFTEEN YEARS, SEVEN MONTHS, AND FIVE DAYS

The 2 sisters are constant companions.
Rebecca, the elder, is the girlfriend of the Schoolmaster who suddenly dies (of T.B.?). For carrying on with him, she is punished by not allowing her to go into town
Ellie goes into town alone and stays a week, during which time R. dies.
The parent's are incapable of showing love to the children - or of understanding them.
(Side sketch of Ellie being taken by Mr. Harmstead.)

UNCLE CHRISTOPHER'S

I

THE NIGHT WAS intensely cold, but not dismal, for all the hills and meadows, all the steep roofs of the farm-houses, and the black roofs of the barns, were white as snow could make them. The haystacks looked like high, smooth heaps of snow, and the fences, in their zigzag course across the fields, seemed made of snow too, and half the trees had their limbs encrusted with the pure white.

Through the middle of the road, and between banks out of which it seemed to have been cut, ran a path, hard and blue and icy, and so narrow that only two horses could move in it abreast; and almost all the while I could hear the merry music of bells, or the clear and joyous voices of sleigh riders, exultant in the frosty and sparkling air.

With his head pushed under the curtain of the window next the road, so that his face touched the glass, stood my father, watching with as much interest, the things without, as I the pictures in the fire. His hands were thrust deep in his pockets; both his vest and coat hung loosely open; and so for a half hour he had stood, dividing my musings with joyous exclamations as the gay riders went by, singly, or in companies. Now it was a sled running over with children that he told me of; now an old man and woman wrapt in a coverlid and driving one poor horse; and now a bright sleigh with fine horses, jingling bells, and a troop of merry young folks.

Then again he called out, "There goes a spider-legged thing that I wouldn't ride in," and this remark I knew referred to one of those contrivances which are gotten up on the spur of a moment, and generally after the snow begins to fall, consisting of two limber saplings on which a seat is fixed, and which serve for runners, fills, and all.

It was not often we had such a deep snow as this, and it carried the thoughts of my father away back to his boyhood, for he had lived among the mountains then, and been used to the hardy winters which keep their empire nearly half the year. Turning from the window, he remarked, at length, "This is a nice time to go to Uncle Christopher's, or some where."

"Yes," I said, "it would be a nice time;" but I did not think so, all the while, for the snow and I were never good friends. I knew, however, that my father would like above all things to visit Uncle Christopher, and that, better still, though he did not like to own it, he would enjoy the sleighing.

"I want to see Uncle Christopher directly," he continued, "about getting some spring wheat to sow."

"It is very cold," I said, "isn't it?" I really couldn't help the question.

"Just comfortably so," he answered, moving back from the fire.

Two or three times I tried to say, "Suppose we go," but the words were difficult, and not till he had said, "Nobody ever wants to go with me to Uncle Christopher's, nor anywhere," did I respond, heartily, "Oh, yes, father, I want to go."

In a minute afterwards, I heard him giving directions about the sleigh and horses.

"I am afraid, sir, you'll find it pretty cold," replied Billy, as he rose to obey.

"I don't care about going myself," continued my father, apologetically, "but my daughter has taken a fancy to a ride, and so I must oblige her."

A few minutes, and a pair of handsome, well-kept horses were champing the bit, and pawing the snow at the door, while shawls, mittens, &c., were warmed at the fire. It was hard to see the bright coals smothered under the ashes, and the chairs set away; but I forced a smile to my lips, and as my father said, "Ready?" I answered "Ready," and the door closed on the genial atmosphere—the horses stepped forward and backward, flung their heads up and down, curved their necks to the tightening rein, and we were off. The fates be praised, it is not to do again. All the shawls and muffs in Christendom could not avail against such a night—so still, clear, and intensely cold. The very stars seemed sharpened against the ice, and the white moonbeams slanted earthward, and pierced our faces like thorns—I think they had substance that night, and were stiff; and the thickest veil, doubled twice or thrice, was less than gossamer, and yet the wind did not blow, even so much as to stir one flake of snow from the bent boughs.

At first we talked with some attempts at mirth, but sobered presently and said little, as we glided almost noiselessly along the hard and smooth road. We had gone, perhaps, five miles to the northward, when we turned from the paved and level way into a narrow lane, or neighborhood road, as it was called, seeming to me hilly and winding and wild, for I had never been there before. The track was not so well worn, but my father pronounced it better than that we had left, and among the stumps and logs, and between hills and over hills, now through thick woods, and now through openings, we went crushing along. We passed a few cabins and old-fashioned houses, but not many, and the distances between them grew greater and greater, and there were many fields and many dark patches of woods between the lights. Every successive habitation I hoped would terminate our journey—our pleasure, I should have said—yet still we went on, and on.

"Is it much farther?" I asked, at length.

"Oh, no—only four or five miles," replied my father; and he added, "Why, are you getting cold?"

"Not much," I said, putting my hand to my face to ascertain that it was not frozen.

At last we turned into a lane, narrower, darker, and more lonesome still—edged with woods on either side, and leading up and up farther than I could see. No path had been previously broken, and the horses sunk knee deep at every step, their harness tightening as they strained forward, and their steamy breath drifting back, and freezing stiff my veil. At the summit the way was interrupted by a cross fence, and a gate was to be opened—a heavy thing, painted red, and fastened with a chain. It had been well secured, for after half an hour's attempts to open it, we found ourselves defied.

"I guess we'll have to leave the horses and walk to the house," said my father; "it's only a little step."

I felt terrible misgivings; the gate opened into an orchard; I could see no house, and the deep snow lay all unbroken; but there was no help; I must go forward as best I could, or remain and freeze. It was difficult to choose, but I decided to go on. In some places the snow was blown aside, and we walked a few steps on ground almost bare, but in the end high drifts met us, through which we could scarcely press our way. In a little while we began to descend, and soon, abruptly, in a nook sheltered by trees, and higher hills, I saw a curious combination of houses—brick, wood, and stone—and a great gray barn, looking desolate enough in the moonlight, though about it stood half a dozen of inferior size. But another and a more cheerful indication of humanity attracted me. On the brink of the hill stood two persons with a small hand-sled between them, which they seemed to have just drawn up; in the imperfect light, they appeared to be mere youths, the youngest not more than ten or twelve years of age. Their laughter rang on the cold air, and our approach, instead of checking, seemed to increase their mirth.

"Laugh, Mark, laugh," said the taller of the two, as we drew near, "so they will see our path—they're going right through the deep snow."

But instead, the little fellow stepped manfully forward, and directed us into the track broken by their sleds.

At the foot of the hill we came upon the medley of buildings, so incongruous that they might have been blown together by chance. Light appeared in the windows of that portion which was built of stone, but we heard no sound, and the snow about the door had not been disturbed since its fall. "And this," said I, "is where Uncle Christopher lives?"

A black dog, with yellow spots under his eyes, stood suddenly before us, and growled so forbiddingly that we drew back.

"He will not bite," said the little boy; for the merry makers had landed on their sled at the foot of the hill, and followed us to the door; and in a moment the larger youth dashed past us, seized the dog by the fore paws, and dragged him violently aside, snarling and whimpering all the time. "Haven't you got no more sense," he exclaimed, "than to bark so at a gentleman and ladies?"

The trip out to Uncle Christopher's on a bitterly cold night.

II

IN ANSWER TO our quick rap, the door opened at once, and the circle about the great blazing log fire was broken by a general rising. The group consisted of eight persons—one man and seven women; the women so closely resembling each other, that one could not tell them apart; not even the mother from the daughters—for she appeared as young as the oldest of them—except by her cap and spectacles. All the seven were very slender, very straight, and very tall; all had dark complexions, black eyes, low foreheads, straight noses, and projecting teeth; and all were dressed precisely alike, in gowns of brown flannel, and coarse leather boots, with blue woollen stockings, and small capes, of red and yellow calico. The six daughters were all marriageable; at least the youngest of them was. They had staid, almost severe, expressions of countenances, and scarcely spoke during the evening. By one corner of the great fireplace they huddled together, each busy with knitting, and all occupied with long blue stockings, advanced in nearly similar degrees toward completion. Now and then they said "Yes, ma'am," or "no ma'am," when I spoke to them, but never or very rarely any thing more. As I said, Mrs. Wright differed from her daughters in appearance, only in that she wore a cap and spectacles; but she was neither silent nor ill at ease as they were; on the contrary, she industriously filled up all the little spaces unoccupied by her good man in the conversation; she set off his excellencies, as a frame does a picture; and before we were even seated, she expressed her delight that we had come when "Christopher" was at home, as, owing to his *gift,* he was much abroad.

Uncle Christopher was a tall muscular man of sixty or thereabouts, dressed in what might be termed stylish homespun coat, trowsers and waistcoat, of snuff-colored cloth. His cravat was of red-and-white-checked gingham, but it was quite hidden under his long grizzly beard, which he wore in full, this peculiarity being a part of his religion. His hair was of the same color, combed straight from his forehead, and turned over in one even curl on the back of the neck. Heavy gray eyebrows met over a hooked nose, and deep in his head twinkled two little blue eyes, which seemed to say, "I am delighted with myself, and, of course, you are with me." Between his knees he held a stout hickory stick, on which, occasionally, when he had settled something beyond the shadow of doubt, he rested his chin for a moment, and enjoyed the triumph. He rose on our entrance, for he had been seated beside a small table, where he monopolized a good portion of the light, and all the warmth, and having shaken hands with my father and welcomed him in a long and pompous speech, during which the good wife bowed her head, and listened as to an oracle; he greeted me in the same way, saying, "This, I suppose, is the virgin who abideth still in the house with you. She is not given, I hope, to gadding overmuch, nor to vain and foolish decorations of her person with ear-rings and finger-rings, and crisping-pins:* for such are unprofitable, yea, abominable. My daughter, consider it well, and look upon it, and receive instruction." I was about replying, I don't know what, when he checked me by saying, "Much speech in a woman is as the crackling of thorns under a pot. Open rebuke," he continued, "is better than secret love." Then pointing with his cane in the direction of the six girls, he said, "Rise, maidens, and salute your kinswoman;" and as they stood up, pointing to each with his stick, he called their names, beginning with Abagail, oldest of the daughters of Rachael Wright and Christopher Wright, and ending with Lucinda, youngest born of Rachael Wright and Christopher Wright. Each, as she was referred to, made a quick ungraceful curtsy, and resumed her seat and her knitting.

A half hour afterward, seeing that we remained silent, the father said, by way of a gracious permission of conversation, I suppose, "A little talk of flax and wool, and of household diligence, would not ill become the daughters of our house." Upon hearing this, Lucinda, who, her mother remarked, had the "liveliest turn" of any of the girls, asked me if I liked to knit; to which I answered, "Yes," and added, "is it a favorite occupation with you?" she replied, "Yes ma'am," and after a long silence, inquired how many cows we milked, and at the end of another pause, whether we had colored our flannel brown or blue; if we had gathered many hickory nuts; if our apples were keeping well, etc.

The room in which we sat was large, with a low ceiling, and bare floor, and so open about the windows and doors, that the slightest movement of the air without would keep the candle flame in motion, and chill

*Crisping pins are iron instruments used to curl or wave hair.

those who were not sitting nearest the fire, which blazed and crackled and roared in the chimney. Uncle Christopher, as my father had always called him (though he was uncle so many degrees removed that I never exactly knew the relationship), laid aside the old volume from which he had been reading, removed the two pairs of spectacles he had previously worn, and hung them, by leather strings connecting their bows, on a nail in the stone jamb by which he sat, and talked, and talked; and talked, and I soon discovered by his conversation, aided by the occasional explanatory whispers of his wife, that he was one of those infatuated men who fancy themselves "called" to be teachers of religion, though he had neither talents, education, nor anything else to warrant such a notion, except a faculty for joining pompous and half scriptural phrases, from January to December.

That inward purity must be manifested by a public washing of the feet, that it was a sin to shave the beard, and an abomination for a man to be hired to preach, were his doctrines, I believe, and much time and some money he spent in their vindication. From neighborhood to neighborhood he traveled, now entering a blacksmith's shop and delivering a homily, now debating with the boys in the cornfield, and now obtruding into some church, where peaceable worshippers were assembled, with intimations that they had "broken teeth, and feet out of joint," that they were "like cold and snow in the time of harvest, yea worse, even as pot-sheds covered with silver dross." And such exhortations he often concluded by quoting the passage: "Though thou shouldst bray a fool in a mortar among wheat, with a postle, yet will not his foolishness depart from him."

More than half an hour elapsed before the youths whose sliding down the hill had been interrupted by us, entered the house. Their hands and faces were red and stiffened with the cold, yet they kept shyly away from the fire, and no one noticed or made room for them. Both interested me at once, and partly, perhaps, that they seemed to interest nobody else. The taller was not so young as I at first imagined; he was ungraceful, shambling, awkward, and possessed one of those clean, pinky complexions which look so youthful; his hair was yellow, his eyes small and blue, with an unquiet expression, and his hands and feet inordinately large; and when he spoke, it was to the boy who sat on a low stool beside him, in a whisper, which he evidently meant to be inaudible to others, but which was, nevertheless, quite distinct to me. He seemed to exercise a kind of brotherly care over the boy, but he did not speak, nor move, nor look up, nor look down, nor turn aside, nor sit still, without an air of the most wretched embarrassment. I should not have written "sit still," for he changed his position continually, and each time his face grew crimson, and, to cover his confusion, as it were, he drew from his pocket a large silk handkerchief, rubbed his lips, and replaced it, at the same time moving and screwing and twisting the toe of his boot in every direction.

I felt glad of his attention to the boy, for he seemed silent and thoughtful beyond his years; perhaps he was lonesome, I thought; certainly he was not happy, for he leaned his chin on his hand, which was cracked and bleeding, and now and then when his companion ceased to speak, the tears gathered to his eyes; but he seemed willing to be pleased, and brushed the tears off his face and smiled, when the young man laid his great hand on his head, and, shaking it roughly, said, "Mark, Mark, Marky!"

"I can't help thinking about the money," said the boy, at last, "and how many new things it would have bought: just think of it, Andrew!"

"How Towser did bark at them people, didn't he, Mark?" said Andrew, not heeding what had been said to him.

"All new things!" murmured the boy, sorrowfully, glancing at his patched trowsers and ragged shoes.

"In three days it will be New Year's; and then, Mark, won't we have fun!" and Andrew rubbed his huge hands together, in glee, at the prospect.

"It won't be no fun as I know of," replied the boy.

"May be the girls will bake some cakes," said Andrew, turning red, and looking sideways at the young women.

Mark laughed, and, looking up, he recognized the interested look with which I regarded him, and from that moment we were friends.

At the sound of laughter, Uncle Christopher struck his cane on the floor, and looking sternly toward the offenders, said, "A whip for the horse, a bridle for the ass, and a rod for the fool's back!" leaving to them the application, which they made, I suppose, for they became silent—the younger dropping his chin in his hands again, and the elder twisting the toe of his boot, and using his handkerchief very freely.

I thought we should never go home, for I soon tired of Uncle Christopher's conversation, and of Aunt Rachael's continual allusions to his "gift;" he was evidently regarded by her as not only the man of the house, but also as the man of all the world. The six young women had knitted their six blue stockings from the heel to the toe, and had begun precisely at the same time to taper them off, with six little white balls of yarn.

The clock struck eleven, and I ventured, timidly, to suggest my wish to return home. Mark, who sat drowsily in his chair, looked at me beseechingly, and when Aunt Rachael said, "Tut, tut! you are not going home to-night!" he laughed again, despite the late admonition. All the six young women also said, "You can stay just as well as not;": and I felt as if I were to be imprisoned, and began urging the impossibility of doing so, when Uncle Christopher put an end to remonstrance by exclaiming, "It is better to dwell in the corner of the housetop, than with a brawling woman, and in a wide house." It was soon determined that I should remain, not only for the night, but till the weather grew warmer; and I can feel now something of the pang I experienced when I heard the horses snorting on their homeward way, after the door had closed upon me.

"I am glad you didn't get to go!" whispered Mark, close to me, favored by a slight confusion induced by the climbing of the six young ladies upon six chairs, to hang over six lines, attached to the rafters, the six stockings.

There was no variableness in the order of things at Uncle Christopher's, but all went regularly forward without even a casual observation, and to see one day, was to see the entire experience in the family.

"He has a great gift in prayer," said Aunt Rachael, pulling my sleeve, as the hour for worship arrived.

I did not then, nor can I to this day, agree with her. I would not treat such matters with levity, and will not repeat the formula which this "gifted man" went over morning and evening, but he did not fail on each occasion to make known to the All-Wise the condition in which matters stood, and to assure him, that he himself was doing a great deal for their better management in the future. It was not so much a prayer as an announcement of the latest intelligence, even to "the visit of his kinswoman who was still detained by the severity of the elements."

It was through the exercise of his wonderful gift, that I first learned the histories of Andrew and Mark; that the former was a relation from the interior of Indiana, who, for feeding and milking Uncle Christopher's cows morning and evening, and the general oversight of affairs, when the great man was abroad, enjoyed the privilege of attending the district school in the neighborhood; and that the latter was the "son of his son," a "wicked and troublesome boy, for the present subjected to the chastening influences of a righteous discipline."

As a mere matter of form, Uncle Christopher always said, I will do so or so, "Providence permitting;" but he felt competent to do anything and everything on his own account, to "the drawing out of the Leviathan with an hook, or his tongue with a cord—to the putting a hook into his nose, or the boring his jaw through with a thorn."

"I believe it's getting colder," said Andrew, as he opened the door of the stairway, darkly winding over the great oven, to a low chamber; and, chuckling, he disappeared. He was pleased, as a child would be, with the novelty of a visitor, and perhaps half believed it was colder, because he hoped it was so. Mark gave me a smile as he sidled past his grandfather, and disappeared within the smoky avenue. We had scarcely spoken together, but somehow he had recognized the kindly disposition I felt toward him.

As I lay awake, among bags of meal and flour, boxes of hickory nuts and apples, with heaps of seed, wheat, oats, and barley, that filled the chamber into which I had been shown—cold, despite the twenty coverlids heaped over me—I kept thinking of little Mark, and wondering what was the story of the money he had referred to. I could not reconcile myself to the assumption of Uncle Christopher that he was a wicked boy; and, falling asleep at last, I dreamed the hard old man was beating him with his walking-stick, because the child was not big enough to fill his own snuff-colored coat and trowsers. And certainly this would have been little more absurd than his real effort to change the boy into a man.

There was yet no sign of daylight, when the stir of the family awoke me, and, knowing they would think very badly of me should I further indulge my disposition for sleep, I began to feel in the darkness for the various articles of my dress. At length, half awake, I made my way through and over the obstructions in the chamber, to the room below, which the blazing logs filled with light. The table was spread, and in the genial warmth sat Uncle Christopher, doing nothing. He turned his blue eyes upon me as I entered, and said, "Let a bear robbed of her whelps meet a man, rather than she who crieth, A little more sleep, and a little more slumber."

"Did he say anything to you?" asked Aunt Rachael, as I entered the kitchen in search of a wash-bowl. "It must have been just to the purpose," she continued; "Christopher always says something to the purpose."

There was no bowl, no accommodations, for one's toilet: Uncle Christopher did not approve of useless expenditures. I was advised to make an application of snow to my hands and face, and while I was doing so, I saw a light moving about the stables, and heard Andrew say, in a chuckling, pleased tone, "B'lieve it's colder, Mark—she can't go home to-day; and if she is only here till New-Years, maybe they will kill the big turkey." I felt, while melting on my cheeks the snow, that it was no warmer, and, perhaps, a little flattered with the evident liking of the young man and the boy, I resolved to make the best of my detention. I could see nothing to do, for seven women were already moving about by the light of a single tallow candle; the pork was frying, and the coffee boiling; the bread and butter were on the table, and there was nothing more, apparently, to be accomplished. I dared not sit down, however, and so remained in the comfortless kitchen, as some atonement for my involuntary idleness. At length the tin-horn was sounded, and shortly after Andrew and Mark came in, and breakfast was announced; in other words, Aunt Rachael placed her hand on her good man's chair, and said, "Come."

To the coarse fare before us we all helped ourselves in silence, except of the bread, and that was placed under the management of Uncle Christopher, and with the same knife he used in eating, slices were cut as they were required. The little courage I summoned while alone in the snow—thinking I might make myself useful, and do something to occupy my time, and oblige the family—flagged and failed during that comfortless meal. My poor attempts at cheerfulness fell like moonbeams on ice, except, indeed, that Andrew and Mark looked grateful.

Several times, before we left the table, I noticed the cry of a kitten, seeming to come from the kitchen, and that when Uncle Christopher turned his ear in that direction, Mark looked at Andrew, who rubbed his lips more earnestly than I had seen him before.

When the breakfast, at last, was ended, the old man proceeded to search out the harmless offender, with the instincts of some animal hungry for blood. I knew its doom, when it was discovered, clinging so tightly to the old hat, in which Mark had hidden it, dry and warm, by the kitchen fire; it had been better left in the cold snow, for I saw that the sharp little eyes which looked on it grew hard as stone.

"Mark," said Uncle Christopher, "into your hands I deliver this unclean beast: there is an old well digged by my father, and which lieth easterly a rod or more from the great barn—uncover the mouth thereof, and when you have borne the creature thither, cast it down!"

Mark looked as if he were suffering torture, and when, with the victim, he had reached the door, he turned, as if constrained by pity, and said, "Can't it stay in the barn?"

"No," answered Uncle Christopher, bringing down his great stick on the floor; "but you can stay in the barn, till you learn better than to gainsay my judgment." Rising, he pointed in the direction of the well, and followed, as I inferred, to see that his order was executed, deigning to offer neither reason nor explanation.

Andrew looked wistfully after, but dared not follow, and, taking from the mantle-shelf Walker's Dictionary, he began to study a column of definitions, in a whisper sufficiently loud for every one in the house to hear.

I inquired if that were one of his studies at school; but so painful was the embarrassment occasioned by the question, though he simply answered, "B'lieve it is," that I repented, and perhaps the more, as it failed of its purpose of inducing a somewhat lower whisper, in his mechanical repetitions of the words, which he resumed with the same annoying distinctness.

With the first appearance of daylight the single candle was snuffed out, and it now stood filling the room with smoke from its long limber wick, while the seven women removed the dishes, and I changed from place to place that I might seem to have some employment; and Andrew, his head and face heated in the blaze from the fireplace, studied the Dictionary. In half an hour Uncle Christopher returned, with stern satisfaction depicted in his face: the kitten was in the well, and Mark was in the barn; I felt that, and was miserable.

I asked for something to do, as the old man, resuming his seat, and folding his hands over his staff, began a homily on the beauty of industry, and was given some patch-work; "There are fifty blocks in the quilt," said Aunt Rachael, "and each of them contains three hundred pieces."

I wrought diligently all the day, though I failed to see the use or beauty of the work on which I was engaged.

At last Andrew, putting his Dictionary in his pocket, saying, "I b'lieve I have my lesson by heart," and, a piece of bread and butter in the top of his hat, tucked the ends of his green woolen trowsers in his cowhide boots, and, without a word of kindness or encouragement, left the house for the school.

By this time the seven women had untwisted seven skeins of blue yarn, which they wound into seven blue balls, and each at the same time began the knitting of seven blue stockings.

That was a very long day to me, and as the hours went by I grew restless, and then wretched. Was little Mark all this time in the cold barn? Scratching the frost from the window pane, I looked in the direction from which I expected him to come, but he was nowhere to be seen.

The quick clicking of the knitting-needles grew hateful, the shut mouths and narrow foreheads of the seven women grew hateful, and hatefulest of all grew the small blue shining eyes of Uncle Christopher, as they bent on the yellow worm-eaten page of the old book he read. He was warm and comfortable, and had forgotten the existence of the little boy he had driven out into the cold.

I put down my work at last, and cold as it was, ventured out. There were narrow paths leading to the many barns and cribs, and entering one after another, I called to Mark, but in vain. Calves started up, and, placing their fore feet in the troughs from which they usually fed, looked at me, half in wonder and half in fear; the horses—and there seemed to be dozens of them—stamped, and whinnied, and, thrusting their noses through their mangers, pressed them into a thousand wrinkles, snuffing the air instead of expected oats. It was so intensely cold I began to fear the boy was dead, and turned over bundles of hay and straw, half expecting to find his stiffened corpse beneath them, but I did not, and was about leaving the green walls of hay that rose smoothly on each side of me, the great dusty beams and black cobwebs swaying here and there in the wind, when a thought struck me: the well—he might have fallen in! Having gone "a rod or more, easterly from the barn," directed by great footprints and little footprints, I discovered the place, and to my joy, the boy also. There was no curb about the well, and, with his hands resting on a decayed strip of plank that lay across its mouth, the boy was kneeling beside it, and looking in. He had not heard my approach, and, stooping, I drew him carefully back, showed him how the plank was decayed, and warned him against such fearful hazards.

"But," he said, half laughing, and half crying, "just see!" and he pulled me toward the well. The opening was small and dark, and seemed very deep, and as I looked more intently my vision gradually penetrated to the bottom; I could see the still pool there, and a little above it, crouching on a loose stone or other projection of the wall, the kitten, turning her shining eyes upward now and then, and mewing piteously.

"Do you think she will get any of it?" said Mark, the tears coming into his eyes; "and if she does, how long will she live there?" The kind-hearted child had been dropping down bits of bread for the prisoner.

He was afraid to go to the house, but when I told him Uncle Christopher might scold me if he scolded any one, and that I would tell him so, he was prevailed upon to accompany me. The hard man was evidently ashamed when he saw the child hiding behind my skirts for fear, and at first said nothing. But directly Mark began to cry—there was such an aching and stinging in his fingers and toes, he could not help it.

"Boo, hoo, hoo!" said the old man, making three times as much noise as the boy—"what's the matter now?"

"I suppose his hands and feet are frozen," said I, as though I knew it, and would maintain it in spite of him, and I confess I felt a secret satisfaction in showing him his cruelty.

"Oh, I guess not," Aunt Rachael said, quickly, alarmed for my cool assertion as well as for the child: "only a leetle frosted, I reckon. Whereabouts does it hurt you, my son?" she continued, stooping over him with a human sympathy and fondness I had not previously seen in any of the family.

"Frosted a leetle—that's all, Christopher," she said, by way of soothing her lord's compunction, and, at the same time, taking in her hands the feet of the boy, which he flung about for pain, crying bitterly. "Hush, little honey," she said, kissing him, and afraid the good man would be vexed at the crying; and as she sat there holding his feet, and tenderly soothing him, I at first could not believe she was the same dark and sedate matron who had been knitting the blue stocking.

"Woman, fret not thy gizzard!" said Christopher, slapping his book on the table, and hanging his spectacles on the jamb. The transient beauty all dropt away, the old expression of obsequious servility was back, and she resumed her seat and her knitting.

"There, let me doctor you," he continued, drawing the child's stocking off. The feet were covered with blisters, and presented the appearance of having been scalded. "Why, boy alive," said he, as he saw the blisters, "these are nothing—they will make you grow." He was forgetting his old pomposity, and, as if aware of it, resumed, "Thou hast been chastised according to thy deserts—go forth in the face of the wind, even the north wind, and, as the ox treadeth the mortar, tread thou the snow."

"You see, Markey," interposed Mrs. Wright, whose heart was really kind,—"you see your feet are a leetle frosted, and that will make them well."

The little fellow wiped his tears with his hand, which was cracked and bleeding from the cold; and, between laughing and crying, ran manfully out into the snow.

It was almost night, and the red clouds about the sunset began to cast their shadows along the hills. The seven women went into the kitchen for the preparation of dinner, (we ate but two meals in the day) and I went to the window to watch Mark as he trod the snow "even as an ox treadeth the mortar." There he was, running hither and thither, and up and down, but, to my surprise, not alone. Andrew, who had returned from school, and found his little friend in such a sorry plight, had, for the sake of giving him courage, bared his own feet, and was chasing after him in generously well-feigned enjoyment. Towser, too, had come forth from his kennel of straw, and a gay frolic they made of it, all together.

I need not describe the dinner—it differed only from the breakfast, in that it had potatoes added to the bread and pork.

I remember never days so long, before nor since; and that night, as the women resumed their knitting, and Uncle Christopher his old book, I could hardly keep from crying like a child, I was so lonesome and homesick. The wind roared in the neighboring woods, the frozen branches rattled against the stone wall, and sometimes the blaze was blown quite out of the fire-place. I could not see to make my patch-work, for Uncle Christopher monopolized the one candle, and no one questioned his right to do so; and, at last, conscious of the displeasure that would follow me, I put by the patches, and joined Mark and Andrew, who were shelling corn in the kitchen. They were not permitted to burn a candle, but the great fire-place was full of blazing logs, and, on seeing me, their faces kindled into smiles, which helped to light the room, I thought. The floor was covered with red and white cobs, and there were sacks of ripe corn, and tubs of shelled corn, about the floor, and, taking a stool, I joined them at their work. At first, Andrew was so much confused, and rubbed his mouth so much with his handkerchief, that he shelled but little; gradually, however, he overcame his diffidence, and seemed to enjoy the privilege of conversation, which he did not often have, poor fellow. Little Mark made slow progress; his tender hands shrank from contact with the rough ears, and when I took his place, and asked him where he lived, and how old he was, his heart was quite won, and he found delight in communicating to me his little joys and sorrows. He was not pretty, certainly—his eyes were gray and large, his hair red, his expression surly, his voice querulous, and his manner unamiable, except, indeed, when talking with Andrew or myself.

I have been mistaken, I thought; he is really amiable and sweet-tempered; and, as I observed him very closely, his more habitual expression came to his face, and he said, abruptly, "I don't like grandfather!" "Why?" I said, smoothing back his hair, for I liked him the better for saying so. "Because," he replied, "he don't like me;" and, in a moment, he continued, while his eyes moistened, "nobody likes me—everybody says I'm bad and ugly." "Oh, Mark!" exclaimed Andrew, "I like you, but I know somebody I don't like—somebody that wears spectaclesses, and a long beard—I don't say it's Uncle Christopher, and I don't say it ain't." Mark laughed, partly at the peculiar manner in which Andrew expressed himself; and when I told him I liked him too, and didn't think him either bad or ugly, he pulled at the hem of my apron as he remarked, that he should like to live with Andrew and me, always.

I answered that I would very gladly take him with me when I went home, and his face shone with pleasure, as he told me he had never yet ridden in a sleigh. But the pleasure lasted only a moment, and, with an altered and pained expression, he said, "I can't go—these things are all I have got," and he pointed to his homely and ill-conditioned clothes.

"Never mind, I will mend them," I said; and, wiping his eyes, he told me that once he had enough money to buy ever so many clothes, that he earned it by doing errands, sawing wood, and other services, for the man who lived next door to his father in the city, and that one Saturday night, when he had done something that pleased his employer, he paid him all he owed, and a little more, for being a good boy. "As I was running home," said he, "I met two boys that I knew; so I stopped to show them how much money I had, and when they told me to put it on the pavement in three little heaps, so we could see how much it made, I did so, and they, each one of them, seized a heap and ran away, and that," said Mark, "is just the truth."

"And what did you do then?" I asked.

"I told father," he answered, "and he said I was a simpleton, and it was good enough for me—that he would send me out here, and grandfather would straighten me."

"Never mind, Markey," said Andrew, "it will be New Year's, day after to-morrow."

And so, sitting in the light of the cob-fire, and guessing what they would get in their stockings, I left them for the night.

I did not dampen their expectations of a good time, but I saw little cause to believe any pleasant dreams of their's would be realized, as I had seen no indications of preparation for the holidays, even to the degree of a plumb cake, or mince-pie. But I was certain of one thing—whatever Mark was, they would not make him any better. As he said, nobody loved him, nobody spoke to him, from morning till night, unless to correct or order him, in some way; and so, perhaps, he sometimes did things he ought not to do, merely to amuse his idleness. In all ways he was expected to have the wisdom of a man—to rise as early, and sit up as late, endure the heat and cold as well, and perform nearly as much labor. So, to say the truth, he was, for the most part, sulky and sullen, and did reluctantly that which he had to do, and no more, except, indeed, at the suggestion of Andrew, or while I was at the house, because it was at my request, and then work seemed only play to him.

The following morning was precisely like the morning that preceded it; the family rose before the daylight, and moved about by the tallow candle, and prepared breakfast, while Uncle Christopher sat in the great arm-chair, and Mark and Andrew fed the cattle by the light of a lantern.

"To-morrow will be New-Year's," said Mark, when breakfast was concluded, and Andrew took down the old Dictionary. No one noticed him, and he presently repeated it.

"Well, and what of it?" replied the old man, giving him a severe look.

"Nothing of it, as I know of," said the boy; "only I thought, maybe we would have something nice."

"Something nice!" echoed the grandfather; "don't we have something nice every day?"

"Well, but I want to do something," urged Mark, sure that he wished to have the dull routine broken in some way.

"Boys will be boys," said Aunt Rachael, in her most conciliatory tone, and addressing nobody in particular; and presently she asked Mark what had become of the potatoes he gleaned. He replied that they were in a barrel in the cellar.

"Eaten up by the rats," added Uncle Christopher.

"No, sir," said Mark, "they are as good as ever—may I sell them?"

"It's a great wonder you didn't let the rats eat them; but, I suppose, it's from no oversight of yours," Uncle Christopher said.

"Yes, sir, I covered them," replied the boy; "and now, may I sell them?—you said I might."

"Sell them—yes, you may sell them," replied the grandfather, in a mocking tone; "why don't you run along and sell them?"

Of course, the boy did not feel that he could sell his little crop, nor did the grandfather intend to grant any such permission.

"Uncle Christopher," said Andrew, looking up from his Dictionary, "do them ere potatoes belong to you, or do they belong to Markey?"

The old man did not reply directly, but said something about busy bodies and meddlers, which caused Andrew to study very earnestly, while Mark withdrew to the kitchen and cried, alone. Toward noon, however, his grandfather asked him if he could ride the old sorrel horse to the blacksmith's, three miles away, and get new shoes set on him, "because," said he, "if you can, you can carry a bag of the potatoes, and sell them."

Mark forgot how cold it was, forgot his ragged trowsers, forgot everything, except that the next day was New-Year's, and that he should have some money; and, mounting the old horse, with a bag of potatoes for a saddle, he was soon facing the north wind. He had no warm cap to turn against his ears, and no mittens for his hands, but he had something pleasant to think about, and so did not feel the cold so much.

When Andrew came from school, and found that Mark was gone to sell his potatoes, he was greatly pleased, and went out early to feed the cattle, first carrying the bundles of oats over the hill to the sheep—a portion of the work belonging to Mark; and he also made a blazing fire, and watched his coming at the window; but no one else seemed to think of him—the supper was served and removed, and not even the tea was kept by the fire for him. It was long after dark when he came, cold and hungry—but nobody made room at the hearth, and nobody inquired the result of his speculation, or what he had seen or heard during the day.

"You will find bread and butter in the cupboard," said Aunt Rachael, after a while, and that was all.

But he had received a dollar for the potatoes; that was fortune enough for one day, and he was careless and thoughtless of their indifference.

There was no light for my patch-work, and Aunt Rachael gave me instead a fine linen sheet to hem. "Isn't it fine and pretty?" said Mark, coming close to me before he went to bed; "I wish I could have it over me."

"Thoughtless child," said the grandfather, "you will have it over you soon enough, and nothing else about you, but your coffin-boards." And, with this benediction, he was dismissed for the night.

I awoke in the morning early, and heard the laughter of Andrew and Mark—it was New Year's—and, in defiance of the gloomy prospect, they were merry; but when I descended the grandson looked grave—he had found nothing in his stockings.

"Put your feet in them," said Uncle Christopher, "and that will be something."

Fresh snow had fallen in the night, and the weather was milder than it had been, but within the house, the day began as usual.

"Grandfather," said Mark, "shall we not have the fat turkey-hen for dinner, to-day? I could run her down in the snow so easy!"

"So could I run you down in the snow, if I tried," he responded, with a surly quickness.

"New-Year's day," said Aunt Rachael, "is no better than any other, that I know of; and if you get very hungry, you can eat good bread and milk."

So, as in other mornings, Andrew whispered over the Dictionary, the old man sat in the corner, and the seven women began to knit.

Toward the noon, a happy thought came into the mind of Uncle Christopher: there would be wine-bibbers and mirth-makers at the village, three miles away—he would ride thither, and discourse to them of righteousness, temperance, and judgment to come. Mark was directed to bring his horse to the door, and, having combed his long beard with great care, and slipped over his head a knitted woollen camp, he departed on his errand, but not without having taken from little Mark the dollar he had received for his potatoes. "It may save a soul," he said, "and shall a wayward boy have his will, and a soul be lost?"

The child, however, was not likely in this way to be infused with religious feeling, whatever Uncle Christopher might think of the subject, and it was easy to see that a sense of the injustice he suffered had induced a change in his heart that no good angel would have joy to see. I tried to appease his anger, but he recounted, with the exactest particularity, all the history of the wrong he had suffered, and would not believe there was the slightest justification possible for robbing him of what was his own, instead of making him, as his grandfather should have done, a handsome present. About the middle of the afternoon Andrew came home from school, having been dismissed at so early an hour because it was a holiday, and to prepare for a spelling match to be held at the school-house in the evening. The chores were done long before sundown, and Andrew was in high spirits, partly in anticipation of the night's triumphs, and partly at the prospect of bringing some happiness to the heart of Mark, with whom he several times read over the lesson, impressing on his memory with all the skill he had the harder words which might come to him. Andrew went early, having in charge the school-house fire, and Mark did not accompany him, but I supposed he would follow presently, and so was not uneasy about him.

As the twilight darkened, Uncle Christopher came in, and, recounting his pious labors, with a conceited cant that was now become disgusting to me, he inquired for Mark, that the "brand" might hear and rejoice at the good accomplished with the money thus applied for the regeneration of the gentiles; but Mark was not to be found, and Aunt Rachael meekly hinted that from what she had overheard, she suspected he had gone with Andrew to the spelling match.

"Gone to the spelling match—and without asking me!" said the good man; "the rod has been spared too long." And taking from his pocket his knife, he opened it with deliberate satisfaction, and left the house.

I thought of the words of Mark, "I don't like my grandfather;" and I felt that he was not to blame. All the long evening the lithe sapling lay over the mantel, while Uncle Christopher knitted his brows, and the seven women knitted their seven stockings. I could not use my needle, nor think of what was being done about me; all the family practised their monotonous tasks in gloomy silence; the wind shrieked in the trees, whose branches were flung violently sometimes against the windows; Towser came scratching and whining at the door, without attracting the notice of any one; and Uncle Christopher sat in his easy-chair, in the most comfortable corner, seeming almost as if he were in an ecstasy with intense self-satisfaction, or, once in a while, looking joyously grim and stern as his eye rested on the instrument of torture he had prepared for poor Mark, for whose protection I found myself praying silently, as I half dreamed that he was in the hands of a pitiless monster.

The old clock struck eleven, from a distant part of the house, and we all counted the strokes, it was so still; the sheet I had finished lay on the settee beneath the window, where the rose-vine creaked, and the mice peered out of the gnawed holes, and the rats ran through the mouldy cellar. There was a stamping at the door, in the moist snow; I listened, but could hear no voices; the door opened, and Andrew came in alone.

"Where is Mark?" asked the stern voice of the disciplinarian.

"I don't know," replied Andrew; "isn't he here?"

"No," said Aunt Rachael, throwing down her knitting, "nor hasn't been these many hours. Mercy on us, where can he be?"

"Fallen asleep somewhere about the house, likely," replied the old man; and taking up the candle, he began the search.

"And he hasn't been with you, Andrew?" asked Aunt Rachael again, in the faint hope that he would contradict his previous assertion.

"No ma'am, as true as I live and breathe," he replied, with childish simplicity and earnestness.

"Mercy on us!" she exclaimed again.

We could hear doors opening and shutting, and floors creaking in distant parts of the house; but nothing more.

"It's very strange," said the old man. "Don't be afraid, girls;" but he was evidently alarmed, and his hand shook as he lighted the lantern, saying, "he must be in the barn!"

Aunt Rachael would go, and I would go, too—I could not stay away. Andrew climbed along the scaffolds, stooping and reaching the lantern before him, and now and then we called to know if he had found him, as if he would not tell it when he did. So all the places we could think of had been searched, and we had begun to call and listen, and call again.

"Hark," said Andrew, "I heard something."

We were all so still that it seemed as if we might hear the falling of flakes of snow.

"Only the howl of a dog," said Uncle Christopher.

"It's Towser's," suggested Andrew, fearfully; and with an anxious look he lowered the lantern to see what indications were in the way. Going toward the well were seen small footprints, and there were none returning. Even Uncle Christopher was evidently disturbed. Seeing the light, the dog began to yelp and whine, looking earnestly at us, and then suddenly down in the well, and when we came to the place everyone felt a sinking of the heart, and no one dared to speak. The plank, on which I had seen him resting, was broken, and a part of it had fallen in. Towser whined, and his eyes shone as if he were in agony for words, and trying to throw all his intelligence into each piteous look he gave us.

"Get a rope, and lower the light," said one of the sisters; but the loose stones of the well were already rattling to the touch of Andrew, who, planting hands and feet on either side, was rapidly but cautiously descending. In a moment he was out of sight, but still we heard him, and soon there was a pause, then the sound of a hand, plashing the water, then a groan, sounding hollow and awful through the damp, dark opening, and a dragging, soughing movement, as if something were drawn up from the water. Presently we heard hands and feet once more against the sides of the well, and then, shining through the blackness into the light, two fiery eyes, and quickly after, as the bent head and shoulders of Andrew came nearer the surface, the kitten leaped from them, and dashed blindly past the old man, who was kneeling and looking down, pale with remorseful fear. Approaching the top, Andrew said, "I've got him!" and the grandfather reached down and lifted the lifeless form of the boy into his arms, where he had never reposed before. He was laid on the settee, by the window; the fine white sheet that I had hemmed, was placed over him; the stern and hard master walked backward and forward in the room, softened and contrite, though silent, except when occasional irrepressible groans disclosed the terrible action of his conscience; and Towser, who had been Mark's dearest playmate, nearly all the while kept his face, from without, against the window pane.

"Oh, if it were yesterday!" murmured Uncle Christopher, when the morning came; "Andrew," he said, and his voice faltered, as the young man took from the mantel the long, limber rod, and measured the shrouded form from the head to the feet, "get the coffin as good as you can—I don't care what it costs—get the best."

The Dictionary was not opened that day; Andrew was digging through the snow, on a lonesome hill-side, pausing now and then to wipe his eyes on his sleeve. Upright on the grave's edge, his only companion, sat the black dog.

Poor little Mark!—we dressed him very carefully, more prettily, too, than he had ever been in his life, and as he lay on the white pillow, all who saw him said, "How beautiful he is!" The day after the funeral, I saw Andrew, previously to his setting out for school, cutting from the sweet-brier such of the limbs as were reddest with berries, and he placed them over the heaped earth, as the best offering he could bring to beautify the last home of his companion. In the afternoon I went home, and have never seen him since, but, ignorant and graceless as he was, he had a heart full of sympathy and love, and Mark had owed to him the happiest hours of his life.

Perhaps, meditating of the injustice he himself was suffering, the unhappy boy, whose terrible death had brought sadness and perhaps repentance to the house of Uncle Christopher, had thought of the victim consigned by the same harsh master to the well, and determined, before starting for the schoolhouse, to go out and drop some food for it over the decayed plank on which I had seen him resting, and by its breaking had been precipitated down its uneven sides to the bottom, and so killed. But whether the result was by such accident, or by voluntary violence, his story is equally instructive to those straight and ungenial natures which see no beauty in childhood, and would drive before its time all childishness from life.

Narrator/observer
forced by weather and adults to stay at Uncle Christopher's house for a few days.
She notes the lack of love and the abuse of little Mark, a grandson.
Mark & Andrew (hired boy)
Mark dies in the well where U.C. had made him throw the kitten.

revenge on fathers
silenced while there, she later tells the story
her father and Mark's father both give their children over to U.C.
practice of child-exchange? Sadism?

WHY MOLLY ROOT GOT MARRIED

I

SOME YEARS AGO there lived in Clovernook a family of the name of Trowbridge—very worthy people, but not without some of the infirmities which belong to human nature. There was scarcely a woman about the village better known than Mrs. Trowbridge, though I have not before had occasion to mention her. And she was as well liked as she was well-known—every body saying, What a dear good woman she is! and I among the rest. I had often said I would like to live with her, for she seemed the most amiable and agreeable person in the world. It was always a good day when she made us a visit. She laughed, when asking if we were well, and laughed when saying she herself was well. She laughed if a common friend were married, and laughed if a common friend were dead; she laughed if her baby was getting teeth, and laughed if her baby was not getting teeth; if her new dress was right pretty she laughed, if it was right ugly she laughed all the same. When she came, she laughed heartily, and when she went she laughed heartily—it was the way she made herself agreeable.

Many a time I had said I should like to live with Mrs. Trowbridge, for she never had anything to fret or worry about, and I liked best of all things an atmosphere of rest. I was delighted therefore when some changes going on in our old homestead led to a decision that I should for a while reside in her family.

But good Mrs. Trowbridge is not to be so much the heroine of this chapter as Molly Root, a relation of her husband. Molly had been driven about the world, poor and homeless, until lodged, at last, in what most of us thought the very bosom of domestic felicity—the domestic circle of this best-natured woman in our society.

For the first two days after my domestication, I was relieved of all suspicion of the real state of things, by one continual flow of laughter. My occupancy of the best room in the house, and of the warmest place at the table, were apparently the most agreeable things that had ever befallen the good Mrs. Trowbridge.

She was a good housekeeper and cook, when she chose to exercise her abilities in that way, but I soon learned that it was only for visitors that she put those admirable accomplishments in requisition, and that for the most part the household duties fell to the girls, Molly, and Catharine, whom they called Kate—her eldest daughter. When I took my first breakfast, she said she was afraid I could not eat *their* breakfast, and she laughed very much; at dinner she said the same thing, and laughed again; at supper she repeated the remark and the laughter; and all these meals were ample and excellent. As they diminished in these respects, the laughter and apologies diminished too.

My fire was burning brightly and mingling its red shadows with the sunset that slanted through the west window—the wind blew the black wintry boughs against the wall, and now and then a snowflake dropt, silently enhancing the in-door comfort, as I sat rocking to and fro, taking soundings as it were of the sea of love, on which I had lately embarked.

All the past week had seen "the girls" busy and cheerful, up with the dawn, and going through all the duties of the day with as much interest and earnestness as though each had been mistress of the family. When the housework was done they sat down to their sewing—Molly sometimes withdrawing to the privacy of her own apartment, an upper chamber, wherein were deposited the accumulations and inheritances of her life: to-wit, an old old-fashioned bedstead and feather bed, a home-made carpet, four or five crippled chairs, an ancient-looking bureau, which contained the wardrobe of her long-deceased and respected grandmother, from her yellow silk wedding dress to the cambric night-cap in which she died; with two barrels of kitchen and table furniture—pots, skillets and gridirons, knives and forks, teapots, and the like; and there was bed-clothing deposited in stacks and heaps of all sizes, spinning-wheels and reels, a side-saddle, and various other articles no less curious than numerous. There, as I said, Molly occasionally retired, to collect her thoughts, or open her band-boxes, perhaps, or bureau drawers—as what woman does not, two or three times in the course of every week, merely to see how things are getting on.

She had gone to this museum on the aforesaid evening, and had been followed, as she usually was, first by Kate with the baby in her arms, next by Hiram, the oldest boy, with a piece of bread and butter, and then by Alexander Pope, also with a similar portion of his evening meal. This last-mentioned son was denominated by the family the preacher, in consequence of an almost miraculous gift of "speaking pieces," which he was supposed to possess.

From the hasty shutting and opening of drawers, I inferred that Miss Molly was making her toilet, for it was Sunday evening, and girls in the country do not always dress for dinner; on the contrary they sometimes delay that duty till after the evening milking.

The creaking of the gate diverted my attention, both from Molly and the conclusion at which I had just arrived, that we may visit and be visited a good while, and not learn much of each other; and looking out, I saw riding towards the house—for he had unlatched the gate without dismounting—a rosy-faced young man, whose chin dropt on his bosom, perhaps to keep it warm. His boots were spurred, and the little sorrel horse he bestrode capered and curvetted to the touch of his heels in a way that was ludicrous to witness; and the more, as the strong wind drifted the mane and tail of the animal strongly in the direction in which he was going. There was a general rushing down stairs—Kate and the baby first, and the two boys, with their bread and butter, following.

"Oh mother, mother, mother! somebody is coming to our house—somebody with a black coat on, somebody on a sorrel horse!"

"Mother, make them hush," said Kate. "I know who it is; it's Will Pell, and he is coming to see Molly."

"Why, Kate, do say Mr. Pell," replied Mrs. Trowbridge; and she added, "I wonder what there is you don't know?"

"Not much of anything," answered the girl, complacently.

Meantime the two boys kept watch at the window, and reported the progress made by Mr. Pell in his preparations to come in. "Now he is hitching his horse," they said; "Now he is coming this way;" "Now he is brushing his boots with his handkerchief;" "Now he is pulling down his waistcoat;" "Now he is going to rap."

"I see, he's got the crape off, already," said Kate, "and it's just a year and two months and three days since his wife died: it was Sunday, about two hours before this very time, that she was buried."

"What a girl you are!" interposed the mother—"I wonder if you couldn't tell how many dresses she had."

"Yes," said Kate; "she had her white wedding dress, and she had an old black silk dress, and she had a blue gingham dress that she had only worn twice—once a visiting at Mrs. Whitfield's, and once at meeting; and she had a"— Here the catalogue was interrupted by the rapping of Mr. Pell.

Kate was a curious combination of shrewdness and vulgarity, of wisdom in little things, and pertinacity of opinion. She was about fourteen years of age, ill-shapen and unshapen—partly grown and partly growing. Her eyes, sparkling and intelligent, were black as the night, and her hair, of the same dye, was combed so low over her forehead and cheeks that they were always in part concealed. Her shoulders were bent down, for that when not engaged in some household drudgery, she was doomed to carry the baby about—it was her relaxation, her amusement. Molly Root was a quiet little woman, who for a considerable number of years had looked pretty much as she did then: I do not know precisely how old she was, but everybody told her she looked young; and when one begins to receive compliments of that sort they are to be understood as delicate intimations that they have once been a good deal younger than they are at present. In dress she was tidy, and now and then she made little attempts at style. Her manner, to speak truth, was what is called affected, so was her conversation—faults which arose from a desire on her part to appear well. She was amiable and good in all ways; the everlasting smile on her face did not belie her heart. In person she was short—chubby, as we say; her arms were short, her neck was short, and her face was short—her forehead being the largest part of it. Her eyes were of a pale blue, gentle, but dull, with scarce an arrow to be shot at any one, however exciting the emergency. Her hair was of a soft brown, and was worn in part in a small knot on the back of her neck, and in part so drawn across the forehead and turned toward the ears as to make an oblong square. She had from time to time received offers, as perhaps most young women do, and every body wondered why she did not get married. At length that happy event was brought about, and then everybody wondered why Molly did get married: "She had such a nice home—just like her own father's house—and Mrs. Trowbridge is so good-natured, anybody could live with her." It was my peculiar fortune to learn, both why Molly did not get married and why she did.

When any especial good luck occurs to our fellow creatures we are apt to balance it with their little faults and infirmities. Now Mr. Pell was rich; that he had come to see Molly there could be no doubt—Kate said he had, and Kate knew; and besides, Molly had put on her best gown, and an extra smile, and straws show which way the wind blows. On the strength of these considerations Mrs. Trowbridge came presently into my room. She held up one finger by way of keeping down the exclamation she evidently expected, as she announced in a whisper that Will Pell was in the other room. "Indeed!" said I, for I felt that it would be a pity to disappoint her altogether, by evincing no surprise.

"Yes, and he is all fixed up, ever so fine spurs on his boots, and a gold chain, as big as Samuel's log-chain, hanging out of his pocket; and he says to Molly, says he, 'I'm pretty well I thank you,' when she had not asked him a blessed word about it; and for my part I think such things mean something."

"That was funny," I said.

"Yes, and Samuel saw how confused he was too: he could hardly keep his face straight."

Samuel was Mr. Trowbridge; and I may say here, that for the most part he kept his face very straight. But of this here after.

"I don't pretend to be a prophet," she went on, "but this day a twelve-month they will be married—mark my words!"

"I don't see how you are to get along," I said.

"I am very willing to try!" she answered, in a way to indicate that Molly's services were of very little importance.

"She seems very industrious, and so motherly to the children."

"Sometimes," said Mrs. Trowbridge; "you see we give her a home.

She has the best room in the house, and does what she pleases and when she pleases, and nothing if she pleases. If she takes a notion, she goes away for weeks at a time—and right in the busiest time, as like as any way."

Here the children, provided with fresh slices of bread and butter, came after their mother. "Molly pushed me off," said one; "I don't care for old Molly," cried another. "Well," said the injured mother, "she is dressed too fine for you to touch her—I wouldn't go near her again for a week." And she put her arm about the little fellow's neck and kissed him. Presently she said, "If a certain person that you know should tie herself up with a certain other person, what should you think of it?"

"Who, mother—who is going to be tied up?" said the children.

"Oh, I don't know—the man in the moon," she replied. Of course I did not think much about it, and she proceeded to say, if it *was* going to be, she hoped it would be soon—that was all: that some folks drove others out of their own house, and that she felt as if she didn't know where to put her head.

"Why mother! Where do you want to put your head?" asked the boys.

"Oh, I don't know: in a bumble-bee's nest, may be." And after a pause—"If Miss you-know-who were to jump into a feather-bed after all this time, it would be right down funny, wouldn't it?"

"Who is Miss-you-know-who?" asked the children, "and what is she going to jump into a feather-bed for? Is it our bed, mother?—say!"

"Little folks must not have big ears," she replied; "do run away and play; go, get your father's knife, and cut sticks in the kitchen; I saw some pretty shingles there—go and cut them up."

Away they ran, at this inducement, and Mrs. Trowbridge was enabled to drop the disguise and speak plainly again. There is no need to repeat all she said: Molly was not perfect, of course; Mrs. Trowbridge and her children were; consequently every unpleasant occurrence in the family was attributable to but one person. She did not say this precisely, but such was a necessary inference from what she did say. Just then, for instance, Molly and her beau were in the way of getting tea. What should she do? She believed she would not have any tea.

I obviated the difficulty by inviting the lovers into my room; and Mrs. Trowbridge no sooner found herself in the presence of Mr. Pell than she resumed her laughter, suspended during the confidential conference with me. As I have said, it was her way of entertaining people, and making herself agreeable.

Mr. Pell, as the reader is informed, was a widower—an exceedingly active and sprightly man, and his natural vivacity was heightened, no doubt, by the general complaisance of the ladies and the prosperous state of his affairs.

"Don't you think," said Molly, dropping her head on one shoulder, in her best style, and addressing me—"don't you think it has been communicated to me that Mr. Pell is going to take a partner for life?" She liked to use good words.

"Pray, who is the happy lady?" I asked.

"Oh, yes, yes, yes, yes, yes! tell us that!" said Mr. Pell, making two series of little taps, the one on the carpet with his foot, and the other on the table with his hand.

"Oh, a little bird told me—a dear little bird!" And the cheek of Molly almost touched her shoulder.

"A love-bird, wasn't it?" And Mr. Pell gave her cheek a light brush with the finger tips of his glove.

"Oh dear, that is too bad!"

"Did you mean that 'oh dear' for me?" asked Mr. Pell, laughing and hitching his chair toward her.

"You provoking fellow!" she replied, tapping his ear with her fan.

"Miss Molly, Miss Molly, Miss Molly!" he exclaimed, putting his hand to his ear, as if it were stung—"have you such a temper?"

"The sky is all obscured—I apprehend a tempestuous night," Molly observed, and turned her eyes away.

"Just see! She can't look at me because she feels so guilty—temper, temper, temper! Oh dear, dear, dear! I should dread to have such a wife!"

"I am just going to run away!" answered Molly—her head reclining lower than before: but she made no attempt to execute her threat.

"I don't think I shall let you," said Mr. Pell, hitching his chair still closer, and taking her hand as if forcibly to detain her.

"Oh you naughty man! Let me go. Please let me go."

"No. No, no, no, no, no, no, no!"

"Well then, give me my hand."

"No, no. I'll keep it, I'll keep it, I'll keep it, for always and ever, and ever and ever!"

"Oh, bad Mr. Pell, what shall I do without a hand?"

"I'll give you mine, I'll give you mine, I'll give you mine; how will that do? how will that do? how will it do, do, do?"

"Oh, your wit is inexhaustible!"

"You flatter me, I have no wit—not a bit, not a bit, not a bit! It's you that are witty and pretty, and pretty and witty."

"I wish I could speak charmingly like you."

"Oh, Miss Molly, Miss Polly Molly, you have charming speech and charming cheeks, and in both respects I am only an admirer; an admirer of your cheeks and speech."

During this conversation, he had kept a constant hitching and rocking about, striking his feet together, curling and uncurling his beard, with other motions that indicated a restless state of mind; and perceiving his condition, I excused myself, on a pretence of assisting Mrs. Trowbridge. To my surprise, I saw no preparations for tea, but instead, she and Samuel, seated in opposite corners of the fireplace, watching the fading of the embers with the greatest apparent interest. She was smiling a slow smile, as Mrs. Browning says, but nevertheless it was a smile that I could see through. She had expected Molly to attend to the tea, as usual; Molly had not proposed so to do; she had made the necessary preparations during the day, and naturally enough supposed she could be excused from service in the evening. Kate was carrying the baby about, and computing the probable cost of Mr. Pell's boots, coat, and hat, and the two boys lay folded up and asleep on the carpet, having, in consequence of not receiving any of the pound-cake which Molly had baked the day previous, cried themselves into forgetfulness of their misfortune.

Mr. Trowbridge never said much in his wife's presence; if he had done so, he would not have had much said in return; her pleasant things were for others. She was not a scold—her sins were rather of omission of speech, when alone with her spouse, or with but her home audience, than commission. No matter what he had done or what he had failed to do, her reply was always a fretful and querulous "well." He might chop wood all day in the snow, and she never thought to have the fire warmer when he should come in half frozen; and if he said, "you have let the fire get low," or anything of that sort, she would merely answer "well." If she baked buckwheat cakes, though her husband—the uncivilized creature—could not eat them, she never put any other bread on the table. If Kate said, "I think you are smart, mother: you know father don't like these," she only answered "well!" Poor man, a cup of weak tea has served him for supper many a time, after a hard day's work. If his coat grew old-fashioned, he had to wear it so, for Mrs. Trowbridge only said "well," fancying, as it seemed, that her gowns were many enough and bright enough to cover all deficiencies in both their wardrobes. From his youth till he was far beyond middle age, he had been industrious and laborious, in years in and out of season, but he never acquired anything beyond the necessities of the day, and he moved about from place to place, always hoping to improve the state of his affairs, but never doing so.

On this evening I remember that he seemed unusually sensible of his condition, and that his wife said "well" an unusual number of times.

The hours went slowly by till nine o'clock; the cat lay on the hearth seemingly very comfortable, and she was the only one that was so. Mr. Trowbridge was looking in the fire, and Mrs. Trowbridge was looking in the fire, and I was looking at them, when Molly, opening the door, inquired whether we were to have any supper.

"Sure enough," said Mrs. Trowbridge, "*are* we to have any?"

Molly understood the reproof, and said she would have prepared tea as she always did, but that the children had destroyed her kindling, and she thought whoever allowed the mischief might repair it. In an under-tone she said something further, about being excused once in her life, and withdrew rather petulantly.

II

THE OLD CLOCK had struck twelve, the embers were deep under the ashes, where the heads of the household had been sitting an hour before; the children had been duly taken up, and duly scolded, and compelled to walk to bed half asleep, as they were, in punishment for being so naughty—when Molly and I, alone by the parlor fire—Mr. Pell having said, half an hour before, "Good bye, good bye, good bye!"—entered on a "private session."

Night, whether moon-light or star-light, summer night or spring night, is favorable to confessions; we feel a confidence and security as we draw together, and the darkness shuts out all the great world. Almost any two persons, under such circumstances, will be more communicative than they would be in the open noonday, and more especially if they feel mutually aggrieved, as did Molly and I on this particular occasion; for, be it remembered, we had not had our supper.

"It is too bad," she said at length; "I have done enough for Mrs. Trowbridge, I am sure, to merit a little favor once in a year or two—haven't I helpt her, week in and week out, from year's end to year's end? I was with her, with Hiram and the *Preacher* and all, and I have helpt to move ten times if I have once, and done time and again what no money would hire me to do, and you see what thanks I get?" She was silent for a moment, and then said abruptly, "Well, I shall not move grandmother's old pots more than once more!"

"Ah, Mrs. Pell," I said laughing, and taking her hand, "allow me to congratulate you!"

Molly did not smile as I had expected, but hid her face in her hands and burst into tears. When the first tumult had subsided, "I calmed her fears and she was calm," and then she "told her love with virgin pride."

"When I was younger than now," she began; "let me see, it must be fif—, no, I don't know how long it is—well, it's no matter"—she could not make up her mind to say it was even more than fifteen years ago—"I lived with my grandmother; it was in a lonesome old house, away from everybody else; from our highest window we could see the smoke of one dwelling and that was all; and living there at the same time was a young man of the name of Philip Heaton. I have always thought Philip the prettiest name in the world, but no matter about that; I thought Philip Heaton the prettiest fellow I had ever seen, as you can guess; he was so good to me, leaving his own work to spade the garden beds, and milking the cows that were refractory, and doing a thousand things that it will not interest you to hear about. When the circuit preacher came once a month, and there was a meeting in the old log schoolhouse, a mile and a half away, we never failed to go, and what pleasant times they were! I think I remember distinctly all the walks and rides we ever had together. Once I call to mind he gathered me three speckled lilies—I know just where they grew in the edge of a pond, where the grass was coarse and heavy, and over which we walked on a log—I have the withered things somewhere yet—the meadow we crossed, and where we climbed the fences, the long strip of woods with its crooked path among decayed leaves and sticks. Oh, I remember all, as though I had been there yesterday; and just where we were when we said so and so: I could go back and recount everything. Well, as I said, I thought Philip was handsome—I thought he was good—in fact I loved him, and I still think he loved me then. When grandmother was dead, and the funeral was over, we first talked seriously of affection and marriage. I ws sitting alone in the great old-fashioned parlor, thinking of one of our neighbors, a poor old woman, who had told me I must not keep the sheet that had been over the corpse—that it would bring ill-luck to me; and I suspected she wished me to give it to her, as I afterwards did; I was alone, thinking of this, and weighed down with a thousand melancholy thoughts connected with the event that had deprived me not only of a home but of the only real friend I had in the world, when Philip joined me; for it was evening, and his work was done. The November winds rattled the sash against which I sat; I saw the vacant chair, and thought of the new grave; and covering my face, I cried a long time; but it was not altogether for the dead that my tears fell: Philip was going into a distant city to make his fortune, I was to live with a distant relative, and we should not see each other for a long time. The cows we had petted and milked together were to be sold, and the garden flowers would not be ours any more. 'Maybe we shall buy back the cows,' said Philip, 'and get roots and seeds of the same flowers,' for he was young and sanguine, and love sees its way through all things; and when he kissed me, and said it should be so, I thought it would. So I packed up the old things that had fallen to me, and went to my new home, with a world of sweet hopes and promises shut close in my heart. It was a hard and lonesome life I led, but when from that home I went to another and a worse one, I was kept up with the old memory and the new hope.

"Philip prospered beyond all his expectations, and there began to be prospects of buying the cows, sure enough, when there came a few tremulous lines to inform me he was very ill. I cannot tell, and it would be useless to do so if I could, what were my sufferings; there never came another word nor sign; I tried to be cheerful and to live on in some way, but the dear charm of life was gone; no new lover ever displaced the old one from my heart; but to-night—what do you think I heard to-night! Why, that Philip Heaton is a rich man, and has been married these—these—oh, a good while! Mr. Pell saw him last summer, and he inquired about me—if I was married—said I deserved to be—I was a good sort of a girl—and a good deal more he said of me in the same way." Alas, for Molly! then and there vanished the last and only romance of her existence.

I have not given the story in her precise language, for I cannot remember that, but I have retained the spirit and the essential facts of her not unparalleled experience. It needed no subsequent observation for me to see how things stood, and how they would end; how in the estimation of Mrs. Trowbridge Molly did what she pleased, and when she pleased, and nothing if she pleased; how she had all the advantages of a home and a mother's care, and how she could get along better without her. And I saw, too, how Molly thought she did herself a thousand things no money would hire her to do; how she took an interest in the house, as though it were all hers—getting small thanks after all; how she sewed for others to earn her scanty clothing; and how she had moved her heirlooms about till she was tired, and had begun to take less romantic and more practical views of things. She never said so precisely, but I saw that a good home and an estimable man to care for her were weighing heavily against an old dream; so that I was not surprised when on entering her room one day I found her standing before her grandmother's narrow looking-glass, carefully dividing hair from hair, and now and then plucking one that had a questionable hue; nor was it any surprise when Kate told me, in a whisper, that in just seventeen days and three hours and ten minutes Molly would become Mrs. Pell. She had made accurate calculation, for the wedding day was in her little life a great day indeed, as in fact it was to Mrs. Trowbridge; whose laughter, for those intervening seventeen days, I think had scarcely a cessation.

Mr. Pell, meantime, became unusually nimble, hopping and balancing about like a spring bird, and more than ever repeating his words in a musical trill;—"wify, wify, wify!" he would say sometimes, assuming the conjugal address before the conjugal ceremony, and he was observed to wear his hat awry, and to go abroad in a red boyish waistcoat which he probably had not worn for years: and Molly I think was even more nice in her choice of words than was her wont.

The night before the marriage, as we sat together before the fire, she took from the shelf, and unfolded from a dozen careful wrappers, an old volume, and shook into the ashes from betwixt the leaves some broken remnants of flowers. She sighed as she did so—they may have been the three lilies; in a moment she smiled again, and twirling the marriage ring, and looking from the window, observed that she could not think of anything but the splendor of the queen of night! I thought it was very likely.

All the preceding day Kate was in the seventh heaven; she wore new calf-skin shoes and a new calico dress, and why should she not be happy? Mrs. Trowbridge said a wedding seemed to her one of the solemnest things in the world, but she laughed all the while; she did not even say "well," that Mr. Trowbridge bought a new hat for the occasion, which he did not once all that day move from his head.

I will not attempt a description of the wedding festivities. It seemed to me half the folks in Clovernook were there. Sally Blake came first, pleasant and useful as ever, and afterward Miss Claverel, Miss Whitfield, poor Mrs. Troost with her ill-omened gossip, and excellent Mrs. Hill, our old friend, with kindlier prophecies of happiness, and Dr. Hayward, the family physician, and a great many others, living in the neighborhood, besides two or three smartish young grocers and produce dealers from the city, with whom Mr. Pell had transactions "agreeable and profitable all round." Mrs. Trowbridge's children were as noisy and ill-mannered as ever, the good woman laughed at every observation made by herself, or the bride and groom, or the guests, and Mr. Pell was smartly dressed and looked unutterable and said incomprehensible things, all with an air of self-satisfaction which gave ample assurance that he was blessed as ever bridegroom should wish to be. As for Molly, she was attired very prettily, and seemed, or tried to seem, the happiest woman in the house; but I could see once in a while an involuntary seriousness in her eyes; and once, after she had suddenly quitted the room for a moment, I thought I saw signs of tears, driven back with a strong will—tears that had come with unbidden memories from scenes where she had walked in summer nights, so long ago—where beautiful hopes were born, and buried, buried forever. As she entered the room, her hand upon her breast, the angels might have heard her say, "Be still, be still, oh turbulent heart!" and when she led off a dance with Mr. Pell, she looked as if she had quite forgot all the dreams ever dreamed by Molly Root.

These marriages of convenience are sad affairs, even among the humble, with whom so many cares divide authority in the heart. It is well when they are contracted by brave natures, with unfaltering wills, looking backward for darkness and forward for light, and never suffering the past to prevent the clutching of every possible good in the present, or to cloud the future so that its farthest joys shall fail of inspiring continual hope and strength.

Mr. and Mrs. Pell are well-to-do in the world; the "rise of property," indeed, has made them rich, and Molly sometimes sends her carriage to bring Mrs. Trowbridge to tea, and gives to Kate occasionally some cast-off dress or last year's finery, which, made over, is to her as good as new. The reader will understand why she remained so long unmarried, why at length she became a wife; and those accustomed much to the conversations of married ladies perhaps might hear without surprise her frequent declaration, that "dear Mr. Pell" was her "first and only love!"

——There they go! How those spanking grays, with their shining harness, and the bright green and yellow barouche, make the dust fly as they whirl by the Clovernook Hotel! Mr. Pell says "It is the thing, *the* thing, precisely the thing! Isn't it Molly, Molly, Molly!"

The sad marriage of Molly Root to the mindless Mr. Pell after being jilted by Philip.

"Why she remained unmarried and why at length she became a wife"

Mrs. Trowbridge's unbearable house hidden by her laughter.

The dialogue betw. Molly and Mr. Pell. 3 x repetitions.

romance vs. realism | the discovery that Philip is not dead, but true but that he is alive and untrue propels

CHARLOTTE RYAN

I

AS THERE IS in every neighborhood a first family, so there is a last family—a family a little behind everybody else—and in Clovernook this family was named Ryan. They did not indeed live very near the village, but rather on the very verge of our neighborhood. A little dingy house, off the main road, and situated in a hollow, was their habitation, and, though they were intelligent, they had no ideas of the elegancies of life, and but meagre ones, indeed, of its comforts.

Charlotte, the eldest daughter, inherited all the cleverness of her parents, with few of their prejudices against modern improvements, so that, now and then, her notions ran out into a sort of flowery border along the narrow way in which she had been taught to walk. Small opportunities had she for the indulgence of refined or elegant tastes, but sometimes, as she brought home the cows at night, she lingered to make a "wreath of roses," or to twist the crimson tops of the iron-weeds with her long black hair; and once I remember seeing her, while she was yet a little girl, with a row of maple leaves pinned to the bottom of her skirt; she was pretending they were the golden fringe of her petticoat.

Clovernook boasted of one or two select schools even at that time, to which most of the people, who were not very poor, contrived to send their daughters: but little Charlotte went down the hollow, across a strip of woods, to the old schoolmaster, who taught in a log house and in an obscure neighborhood for the summer, and made shoes in the winter, and I suspect he was but imperfectly skilled in either vocation, for I remember it used to be said that he had "taken up both trades out of his own head." The girls of the "high school" were in her eyes "privileged beyond the common run—quite on the verge of heaven." And no wonder she regarded them so: the ribbons that tied their braids, were prettier than the two or three teeth of horn comb that fastened her own hair, and her long checked-apron compared unfavorably with their white ones. But with this period of her life I have little to do, as the story I am going to relate is limited to the circle of a few days, when Charlotte had ceased to pin maple leaves on her petticoat, and wore instead ornaments of glass and pinchbeck.*

"Here is a letter for Miss Ryan: it will not be much out of your way, if you will be so kind," said the post-master to me one evening, as I received my own missives, for at that time the postmaster of Clovernook knew all the persons in the habit of receiving letters, and as one for Miss Ryan had never been there before, I, as well as he, naturally supposed it would be a surprise, probably an agreeable one to her, and I therefore gladly took charge of it, choosing instead of the dusty highway, a path through the meadows, and close under the shadow of the woods, which brought the home of Charlotte directly in my way, though the duty I undertook added more than a mile to my walk homeward. It was in the late autumn, and one of those dry, windy, uncomfortable days which brings thought from its wanderings to hover down about one's home; so, as the night fell, I quickened my steps, pausing now and then to listen to the roar down deep in the woods, which seemed like the moan of the sea—which I had heard only in imagination then—or to mark the cabin homes, peering out of the forest, and calculate the amount of comfort or discomfort in them or about; and I remember to this day some particular facts from which inferences were drawn. Before one door, a dozen dun and speckled pigs were feeding from a trough, and sunken in mud knee deep, and near them, barefooted, and wearing a red flannel shirt, stood a ragged urchin, whose shouts of delight would have been pleasant to hear, but for the harsh,

* Pinchbeck is an alloy of zinc and copper used to imitate gold.

scolding voice that half drowned them. Both the joy and the anger were a mystery at first, but I presently saw by what they were caused.

"I'll come out and settle with you, my boy, if you don't quit that—mind I tell you!" screamed an old woman, leaning over the low rail fence of the door-yard, her cap-border flapping like a flag of war, and with one foot on the ground and one in the air, as she bent eagerly forward, gesticulating vehemently, but chiefly in the direction of an old cat, which the boy had put in a slender harness of twine—his own ingenious workmanship, I suspect. He laughed heartily, in spite of the threatened settlement, calling out in high glee, as pussy ran up a tree to escape him, "Jementallies! how she goes it!"

"I'll go you," continued the monitor, "as sure as you're born, if you don't ungear the poor sarpent before you're a minute older!" And so I passed out of hearing and out of sight, and I have never since been enlightened as to the adjustment of the pending difficulty.

It was quite night, and the candle-light streamed bright through the dead morning-glory vines which still hung at the window, when my rap at the door of Mr. Ryan was answered by a loud and clear "Come in!" so earnest that it seemed half angry.

Homely, but still home-like, was the scene that presented itself—the hickory logs were blazing in the deep wide fire-place, the children were seated quietly on the trundle-bed, for their number had grown faster than that of the chairs, and talking in an under-tone about "choosing sides" at school, and what boys and girls were "first-rate and particular" as choosers, and what ones were big dumb-heads: they presently changed their tone from a low key to a sharp whisper, much more distinct, but my entrance did not interrupt their discussion.

Mr. Ryan, wearing a coat and trowsers with patches at elbow and knee of a dissimilar color, was seated on a low stool in the corner, engaged in softening with melted tallow the hard last year's shoes of the children, which had been put aside during the summer season.

"A young winter," he said, by way of welcoming me, and then continued apologetically, and as though it was almost a disgrace to wear shoes, "the wind to-day makes a body feel like drawing their feet in their feathers."

I said the winter brought its needs, or something of that sort, implying that we regarded things in the same way, and he resumed and continued the mollifying process without speaking another word.

Golden rings of dried pumpkins hung along the ceiling, bags of dried apples and peaches, bunches of herbs, and the like, and here and there from projections of framework, hung stockings, by dozens, and other garments suited to the times. A limb of bright red apples, withering in the warmth and smoke, beautified the jamb, beneath the great "bake oven," and such were all the ornaments of which the room could boast, I think.

Mrs. Ryan was busy at the kneading trough, making shortcakes for breakfast—silent mostly, and wearing a look of severity, as though she knew her duty and did it. Only Charlotte came forward to meet me, and smiled her welcome. The Methodist "Advocate" lay open on the table, and some sewing work dropped from her lap as she rose. She politely offered me the chair with the leather bottom, and added to the sticks on the fire, manifesting her good will and courtesy in the only ways possible.

She had grown beautifully into womanhood, and though her dress was neither of choice material, nor so made as to set off her person very advantageously, it was easy to perceive that under the hands of an artist in waists, skirts, &c., her form would seem admirable for its contour and fine proportion, while her face should be a signal for envy or for admiration to youthful women and men, if she were "in society." And she had in some way acquired, too, quite an agreeable manner of her own, only wanting a freedom from restraining influences to become really graceful and captivating; and I could not help wishing, as I looked on her, that she could find a position better suited to her capacities and inclinations. A foolish wish.

The letter elicited expressions of surprise and curiosity from all members of the family, except Charlotte, who suppressed her interest for the time. "Let me see it, let me see it," exclaimed the children, but the stamp of the father's foot brought silence into the room, on which he arose, and wiping his hands on his hair, prepared to read the letter, for Charlotte did not think of breaking the seal herself.

"It's from down the river I reckon," said the mother, "and tells us all about Peter's folks." Charlotte blushed and looked annoyed. "I'll just bet!"

said one of the boys, a bright-looking lad of nine or ten years, "that a queen gets letters every day; yes, and written on gold paper, likely enough," he continued, after a moment, and in response to himself as it were.

"I wish I was there," said a younger sister, smiling at the pleasant fancy, "and I'd climb away up on her throne some time when she was gone to meeting, and steal some of her things."

"And you would get catched and have your head chopped off with a great big axe," replied the brother.

The little girl continued musingly, "I expect Charlotte's new Sunday dress is no finer than a queen wears every day."

"Every day!" exclaimed the mother in lofty contempt, "she wears as good washing-day in the kitchen." In the midst of these speculations I took leave. A day or two afterwards, I learned that Charlotte was gone to pass a month or two with some relations near the city.

II

THESE RELATIVES were but recently established in a country home, having belonged originally to one of the northern seaport towns. The family embraced but three persons, the father, whose life had in some capacity been passed mostly at sea, and two daughters—all unfitted by education and habit for their new position.

Of course Charlotte had heard much of her uncle, Captain Bailey, and his daughters, and in childish simplicity supposed them to be not only the grandest but also the most excellent people in the world. They dwelt in her thoughts on a plane of being so much above her, that she involuntarily looked up to them and reverenced them as if they were of a fairer and purer world.

Through all her childhood it had been a frequent wish that some of uncle John's folks would come, but uncle John's folks never came, and so she grew into womanhood without being much disenchanted. Nobody about Clovernook was at all comparable to them in any respect, as they lived in the beautiful region of her dreams.

Mrs. Ryan and Mrs. Bailey were sisters, who in early life were all in all to each other. Marriage had separated them, by distance much, by circumstances more. Mrs. Bailey went to an establishment in town, and after a round of dissipations and gaieties, became a small link in the chain of fashion, having married out of, and above her previous and fit position. Mrs. Ryan, who as a girl was the less dashing and spirited of the two, became a farmer's wife, and with the energy and determination which characterized her always, struck at once into the wilderness in search of a new home.

Sad enough was the parting of the sisters, and many the promises to write often, and to visit each other as soon as might be; but these promises were never kept, and perhaps it was well they never were, for far outside of the blessed oneness of thought and feeling in which they parted, would have been their meeting! Absence, separate interests, different ways of life, soon did their work.

As I said, they never met, and so never knew that they had grown apart, but each lived in the memory of the other, best and most beautiful to the last. But though each mother taught her children to love and reverence the good aunt that lived far away, and whom possibly they would see some time, the young Baileys failed to be impressed with that respect and admiration for their country relations, which the country relations felt for them.

After a series of successes came adverse fortune to the Baileys, then the death of the wife and mother, and so, partly in the hope of bettering their condition, and partly to escape mortification, the broken and helpless family removed from their statelier home and settled in the neighborhood of our beautiful city in the west. For they fancied, as many other people do who know nothing about it, that the farmer's is a sort of holiday life; that after planting the crop he may sleep or play till the harvest time; that then the labor of a day or two fills the barn with bright sheaves and sweet hay; and that all the while, and without any effort, cattle and sheep and horses are growing and fattening, and plenty flowing in. A little experience sufficed to cure the Baileys of this pleasant conceit. In truth, they didn't go to work in the right way, with an honest determination that compels success. Farming and housekeeping were begun as delightful experiments, and when the novelty was lost, they fell back into lamentations and repinings for the opulence they had lost. Briers made sorry work with Captain Bailey's ruffles, and the morning dew was unfavorable to the polish of his boots; the corn didn't fall into baskets of itself, nor the apples come home without having been first shaken from the trees, and picked up, one by one. Weeds and burs ran over the garden and choked the small vegetables; the cows grew lean, and their milk dried away, to the astonishment of all parties—for nobody suspected they were not milked regularly and rightly, or that their wants were not attended to, and some fearful distemper was supposed to have attacked them, as day after day flocks of buzzards and crows were seen settling in hollows where the poor creatures had died. But Captain Bailey's troubles were trifles compared with the afflictions of his daughters, who not only sighed and cried, but wished themselves dead, a dozen times a day. The hard, yellow balls of butter, which they fancied would be so nice, required more labor and care in the making than they were willing to bestow; bread was taken from the oven black and heavy; and, in fact, the few things that were done at all were not done well, and general weariness and dissatisfaction was the consequence.

"I wish I was in heaven!" exclaimed Miss Sally Bailey, one day, more wrathfully than piously, turning at the same time from the churn and hiding her eyes from the great splash of cream that soiled the front of her lavender colored silk.

"It's no use for us to try to live like anybody," answered Kate, "and we might as well give up first as last, and put on linsey, and work, and work, and work till we die!"

And both girls sat down and bent their eyes on the floor, either not seeing, or affecting not to see, the discomfort in which their father was; poor man, he had come in from the field with a thorn in his hand, and with the blood oozing from the wound, was vainly searching under chairs and tables, and shoving his hand one way and the other across the carpet, for the needle lost in his endeavor to perform with it a surgical operation.

"*I do* wish," he said at last, a little petulantly, "I could ever have any body to do any thing for me."

"I am sure I am sorry for the accident," said one of the girls, "if that will do you any good."

"I don't think it will," was the reply; and the other sister offered assistance, assuring her father, and as though he were responsible for it, that she could feel nothing less than the broomstick in her clumsy fingers, so it was useless to try to handle a needle.

Having survived the operation, Captain Bailey, who was really disposed to do the best he could, pinned a towel against his vest, and took hold of the churn, saying, "Now, my dears, I'll make the butter, while you arrange the dinner."

"I would like to know what we are to arrange," said Kate, tossing her head, "there is nothing in the house that I know of."

"Surely there is something," the father said, working the dasher most energetically; "there is pork, and flour, and apples, and cream, and butter, and potatoes, and coffee, and tea, and sugar"—there the girls interrupted him with something about a meal suitable for wood-choppers.

Captain Bailey was now seriously discouraged, and without speaking again, continued to churn for two hours, but the cream was cold and thin, and at the end of that time looked no more likely to "come" than at first, so giving the churn a jostle to one side, with something that sounded very like an oath, the gentleman removed the towel which had served him for an apron, and taking down his gun from the wall, walked hurriedly in the direction of the woods. But he was one of those men who are called good-hearted, and though he managed badly, never doing either himself or anybody else any good, still, every one said, "he means well," and "what a good-hearted fellow he is." So, of course, his amiability soon returned, and having brought down two squirrels and a wood-cock, whistling out the hope and good-nature that were in his heart. "Well, Sally," he said, throwing down the game, "here is something for dinner."

"Very well," she replied, but without looking up, or ceasing from her work of rubbing chalk on the cream-spot of her dress.

Kate, since her father's departure, had bestirred herself so much as to pin a towel about the churn, set it one side, and fill the tea-kettle, after which she seated herself with the last new novel.

"Well my dear, what is the news with you?" asked the captain, punching the fire at the same time, in an anxious way.

"The news is," she answered, "that two chickens have drowned themselves in a pail of dish-water, and the pig you bought at the vendue is choked to death with a loaf of burnt bread—when I found it, it was in the last agonies," she continued, laughing, "and I don't see what we *are* to do."

"An idea strikes me," answered the father, in no wise discouraged. "Write to your cousin—what's her name? who lives out in Clovernook—she's a housekeeper, I'll warrant you; write to her to come and visit you for a month or two, and initiate you in the ways of the woods."

"A good notion," said Kate, throwing down her book, and the dinner went forward better than any one had done since the housekeeping began.

The farm selected by Captain Bailey, was east of the Queen City—not so far, however, but that some of the spires, and it is a city of spires, were clearly visible from its higher elevations. Both house and grounds were seriously out of repair, having been abandoned by the person who purchased and fitted them up, and sold ultimately at a sacrifice. They were well suited for the present proprietor; the spirit of broken-down assumption reigned supreme everywhere: you might see it perched on the leaning posts of the gateway, and peering from under the broken mullions of the great windows. It had been a fine place, when the forest land was first trimmed up and cleared, when pebbles and flowers bordered the rivulets, and the eminence on which stood the house was terraced into green stairs. The tall red chimneys were some of them fallen partly down now, and the avenue leading from the gate to the hall was lost in weeds and grass, through which only a wagon-track was broken.

One or two trellised summer-houses stood pitching down the hill, and here and there a rose-bush or lilac lopped aside devoid of beauty, except the silver sieves woven amongst them by the black and yellow spiders.

III

THE LITTLE CART in which Charlotte Ryan rode with her father rattled terribly; it seemed never to have made so much noise till then; it would betray their poverty, but if her father would only drive softly and leave the cart at the gate, it doubtless would be supposed that they had come in a more stylish way. Mr. Ryan, however, was a plain blunt farmer, and would have driven his little cart up to the White House, and elbowed his way through the Cabinet without a fear or a blush for his home-spun dress or country breeding, if he had felt inclined to pay his respects to the President—and why indeed should he not? He was a yeoman, and not ashamed of being a yeoman—what cause had he to be? But a pride of despising all innovation, all elegance, were peculiarities that stood in his light. So, as I said, he dashed forward at a rapid and noisy rate, feeling much, honest man, as though the sound of his wagon wheels would be the gladdest one his friends ever heard. Nor did he slacken rein till the feet of his work horses struck on the pavement before the main entrance of the house, and with their sides panting against the wide bands of faded leather composing their harness, stood champing the bit, and foaming as though they had run a race.

Poor Charlotte! she could scarcely rise out of the straw in which she was imbedded, when the hall-door opened, and Captain Bailey, followed by his two daughters, came forward to meet her and her father, with self-possession and well-bred cordiality. The young women not only kissed her, but imposed a similar infliction on the dear uncle, making many tender inquiries about the aunt and sweet little cousins at home; but when Captain Bailey offered his arm, saying, "This way, my dear," the discomfiture of the niece was completed, and slipping two fingers over his elbow, and at arm's length from him, she entered the hall, trying her best not to hear her father say—"Bless your souls, gals, I don't want your sarvant man," as he went lustily to unharness his horses, just as he would have done at home.

"We are so glad you are come," said the cousins; "we want you to teach us so many things," but Charlotte felt that though the last part of the sentence might be true, the first was not—for we instinctively recognize the difference between formal politeness and real heartiness. Partly because she thought she ought to do so, and partly because her conflicting emotions could find vent in no other way, she began to cry.

"Are you sick?" asked the girls, really concerned, for their sense of propriety would not have allowed of such an ebulition of feeling on any occasion, much less on one so trivial. They could not imagine why she cried—models of propriety that they were—unless indeed, she were in great bodily pain.

Presently Mr. Ryan, having attended to the duties of the groom, came in, bearing in each hand a small budget,* containing presents of his choicest apples, saying as he presented them, "These apples my daughter here helped me to gather, and we have a hundred bushels as fine at home."

The father was now appealed to for an explanation of Charlotte's conduct, for she had covered her face with her hands, and sat in an obscure corner, sobbing to herself.

"She sees so many strange, new, and fine things that she is not used to," he said, for he could understand her; "they make her feel kind of bad and home-sick like. Charlotte," he continued, speaking as he would to a child, "wipe up your eyes, and let's see how much better your uncle's stock is than ours."

Glad of any excuse to escape from the cold speculation of the eyes that were on her, the daughter obeyed, making neither excuse nor apology for the abrupt and somewhat inquisitive procedure.

The sunshine soon dried up her tears, for her spirit was healthful, and though she had given way to a brief impulse of sorrow, it was not an expression of habitual sickliness of feeling. Her father's repeated exclamations of surprise and contempt for the bad culture and bad stock, helped, too, to reassure her, and she returned at length to the house, her crushed self-esteem built up in part, at least; but contrasts unfavorable to herself would present themselves, in spite of efforts to keep them down, whenever her brown hands touched the lily ones of her cousins, or when the noise of her coarse shoes reminded her of their delicate slippers; and when toward sunset the horses were brought out, feeling smart, for they had had a visitor's portion of oats, she half wished she was to go back, especially when she remembered the contents of the little bundle she had brought with her, containing what she considered the choice portion of her wardrobe.

But I need not dwell longer on this phase of her experience. In education, in knowledge of the world, in the fashionable modes of dress, the Misses Bailey were in the advance of her, as much as she, in good sense,

*A budget is a workman's bag, pack, or wallet, generally made of leather; the leather pouch in which a mower carries his whetstone; a bag or wallet in which Indians carried their totems, weapons, etc.

natural refinement, and instinctive perceptions of fitness, was superior to them. But unfortunately she could see much more clearly their advantages than her own. Falling back on the deficiencies of which she was so painfully aware, she could not think it possible that she possessed any advantage whatever, much less any personal charms.

All the while the envied cousins were envious of her roseate complexion, elasticity of movement, and black heavy braids of hair, arranged, though they were, something ungracefully. The books which they kept, to be admired rather than read, afforded her much delight, and alone with these or with her uncle, the homesick and restless feeling was sometimes almost forgotten; for Captain Bailey was kind from the impulses of his nature, and not because he thought it duty or policy. The cheerful and natural aspect which things assumed under the transforming hands of Charlotte gave him excessive delight, and then when her work was done, she would tie on her sunbonnet, and accompany him in his walks through the fields and woods, making plans with him for the next year's culture and improvements. In the evenings she read to him, or listened to stories of the sea, which it gave him pleasure to relate; while the young ladies mourned at one side of the room over their hapless fate—wishing themselves back in their old home, or that Mrs. so, or so, would come out to the West, and give such parties as she used.

"But then," said they, "there is nobody here that is anybody," and so the mere supposition that a fashionable lady might come West and give parties, hops, re-unions, &c., was but a new source of discontent.

Sometimes they recounted, partly for the pleasure of hearing themselves, and partly to astonish and dazzle their country cousin, the various elegant costumes they had worn, on what, to them, were the most interesting occasions of their lives; and after all, they were not so much to blame—it was natural that they should pine for their native air, and for the gaieties to which they had been accustomed. But to Charlotte, whose notions of filial respect were almost reverent, it was a matter of painful surprise that they never mentioned their mother, or in any way alluded to her, except in complaints of the mourning clothes, which compelled them to be *so* plain. Neither brain nor heart of either was ample enough for a great sorrow.

At first Charlotte had lent her aid in the management and completion of household affairs with hearty good will, but the more she did the more seemed to be expected of her—the ladies couldn't learn because they paid no attention to her teaching, and took no interest in it, though never was there a more painstaking instructor. All persons are not gifted alike, they said, "it seems so easy for you to work." But in what their own gifts consisted it were hard to tell.

"Really, cousin Charlotte is quite companionable sometimes," said Sally, one day—laying emphasis on the word cousin—after partaking of some of her fresh-baked pumpkin pies.

"But it's a pity," replied Kate, "that she only appears to advantage in the kitchen. Now what in the *world* would you do if Dr. Opdike, or Lawyer Dingley, or any of that set were to come?"

"Why," said Sally, laughing, "I always think it's as well to tell the truth, when there is no particular advantage to be gained by telling anything else, so I should simply say—'A country cousin, whom father has taken a fancy to patronize.'"

Kate laughed, and taking with them some light romance, fit suited to wile the way into dreamland, they retired to their chamber.

"Suppose we steal a march on the girls," said Captain Bailey, entering the room where Charlotte was engaged in idle endeavors to make her hair curl—"what say you to riding into town?"

Charlotte hesitated, for nothing called her to town except the search for pleasure, and she had been unaccustomed to go out of her way for that; but directly yielding to persuasion, she was tying on her bonnet, when the Captain, desirous of improving her toilet, suggested that she should not wear her best hat, but the old hack of Kate or Sally. The little straw bonnet, which looked smart enough at the prayer meetings and "circuit preachings" of the log school-house, became suddenly hateful, and the plain white ribbon, crossed about the crown, only in keeping with summer, and seventy years. Her cheeks flushed as her trembling hands removed her favorite bonnet, and the uncle continued—"just bring along Kate's white cashmere, while you are about it—yours will be too warm to-day, I think."

The shawl which Charlotte proposed to wear was a coarse black woolen one, which had already been worn by her mother for twenty years, or thereabouts, and though she had never looked so well in her life, as in the old bonnet and shawl belonging to Kate, still she felt ill at ease, and could not suppress a wish that she had at once declined the invitation. Captain Bailey, who was really a kind-hearted man, exerted himself to dissipate the cloud which weighed down her spirit, but ever and anon she turned aside to wipe the tears away. My wish was being fulfilled—Charlotte had attained a new position.

"Now, my dear," said the uncle, as he assisted Charlotte out of the carriage, before the most fashionable dry-goods shop of the city, "you must favor me by accepting a new gown and hat, and whatever other trifles you may fancy to have."

"Oh, no, no!" she said, blushing, but dissent was not to be listened to—she was merely desired to select one from among the many varieties of silks thrown on the counter.

Now the purchasing of a silk dress was in the estimation of Charlotte, a proceeding of very grave importance, not to be thus hastily gone into. She would consent to accept of a calico—positively of nothing more—and on being assured by the clerks, as they brought forward some highly colored prints, that they were the patterns most in vogue, she selected one of mingled red and yellow, declined to receive anything further, and returned home, saddened and injured, rather than glad and grateful. She could not help wishing she had remained in her old haunts instead of going where people were ashamed of her—and then would come the more crushing and bitter thoughts which justified the feelings with which they regarded her; and so, in alternate emotions of self-contempt and honest and indignant pride, she continued to think and think—sometimes disregarding and sometimes answering briefly and coldly the various remarks of her kind relative. The sun had set an hour when the white walls of his house appeared in the distance, and as they approached nearer, it was evident from the lights and laughter within, that the occasion with the inmates was an unusually joyous one.

At the sound of footsteps in the hall, Kate came hurriedly forth to communicate the intelligence of the arrival of a friend, "Mr. Sully Dinsmore, a young author of rising eminence, and a man whose acquaintance was worth having"—and she continued, as her father observed—"glad to have you know him, Charlotte"—"Of course you will like to make some change in your toilet—the dress you have on affects your complexion shockingly."

Charlotte assented, not knowing how she was to improve her appearance, inasmuch as she then wore the best clothes she possessed.

Once in the dressing room, she threw indignantly aside what appeared to her but borrowed finery, and gave way to such a passion of tears as never before had dimmed her beautiful eyes.

She was disturbed at length by a light tap at the door, followed by an inquiry of her uncle whether she were not ready to go below. "Thank you, I don't wish to go," she replied, with as much steadiness of voice as she could command; but her sorrow betrayed itself, and the kindly entreaties which should have soothed, only aggravated it.

"Well, my dear," said the uncle, as if satisfied, seeing that she was really unpresentable, "if you will come down and make a cup of tea, you and I will have the pleasure of partaking of it by ourselves."

This little strategem succeeded in part, and in the bustling preparation of supper, the smile of resignation, if not of gaiety, came back; for Charlotte's heart was good and pure, and her hands quick always in the service of another. The benevolent uncle prudently forbore any reference to guest or drawing-room for the evening, and leading the conversation into unlooked-for channels, only betrayed by unusual kindness of manner a remembrance of the unhappy incidents of the day. A practiced observer, however, might have detected the tenor of his thoughts, in the liberal amount of cream and sugar—twice as much as she desired—infused into the tea of the gentle niece, whose pained heart throbbed sensitively, while her lips smiled thanks.

IV

THE ORANGE LIGHT of the coming sunrise was widening among the eastern clouds, and the grass that had till then kept green, stood stiff in the white frost, when the quick step of Charlotte broke rather than bent it down, for she had risen early to milk the spotted heifer ere any one should be astir. She tripped gracefully along, unconscious that earnest eyes were on her, singing snatches of rural songs, and drinking the beauty of the sunrise with the eyes of a poet. Half playfully, and half angrily, the heifer shook her horns of pearly green for such untimely rousing from the warm grassy hollow in which she lay, but the white pine pail was soon brimming with milk.

The wind blew aside Charlotte's little hood, and with cheeks, flushed with the air, and the exercise, gleaming through the tangles of her black hair, she really presented a picture refreshing to look on, especially to eyes wearied with artificial complexions and curls. As she arose the hues deepened, and she drew the hood quickly forward—for standing midway in the crooked path leading from the door-yard to the cow-yard, and shelling corn to a flock of chickens gathered about him, was Mr. Sully Dinsmore—a rather good looking, pleasant-faced young man of thirty or thereabout. He bowed with graceful ease as the girl approached, and followed his salutation by some jest about the fowl proceeding in which he had been detected, and at the same time took from her hand the pail with an air and manner which seemed to say he had been used to carrying milk-pails all his life—there was nothing he liked so well, in fact. Charlotte had no time for embarrassment—deference was so blended with familiarity—and beside, the gentleman apologized so sweetly and sadly for the informal introduction he had given himself; the young lady looked so like one—he hesitated—like his own dear wife—and he continued with a sigh, "she sleeps now among the mountains." He was silent a moment, and then went on as if forcibly rallying, "This is a delightful way to live, is it not? We always intended, poor Florence and I, to come to the West, buy a farm, and pass the evening of our days in quiet independence; but," in a more subdued tone, "I had never money enough till dear Florence died, and since that I have cared little about my way of life—little about life at all."

Charlotte's sympathies were aroused. Poor man, his cheek did look pale, and doubtless it was to dissipate his grief that he was there; and with simple earnestness she expressed a hope, that the bright hills and broad forests of the West might restore something of the old healthiness of feeling in his heart.

His thanks were given with the tone and manner of one sincerely grateful; the gay worldlings, he said, with whom he had been fated mostly to mingle, could not appreciate his feelings. All this required much less time than I have taken to record it, for the gentleman made the most of the brief walk.

At the door Captain Bailey met them, and with a look of mingled surprise and curiosity, was beginning a formal presentation, when Mr. Dinsmore assured him such ceremony was quite unnecessary—each had recognized a friend in the other, he said, and they were already progressing toward very intimate relations. No sooner had Charlotte disappeared, with her pail and strainer, than, abruptly changing tone and manner, he exclaimed, "Dev'lish pretty girl—I hope she remains here as long as I do!"

The Captain, who was displeased, affected ignorance of what had been said, and bent his steps in rather a hurried way toward the barn.

"Propose to fodder the stock, eh?" called out Mr. Dinsmore: "allow me to join you—just the business I was brought up to do." And coming forward, he linked his arm through that of the stout Captain, and brought him to a sudden standstill, saying, with the delightful enthusiasm of a voyager come to the beautiful shore of a new country, "What a wonderful scene—forest and meadow, and orchards and wheat-fields! why, Captain, you are a rich man; if I owned this place I shouldn't want anything beside—no other place half so good about here, I suppose?—in fact, it seems to me, in all my travels, I never saw such a farm—just enough of it—let's see, what's its extent? Yes, I thought you must have just about that much; and, if I had never seen it, I could have sworn it was the best farm in the country, because I know the soundness of your judgment, you see!"

The Captain drew himself up, and surveyed the prospect more proudly than he had done before, saying he ought to know something of good land, and favorable localities—he had seen something of the world.

"Why," answered Mr. Sully Dinsmore, as though his host had not done half justice to himself, "I guess there is not much of the world worth seeing that you have not seen; you have been a *great* traveler, Captain; and you know what you see, too," he added in a tone acceptably insinuating.

"Yes, yes, that is true: few men know better what they see than Captain Bailey," and he began pointing out the various excellencies and attractions of his place which the young man did not seem to have observed.

"No wonder," Mr. Dinsmore proceeded, "my vision was too much dazzled to take all in at once; you must remember, I am only used to rugged hills and bleak rocks, where the farmers fasten the grain down with stones, lest being indignant at the poor soil, it should *scrabble* out, you see." This word was coined with special reference to the Captain, who sometimes found himself reduced to such necessities. An approving peal of laughter rewarded his pains, and he repeated it, "Yes, the grain would actually scrabble out but for the stones; so you see it's natural my eyes failed to perceive all those waves of beauty and plenty." Where he saw the waves referred to, only himself could have told, for the stubble land looked bleak enough, and the November woods dark and withered to dreariness. "Well, Captain," he said at last, as though the scene were a continual delight to his eyes, "it's of no use—I could stand gazing all day—so let us fodder those fine cattle of yours."

With good will he entered upon the work—seizing bundles of oats and corn-blades, and dusty hay, regardless of broadcloths and linen; now patting the neck of some clumsy-horned, long-legged steer, calling to the Captain to know if he were not of the full blood; and now, as he scattered the bushel of oats among the little flock of thin and dirty sheep, inquiring, with the deepest interest apparently, if they were not something superior to the southdowns or merinos—for the wool was as fine as could be.

The "chores" completed, they returned to the house, but Mr. Dinsmore found so many things to admire by the way that their progress was slow; now he paused at the gateway to remark what nice strong posts they were—he believed they were of cedar; and now he turned in admiration of the smoke-house—a ruinous and exceedingly diminutive building of bricks, of which the walls were overgrown with moss, the roof sunken, and the door off its hinges: they seemed to him about the best bricks he ever saw—moss wouldn't gather over them if they were not solid as a rock—"what a pleasing effect it has," he said.

"A little out of repair," said the Captain, "and too small—too small! I think of enlarging," and he attempted to urge his companion forward.

"But," interposed the guest, still gazing at the smoke-house, "that is one of your few errors of judgment: I wouldn't have it an inch bigger, nor an inch less; and besides, the moss is prettier than any paint."

"I must put up the door, at least," interrupted the Captain.

"Ay, no sir, let me advise you to the contrary. Governor Patterson, of New Jersey, smokes all his meat, and has for twenty years, in a house without a door—it makes the flavor finer—I thought it was built so on purpose—if ever I have a farm I should make your smoke-house a model."

This morning all the household tasks had fallen on Charlotte. "She went to bed early," said the cousins, "and can afford to get up early—besides, she has no toilet to make, as we have."

But though they gave her the trouble of delaying the breakfast, after she had prepared it, Charlotte was amply repaid for all, in the praises bestowed on her coffee and toast by Mr. Sully Dinsmore. Her uncle, too, said she had never looked so pretty, that her hair was arranged in most becoming style, and that her dress suited her complexion.

"Really, Lotty, I am growing jealous," said Kate, tossing her head in a way meant to be at once irresistibly captivating, and patronizing.

Kate had never said "Lotty" before, but seeing that Mr. Dinsmore was not shocked with the rural cousin, she thought it politic to make the most of her, and from that moment glided into the most loving behavior. Lotty was a dear little creature, in her way, quite pretty—and she was such a housekeeper! Finally, it was concluded to make a "virtue of necessity," and acknowledge that they were learning to keep house themselves—in truth, they thought it fine fun, and preferred to have as few troublesome servants about as possible.

So a few days glided swiftly and pleasantly to Charlotte, notwithstanding that most of the household labor—all its drudgery—devolved on her. What cared she for this, while the sunrise of a paradisal morning was glorifying the world. Kate and Sally offered their assistance in making the new dress, and contrived various little articles, which they said would relieve the high colors, and have a stylish effect. These arts, to the simple-minded country girl, were altogether novel—at home she had never heard of "becoming dress." She, as well as all the girls whom she knew, had been in the habit of going to town once or twice a year, when the butter brought the best price, or when a load of hay or a cow was sold, and purchasing a dress, bonnet, &c., without regard to color or fashion. A new thing was supposed to look well, and to their unpractised eyes always did look well.

"Come here, Lotty," said Kate, one evening, surveying her cousin, as she hooked the accustomed old black silk. "Just slip off that old-womanish thing," she continued, as Charlotte approached—and ere the young girl was aware, the *silk* dress that had been regarded with so much reverence was deprived of both its sleeves. "Oh mercy! what will mother say?" was her first exclamation; but Kate was in no wise affected by the amputation she had effected, and cooly surveying her work, said, "Yes, you look a thousand dollars better." And she continued, as Charlotte was pinning on the large cape she had been used to wear, "Have you the rheumatism in the shoulders, or anything of that sort, or why do you wrap up like a grandmother at a woods-meeting?"

Charlotte could only say, "Just because"—it was, however, that she desired to conceal as much of her bare arms as possible; and it was not without many entreaties and persuasions that she was induced to appear with arms uncovered and a simple white frill about her neck.

"What a pity," said the cousins, as they made up the red calico, "that she had not consulted us, and spent her money the other day for ruffles and ribbons instead of this fantastic thing!"

They regarded her in a half-pitying, half-friendly light, and, perhaps, under the circumstances, did the best they could; for though Charlotte had many of the instincts of refinement, she had been accustomed to a rude way of living, and a first contact with educated society will not rub off the crust of rusticity which has been years in gathering.

"I have been too sensitive," thought Charlotte, or she tried to think so, and if her heart ever throbbed wildly against some delicate insinuation or implied rebuke, she crushed it down again, blaming her own awkwardness and ignorance rather than the fine relations who had stood preeminent in her childish imagination. She might not so readily have reconciled herself to the many mortifications she endured, but for the sustaining influence of Mr. Dinsmore's smiles and encouraging words. Ever ready to praise, and with never a word of blame, he would say to the other ladies, "you are looking shocking to-night," and they could afford to bear it—they never did look so; but whatever Charlotte wore was in exquisite taste—at least he said so. And yet Mr. Dinsmore was not really and at heart a hypocrite, except indeed in the continued and ostentatious display of private griefs. Constitutionally, he was a flatterer, so that he could not pass the veriest mendicant without pausing to say, "Really, you are as fine a looking old beggar-man as I have met this many a day!" Whether he was disinterested and desired only to confer pleasure upon others, or whether he wished to win hearts to himself, I know not—I only know, no opportunity of speaking gracious words ever escaped him.

However or whatever this disposition was, Charlotte interpreted all his speeches kindly. "She had eyes only for what was good," he said, and the sombre shadow of affliction in which he stood, certainly gave him an appearance of sincerity. When the Misses Bailey were thrown, or rather when they threw themselves in his way, he said his delight could not be expressed—they seemed to have the air of the mountain maids about them that made him feel at home in their presence. But when he praised one, generally, he disparaged another, and he not unfrequently said on these occasions, "I have been sacrificing an hour to that country cousin of yours," or, "I have been benevolently engaged," pointing toward Charlotte. Then came exchanges of smiles and glances, which seemed to say, "We understand each other perfectly—and nobody else understands us." One day, while thus engaged in playing the agreeable, Charlotte having finished her dish-washing, came in, her hands red and shining from the suds. Mr. Dinsmore smiled, and, with meaning, added, "Do you remember where Elizabeth tells some clodhopper, the reputed husband of Amy Robsart, I think, that his boots well nigh overcame my Lord of Leicester's perfumery!"* and in the burst of laughter which followed, the diplomatist rose and joined the unsuspecting girl, saying, as he seated himself beside her, and playfully took two of her fingers in his, "You have been using yellow soap, and the fragrance attracted me at once—there is no perfume I like half so well. Why, you might spend hundreds of dollars for essential oils, and nice extracts, and after all, if I could get it, I would prefer the aroma of common yellow soap—it's better than that of violets."

"I have been talking to those frivolous girls," he continued, after a moment, and with the manner of one who had been acting a part and was really glad to be himself again: "rather pretty," in a soliloquising sort of way, "but their beauty is not of the fresh, healthful style I admire."

"I thought," said Charlotte, half pettishly, "you admired them very much!"

"Yes, as I would a butterfly," he said, "but they have not the thrifty and industrious habits that could ever win my serious regard—my love;" and his earnest tone and admiring look were more flattering than the meaning of his words. Charlotte crushed her handkerchief with one hand and smoothed her heavy black hair with the other, to conceal the red burning of her cheek. Mr. Dinsmore continued, "Yes, I have been thinking

*The reference is to a scene from Sir Walter Scott's *Kenilworth* (1821).

since I came here, that this is the best way in the world to obtain health and happiness—this rural way of life, I mean. Just see what a glorious scene presents itself!" and he drew the young girl to the recess of a window, and talked of the cattle and sheep, the meadow and woodland, with the enthusiasm of a devoted practical farmer.

"Of course," said Charlotte, "my predilections are all in favor of the habits to which I have been used."

"Another proof of your genuine good sense," and Mr. Dinsmore folded close both the little red hands of Charlotte within his own soft white ones, but with less of gallantry than sincere appreciation of her sweet simplicity and domestic excellencies. And he presently went on to say, that if he ever found any happiness again, it must be with some such dear angel as herself, and in the healthful, inspiriting occupation of a farmer. True, he did not say in so many simple words, "I should like to marry you, Charlotte," but the nameless things words cannot interpret, said it very plainly to the unsophisticated, simple-minded, true-hearted Charlotte. Poor man, he seemed to her so melancholy, so shut out from sympathy, it was almost a duty to lighten the weary load that oppressed him.

But I cannot record all the sentiment mingled in the recess of that window. I am ignorant of some particulars; and if I were not, such things are interesting only to lovers. But I know a shadow swept suddenly across the sweetest light that for Charlotte had ever brightened the world. The window, beside which these lovers sat, if we may call them lovers, overlooked the highway for half a mile or more; and as they sat there it chanced that a funeral procession came winding through the dust and under the windy trees far down the hill. It was preceded by no hearse or other special carriage for the dead, for in country places the coffin is usually placed in an open wagon, and beneath a sheet, carried to the grave-yard. So, from their elevated position, they could see, far off, the white shape in the bottom of the wagon. Mr. Dinsmore's attentions became suddenly abstracted from the lady beside him, and the painful consciousness of bereavement, from which he had almost escaped, weighed on him with tenfold violence. "Hush, hush," he said, in subdued and reproachful accents, as she made attempts to talk of something besides shrouds. "Florence," he continued, burying his face in his hands, and as though swept by a sudden passion from the consciousness of a living presence, "why was I spared when you were taken, and why am I not permitted to go voluntarily"—he abruptly broke off the sentence, and, rising, rushed from the house. Charlotte arose, too, her heart troubled and trembling, and followed him with her eyes, as he staggered blindly forward to obtain a nearer view of the procession, every now and then raising himself on tiptoe, that he might see the coffin more distinctly.

In the suburbs of the city, and adjoining the grounds of Captain Bailey, lay the old grave-yard termed the Potter's Field, and across the sloping stubble land, toward this desolate place, Charlotte bent her steps, and seated on the roots of a blasted tree, on a hill-side, waited for the procession. Gloomy enough was the scene, not relieved by one human figure, as perhaps she had hoped to find it. To the South hung clouds of smoke over crowded walls, with here and there white spires shooting upward, and in one opening among the withered trees, she caught a glimpse of the Ohio, and over all and through all sounded the din of busy multitudes. In the opposite direction were scattered farm-houses, and meadows, and orchards, with sheep grazing and cattle pasturing, and blue cheerful columns of smoke drifted and lifted on the wind. And just at her feet, and dividing the two pictures, lay this strip of desolated and desecrated ground, the Potter's Field. It was inclosed by no fence, and troops of pigs and cows eked out a scanty sustenance about the place. One of these starved creatures, having one horn dangling loosely about her ear—in consequence of some recent quarrel about the scanty grass perhaps—drew slowly toward the hollow nearest the place where Charlotte sat, and drank from a little grave which seemed to have been recently opened. The soil was marshy—so much so that the slightest pit soon filled with water. The higher ground was thickly furrowed with rows of graves, and two or three, beside this open one, had been made in the very bottom of the hollow. Nearer and nearer came the funeral train. It consisted of but few persons—men, and women, and children—the last looking fearfully and wonderingly about, as led by the hands of their parents they trod the narrow path between the long lines of mounds. Forward walked a strong stalwart middle-aged man, bearing in his arms the coffin—that of a little child; and Charlotte shuddered to think of the cold damp bed which was waiting for it. There seemed to be no clergyman in attendance; and without hymn or prayer, the body that had slept always in its mother's arms till now, was laid in the earth, and in the obscurest and lonesomest corner of the lonesomest of all burial places, left alone. Closer than the rest, even pressing to the edge of the grave, was a pale woman, whose eyes looked down more earnestly than the eyes of the others; and that it was, and not the black ribbon crossed plainly about the straw bonnet—which indicated the mother. Hard by, but not so near the grave, stood a man holding in his arms a child of some two years, very tightly, as though the grave should not get that; and once he put his hand to his eyes; but he turned away before the woman, and as he did so, kissed the cheek of the little child in his arms—she thought only of the dead.

The sun sunk lower and lower, and was gone; the windy evening came dimly out of the woods, shaking the trees and rustling the long grass; the last lengths of light drew themselves from the little damp heap, and presently the small grey headstones were lost from view. And, scarcely disturbing the stillness, the funeral people returned to their several homes—for the way was dusty and they moved slowly—almost as slowly as they came. There were no songs of birds in the twilight—not even a hum of insects; the first were gone, and the last, or such of them as still lived, were crept under fallen leaves, and were quietly drowsing into nothingness. No snakes slipt noiselessly along the dust-path, hollowing their slow ways. They too were gone—some dropping into the frosty cracks of the ground, and others, pressed flat, lay coiled under decaying logs and loose stones. So, at such a time and in such a place, the poor little baby was left alone, and the parents went to their darkened cottage, the mother to try to smile upon the child that was left, while her eyes are tearful and she sees only the vacant cradle,—and the father to make the fire warm and cheerful, and essay with soft words to win the heavy-hearted wife from their common sorrow. They are poor, and have no time to sit mourning, and as the mother prepares the scanty meal, the father will deal out to the impatient cows hay and corn, more liberally than his garners can well afford, for to-night he feels like doing good to everything.

Something in this way ran the thoughts of Charlotte, as slowly and sadly she retraced her steps, trying to make herself believe she would have felt no less lonely at any other time if she had witnessed so mournful a scene. And in part she deceived herself: not quite, however, for her eyes were wandering searchingly from side to side of the path, and now and then wistfully back, though she could scarcely distinguish the patches of fading fennel from the thick mounds of clay. Perhaps she fancied Mr. Sully Dinsmore still lingered among the shadows to muse of the dead.

Nothing like justice can here be done to the variously accomplished Sully Dinsmore. Charlotte requires no elaborate painting; a young and pretty country girl—with a heart, except in its credulity, like most other human hearts, yearning and hopeful—as yet she had distilled from no keen disappointment a bitter wisdom. Little joys and sorrows made up the past; her present seemed portentous of great events.

"Where is Kate?" she asked one day, in the hope of learning what she did not dare to ask; and Sally replied in a way that she meant to be kindly, and certainly thought to be wise, by saying, "She is in some recess, I suppose, comforting poor Mr. Dinsmore, who seems to distribute his attentions most liberally. It was only this morning," she added, "that against a lament for the dead Florence, he patched the story of his love for me."

Charlotte joined in the laugh, but with an ill grace, and still more reluctantly followed when Sally led the way toward the absentees, saying in a whisper, "Let us reconnoitre—all stratagems fair in war, you know."

But whether the stratagem was fair or not, it failed of the success which Sally had expected, for they no sooner came within hearing of voices than Mr. Dinsmore was heard descanting in a half melancholy, half enthusiastic tone, of the superiority of all western products. "Why, Captain Bailey," said he, speaking more earnestly than before, "I would not live east of the mountains for anything I can think of—not for hardly anything in the world!" Such childish simplicity of speech made it difficult to think him insincere; and Charlotte, at least did not, but was the more confirmed in her previous notions, that he was a weary, broken-hearted man, sick of the world and pining for some solitude, "with one sweet spirit for his minister."

Whether Sally's good intentions sprang from envy and jealousy, it might be difficult to decide; but Charlotte attributed only these feelings to her, as she petulantly turned away with the exclamation—"Pshaw! Kate has left him, and he is trying to make father believe the moon is made of green cheese!"

From that day the cousins began to be more and more apart; the slight disposition to please and be pleased, which had on both sides been struggling for an existence, died, and did not revive again.

It was perhaps a week after this little scene, and in the mean time Mr. Dinsmore had been no unsuccessful wooer; in truth, Charlotte began to feel a regret that she had not selected a white instead of a red dress; all the world looked brighter to her than it had ever done before, dreary as the season was.

The distance between the cousins and herself widened every day; but what cared she for this, so long as Mr. Dinsmore said they were envious, selfish, frivolous, and unable to appreciate her. I cannot tell what sweet visions came to her heart; but whatever they were, she found converse with them pleasanter than friends—pleasanter than the most honeyed rhymes poet ever syllabled. And so she kept much alone, busy with dreams—only dreams.

V

IT WAS ONE of the mildest and loveliest of all the days that make our western autumns so beautiful. The meadow sides, indeed, were brown and flowerless; the lush weeds of summer lopped down, black and wilted, along the white dry dust of the roadside; the yellow mossy hearts of the fennel were faded dry; the long, shriveled iron-weeds had given their red bushy tops for a thin greyish down, and the trees had lost their summer garments; still, the day was lovely, and all its beauties had commended themselves with an unwonted degree of accuracy to the eyes of Charlotte—Mr. Dinsmore had asked her to join him in an autumn ramble and search for the last hardy floweres. All the morning she was singing to herself,

"Meet me by moonlight alone,
And then I will tell thee a tale."

It had been stipulated by Mr. Dinsmore, "so as not to excite observation," he said, that they should leave the house separately, and meet at an appointed place, secure from observation. Why a ramble in search of flowers should be clandestine, the young lady did not pause to inquire, but she went forth at the time appointed, with a cheek bright almost as the calico she wore.

On the grassy slope of a hollow that ran in one direction through a strip of partly cleared woodland, and in the other toward an old orchard of low heavy-topped trees, she seated herself, fronting the sun, which was not shining, but seemed only a soft yellow spot in the thick haze that covered all the sky. A child might have looked on it, for scarcely had it more brightness than the moon. The air was soft and loving, as though the autumn was wooing back the summer. The grass was sprouting through the stubble, and only the clear blue sky was wanting to make the time spring-like, and a bird or two to sing of "April purposes." It was full May-time in the heart of Charlotte, and for a time, no bird could sing more gaily than she, as she sat arranging and disarranging the scarlet buds she had twined among her hair; now placing them on one side, now on the other: now stripping off a leaf or two, and now adding a bud or blades of grass.

So an hour was wiled away; but though it seemed long, Charlotte thought perhaps it was not an hour after all; it could not be, or surely Mr. Dinsmore would have joined her. The day was very still, and she knew the time seemed longer when there were no noises. And yet when she became aware of sounds, for a cider-mill was creaking and grating in the edge of the orchard, they seemed only to make the hours more long and lonesome.

Round and round moved the horse, but she could not hear the crushing and grinding of the apples—only the creaking of the mill. Two or three little boys were there, whistling and hopping about—now riding the horse, and now bending over the tub and imbibing cider with a straw. An old man was moving briskly among bundles and barrels, more from a habit of industry, it seemed, than because there was anything to do. But, try as she would, Charlotte could not interest herself in their movements. An uneasy sensation oppressed her—she could not deceive herself any longer—it was time, and long past the time appointed. At first she looked back on the way she had come, long and earnestly; then she arose and walked backward and forward in the path, with a quick step at first, then more irresolutely and slowly. The yellow spot in the clouds had sunken very low and was widening and deepening into orange, when she resumed the old seat, folded her hands listlessly in her lap, and looked toward the cider-mill. The creaking was still, the horses harnessed, and barrels, and bundles of straw, and boys, all in the wagon. The busy farmer was making his last round, to be sure that nothing was amiss, and this done he climbed before the barrels and bundles and boys, cracked his whip, and drove away toward the orange light in the clouds. Mr. Dinsmore was not coming—of that she was confident, and anger, mortification, and disappointment, all mingled in her bosom, producing a degree of misery she had never before experienced.

Not till night had spread one dull leaden color all over the sky, did she turn her steps homeward, in her thoughts bitterly revolving all Mr. Dinsmore had said, and the much more he had suggested. And, as she thus walked, a warm bright light dried up the tears, and she quickened her step—she had fallen back on that last weakness—some unforeseen, perhaps terrible event, had detained him, and all the reproaches she had framed were turned upon herself; she had harshly blamed him, when it was possible, even probable, that he could not come. The world was full of accidents, dangers, and deaths—some of these might have overtaken him, and he perhaps had been watching as anxiously for her as she for him. At this thought she quickened her steps, and was soon at the house. The parlor was but dimly lighted, and, with a trembling and anxious heart, she entered, and recognizing Mr. Dinsmore in one of the recesses of the windows, she obeyed the first impulse, hurried toward him, and parting the heavy and obscuring draperies, said, in an earnest whisper, "Why did you not come?"

"Come—where?" he replied, indolently; and added, in a moment, "Ay, yes, really, I forgot it."

A half sigh reached her, and turning, she became aware that a young and pretty lady occupied the corner of the window opposite. No further explanation was needed.

With feelings never known before, pent in her heart, Charlotte sought the chamber in which she was used to sleep—the lamp was faintly burning, and the bright carpet and the snowy counterpane and curtains, and low cushioned seats, looked very comfortable; and as Charlotte contrasted all with the homely garret in which she had slept at home, the contrast made it luxury.

In her heart, she wished she had never slept any where else but under the naked rafters of her father's house. "I should have known better than to come," she thought; "it is no wonder they think the woods the best place for me." Now, no one had said this, but she attributed it and many such thoughts to her *rich* friends, as she called them, and then set herself as resentfully against them as though they had said they despised her.

Her eyes turned toward the night; she was sitting very still, with all bitter and resentful and sorrowful feelings running through her heart, when a soft tap on the door summoned her to answer. With a haughty step and repellant manner she went forward; and when, opening the door, she saw before her the pleasant-faced little lady she had seen in the window, below, she said, very coldly, "you have mistaken the apartment, I think," and was turning away, when the intruder eagerly but artlessly caught up both her hands, saying, in a tone of mingled sweetness and heartiness, "No, I am not mistaken; I know you, if you do not know me—I could not wait for a formal introduction, but commissioned myself to bring you down to tea. My name," she added, "is Louise—Louise Herbert."

Charlotte bowed stiffly, and saying, "You are very obliging, but I don't want any tea," closed the door abruptly, and resumed her old seat, looking out into the night as before.

"I suppose it was mere curiosity that brought her here," she said, by way of justifying her rudeness; "of course, she could feel no interest in me." And further, she even tried to approve of herself by saying she always hated pretence, and for a fine lady like Miss Herbert, who had evidently been accustomed to all the refinements of wealth, to affect any liking for a poor ignorant country girl, as she chose to call herself, was absurd. In truth, she was glad she had shown independence at least, and let the proud creature know she would not cringe because of her silk dress, or white hands, or pretty face. She didn't want anything of her—she could live without her, and she would. And rising and pacing the room, she made what she thought a very wise and dignified resolve. When they were asleep she would tie in a bundle what few things she had, and walk home; she would not ask her uncle to take her—she would not tell him she was going—he might find it out the best way he could. This decision made, she undressed and went to bed, as usual, and tried to compose herself to sleep by thinking that she was about as ugly and ill-bred, and unfortunate in every way, as she could be; that everybody disliked and despised her, and that all who were connected with her were ashamed of her. There was one thing she could do, nevertheless, and that she would do—go back and remain where she belonged. Thus she lay tossing and tumbling, and frightening the drowsy god quite from the neighborhood of her pillow, when Kate entered, accompanied by the agreeable looking little woman, who, being introduced, begged in a jocular way, that she would afford her sleeping-room for only one night. "I could not," she added very sweetly, "give my friends the trouble of making an extra bed, if you would allow me to share yours."

Charlotte answered, coldly and concisely, that she was ready to do anything to oblige, and placing herself close against the wall, buried her face in the pillow, and lay stiff and straight and still. But Miss Herbert, singularly oblivious of the young woman's uncivil behavior, prepared for sleep,

"And lay down in her loveliness."

"How cold you are," she said, creeping close to her companion, and putting her arm around her. Charlotte said nothing, and gave a hitch, which she meant to be from, but, somehow, it was toward the little woman. "Oh, you are quite in a chill," she added, giving her an embrace, and in a moment she had hopped from the bed, and in her clean, white, night dress, was fluttering out of the room.

"I never had such a night-gown," thought Charlotte, "with its ruffles and lace trimming—I never had any at all," and she resumed her old position, which, however, she had scarcely gained, when the guest came fluttering back, and folding off the counterpane, wrapt, as though she were a baby, her own nicely warmed woollen petticoat about her feet, and having tucked the clothing down, slipt under it and nestled Charlotte in her arms, as before, saying, "There, isn't that better?"

"Yes—thank you," and her voice trembled, as she yielded to this determined kindness.

"Another night we must have an additional blanket," said the lady; "that is, if I succeed in keeping you from freezing to-night," and pressing the chilly hands of Charlotte close in her bosom, she fell asleep. And Charlotte, thinking she would be at home the next night, fell asleep too, and woke not till along the counterpane ran the shadows of the red clouds of morning.

But I am lingering, and must hasten to say, that Louise Herbert was one of the most lovable, generous, and excellent of women; that she had been accustomed to affluence was true, and that she could not know the feelings of Charlotte, who had been born and bred in comparative poverty, was not her fault; from her position in life, she had naturally fallen into certain agreeing habits and ways of thinking, but her soul was large, her heart was warm, and her apprehensions quick; and when she saw Charlotte, and heard the trembling inquiry, and the answer of indifference, she read the little history, which to the young girl was so much, and appreciating, so far as she might, her sorrows, determined to win her love; for at once her heart went out toward her—for she was unsuspicious and unhesitating, always ready to find something good in every one.

Even Charlotte found it impossible not to love her. She didn't know why, but she could get on a stool at her feet, lay her head on her lap, and forget that Louise was not as poor and humble as herself; or, if she remembered it, the silks and plumes and jewelry worn by her, didn't make her envious or jealous—it gave her pleasure to see Louise look pretty.

Mr. Dinsmore, after some vain attempts to coquette and flirt with Miss Herbert, who had too much tact, or was too indifferent to him, to pay much regard to his overtures, departed rather abruptly, merely sending his adieus to Charlotte, who was engaged in the kitchen at the time, and who had been in the shade since the coming of Miss Herbert.

And after a month of eating and sleeping, talking and laughing, baking and making and mending, Louise was joined by her party, who had left her with her friends, the Baileys, while they continued a ruralizing tour through the West, and Charlotte's heart grew desolate at the thought of separation from her. But such a misfortune was not yet to be; for before the departure of the young lady, she persuaded the parents of Charlotte (who could not help liking, though they regarded her very much as they would a being from another sphere) to allow their daughter to accompany her home.

With a heart full of curious joy, but with tears in her eyes, Charlotte took leave of the old home that she had so despised, and yet loved so well.

VI

A YEAR or two afterwards, changes and chances brought me for a moment within the circle in which she moved as the admired star. The rooms were brilliant with lights and flowers, and gaiety and beauty, and intellect; and the lately shrinking country girl was the cynosure of all eyes—the most envied, the most dreaded, the most admired, the most loved.

When my attention was drawn first toward her, there were some voices that had sounded at least through the length and breadth of their own country, softened to the most dulcet of tones, for her sake; and she seemed to listen indifferently, as though her thoughts were otherwhere.

I naturally recalled the humble life she had led—my walk to her house along the autumn woods—the letter which had been the key opening a new life to her—and while I was thus musing, I heard a voice which seemed not altogether unfamiliar—so low, and soft, and oily,—"Really, Miss Herbert, I was never so proud as to-night—that *you* should have remembered me on such an occasion as this! I cannot express the honor I feel, the obligations you have placed me under."

And then, as if constrained to throw aside all formality, and express himself with simple sincerity, he continued—"Why, how in the world did you get all these great folks together! I don't believe there is a house in the United States, except yours, that ever held at once so many celebrities."

Before my eye fell on him, I recognized Mr. Dinsmore, and observed him with increasing interest as he made his way to Miss Ryan, who appeared not to see him, till having pushed and elbowed his way, he addressed her with the familiarity of an old and intimate friend, and as though he were not only delighted himself, but felt assured that she must be much more so. But she hesitated—looked at him inquiringly—and seemed to say by her manner, as plainly as possible, "What impudent fellow are you—and what do you want?"

"Surely, you remember meeting with me," the gentleman said, a little discomfited, but in his most insinuating tone.

"When—where?" she asked, as if she would remember him if she could.

"Don't you remember," he said, "a month with Sully Dinsmore at Captain Bailey's?"

"Ah, yes," she replied, quoting his own words on a former occasion; "Really, I had forgotten it."

He shrunk a head and shoulders in stature, and slipt aside like a detected dog; and after one or two ineffectual attempts to rally, took leave in modest and becoming silence.

An hour afterward we sat alone—Charlotte and I—in the dim corner of a withdrawing room; and as I was congratulating her on her new position, especially on the beauty of her appearance that night, she buried her face in my lap, and burst into tears; and when I tried to soothe her, but wept the more. At length, lifting herself up, and drying her eyes, she said: "What would mother think, if she saw me here, and thus?"—And she scanned her gay dress, as though it were something neither right nor proper for her to wear. "And dear little Willie and sturdy Jonathan," she continued: "I suppose they sleep in their little narrow bed under the rafters yet, and I—I—would I not feel more shame than joy if they were to come in here to-night! Oh, I wish I had staid at home and helped mother spin, and read the sermon to father when the weekly paper came. His hair is getting white, isn't it?" she asked, pulling the flowers out of her own, and throwing them on the ground.

My wish was fulfilled—Charlotte had attained the position I had thought her so fitted to adorn; but was she happier? In the little gain was there not much loss—the fresh young feeling, the capacity to enjoy, the hope, the heart, which, once gone, never come back. character traits-

I cannot trace her biography all out: since that night of triumph and defeat, our paths have never crossed each other.

The story of a poor girl who makes it into society in a series of steps-up. Class reduced to rural/urban split, and the good-hearted rich girl attains for Charlotte a position.

The final question - is she better off - directs the moral of being happy with your station. Conflict is not about class, but is displaced onto character traits.

The Bailey's farm with cousins Mr. Solly Dinsmore, the rake.

Position of the narrator - delivers the letter - importance in the chain.

CONCLUSION TO CLOVERNOOK, SECOND SERIES

ALL THINGS ARE beautiful in their time. Even Death, whom the poets have for ages made hideous, painting him as a skeleton reaper, cutting down tender flowers and ripe grain, and binding them into bundles for his dark garner, heedless of tears and prayers, is sometimes clothed with the wings and the mercy of an angel. It was one of the most beautiful conceptions of Blake, displayed in those illustrations of the Night Thoughts which forever should cause his name to be associated with the poet's, that his countenence who is called the Last Enemy was all sweetness and pitying gentleness; and how many, who have trembled with terror at his approach, have found the dearest rest in his embraces, as a frightened child has forgotten fear in wildest joy on discovering that some frightful being was only its mother, masqued for playing. Through this still messenger "He giveth his beloved sleep." How pleasant to the old and worn to resign all their burdens in his hands, to lay by the staff, and lie down under canopies of flowers, assured that even through the night of the grave the morning will break! Thrice pleasant to the old, assured of having fought the good fight, and who feel, beneath the touch of Death, their white locks brightening with immortal crowns. They have done their work, and only Death can lead them up to hear from the master, "Well done, good and faithful servant." To the little child who has never sinned, he comes like a light slumber, and the tempter, through the long bright ages, has no power. Only through the narrow and dark path of the grave could the tender feet have escaped the thorns—only to the bed which is low and cold may the delirium of passion and the torture of pain never come; so to the child the foe is the kindest of friends—dearest of friends!

One of the loveliest pictures that ever rises before me—I see it as I write—is that of a fair creature whose life was early rounded by that sleep which had in it the "rapture of repose" nothing could disturb forever. She had lain for days moaning and complaining, and we who loved her most could not help her, though she bent on us her mournfully beseeching eyes never so tenderly or imploringly. But when the writhing of anguish was gone, death gave to her cheek its beauty, and to her lips the old smile, and she was at rest. She had been lovely in her life and now she was transformed into an angel of the beautiful light, the fair soft light of the good and changeless world.

And for the wicked, looking over ruins they have made of life's beauty, friends they have changed to foes, love they have warped to hatred, one agonized moment of repentance has stretched itself up to the infinite mercy, and through radiance streaming from the cross, has sounded the soul-awakening and inspiring sentence, "Thy sins are forgiven!" What divine beauty covers the darkness that is before and around him! how blest to go with the friend who has come for him down into the grave, away from reproachful eyes—away from haughty and reviling words—away from the gentle rebuking of the injured, hardest of all to bear, and from the murmuring and complaining of a troubled conscience!

Whatever is dreariest in nature or saddest in life may in its time be bright and joyous—winter itself, with its naked boughs and bitter winds, and masses of clouds and snow. Poverty, too, with whom none of us voluntarily mate ourselves, has given birth to the sweetest humanities; its toils and privations have linked hand with hand, joined shoulder to shoulder, knit heart to heart; the armies of the poor are those who fight with the most indomitable courage, and like dust before the tempest are driven the obstacles that oppose their march; is it not the strength of their sinews that shapes the rough iron into axe and sickle? and does not the wheat-field stand smiling behind them and the hearth-light reach out from the cabin to greet their coming at night? Poverty is the pioneer about whose glowing forges and crashing forests burns and rings half the poetry that has filled the world. Many are the pleasant garlands that would be thrown aside if affluence were universal, and many the gentle oxen going from their plowing that would herd in wild droves but for men's necessities. The burdens of the poor are heavy indeed, and their tasks hard, but it has always seemed to me that in their modest homes and solitary by-paths is a pathos and tenderness in love, a bravery in adversity, a humility in prosperity, very rarely found in those conditions where character is less severely tried, and the virtues, if they make a fairer show, grow less strong than in the tempest, and the summer heat, and the winter cold.

It has been objected by some critics to the former series of these sketches of Western rural life, that they are of too sombre a tone; that a melancholy haze, an unnatural twilight, hangs too continually over every scene; but I think it is not so; if my recollections of "Clovernook" fail to suggest as much happiness as falls to the common lot, my observation has been unfortunate. I have not attempted any descriptions of the gay world; others—nearly all indeed of those writers of my sex who have essayed to amuse or instruct society—have apparently been familiar only with wealth and splendor, and such joys or sorrows as come gracefully to mingle with the refinements of luxury and art; but my days have been passed with the humbler classes, whose manners and experiences I have endeavored to exhibit in their customary lights and shadows, and in limiting myself to that domain to which I was born, it has never been in my thoughts to paint it as less lovely or more exposed to tearful influences than it is. If among those whose attention may be arrested by these unambitious delineations of scenes in "our neighborhood," there be any who have climbed through each gradation of fortune or consideration up to the stateliest distinctions, let them judge whether the "simple annals of the poor" are apt to be more bright, and the sum of enjoyment is greater in even those elevations, to attain to which is so often the most fondly cherished hope of youth and maturity.

In our country, though all men are not "created equal," such is the influence of the sentiment of liberty and political equality, that

"All thoughts, all passions, all delights,
Whatever stirs this mortal frame,"

may with as much probability be supposed to affect conduct and expectation in the log cabin as in the marble mansion; and to illustrate this truth, to dispel that erroneous belief of the necessary baseness of the "common people" which the great masters in literature have in all ages labored to create, is a purpose and an object in our nationality to which the finest and highest genius may wisely be devoted; but which may be effected in a degree by writings as unpretending as these reminiscences of what occurred in and about the little village where I from childhood watched the pulsations of surrounding hearts.

on class and nationalism

HAVING OUR WAY

THE HARVESTERS were busy with mowing; it was a bright, sunshiny day, but whether June or July, I don't remember; the roses were all gone from the bushes, I know, and the little brown bird, that had her nest in the sweet-brier, was teaching her young ones to fly. Rosalie, my older sister, whose eyes and hair were blacker than a crow's, had climbed on a chair, against the window by the brier-bush, and was watching the old bird as she fluttered in and out of the bush, twittering and chirping, as if she said to the young ones, "Come, you can fly as well as I can!"

All at once Rosalie clapped her hands, and called me to see; one of the little birds had made its way through the bush, and was fluttering right against the window. I ran, but had only caught an imperfect view of it, when the gray cat, that had been watching under the bush, leaped nimbly up, and the little bird was gone.

The old bird flew in and out from her nest, and hopped to the ground, and then to the fence, and then up in the tree, making a noise as if she were crying—for it was unlike any singing she had ever done before.

As fast as we could we ran out of the house, and, lying flat on the ground, lifted up the long limbs of the bush, and looked under. We were too late; there stood the cat, twisting her tail, and beating the ground with it, as she held down the bird with one paw—its little wings outspread and quite still. Rosalie cried, and she well might cry, for it was piteous to see the little dead bird, and to hear the moaning of the mother.

We brought crumbs and scattered them on the ground, but she would not pick them as she had done many a time before. Poor thing! in her anguish she seemed to quite forget that there were living birds in the nest that she must care for still. I think it was to divert our attention, and to pacify us, that our mother called to us that she wished a coffee-pot of water carried to the meadow. Wiping our eyes, we tied on our sun-bonnets, and were soon on the way, the water standing in bright drops on the coffee-pot's lid and sides.

It was a deep, narrow path in which we walked, one right behind the other, and saying nothing, for we were both thinking very sadly of the dead bird. Another time we would have walked on the short, cool grass, that, sprinkled with yellow dandelions, grew along each side of the hot, dusty path; but now we were not thinking of our own comfort at all.

The hay-makers saw us as soon as we reached the fence, and, placing the coffee-pot in the shade of a large stump, to keep the water cool, we sat down in the edge of the meadow, and waited for their approach. We could hear the strokes, and see the grass falling very fast before their scythes, which never once did they stop to whet, but bending low, and step by step, they came nearer and nearer. On reaching the place, one of them said that we were little women, I remember; and another told Rosalie that at home he had a little girl with eyes and hair as black as hers; and another—a brawny-armed man, with drops of sweat among his gray whiskers, who drank the most, and seemed to enjoy it the most—said, as he drew a long breath, and turned the coffee-pot bottom side up, that he could tell us where we could fill it with berries, and that we deserved so much for our pains.

We forgot the gray cat and the poor bird, and were in a moment tripping lightly over the green swaths, smelling sweet in the sunshine. Peter, whom I have mentioned before, was loading the hay that was made, and already there was such a great heap of it in the rack, that the horses drawing the wagon were almost hidden by it. Very smooth and even he laid it, all around, for Peter had skill in some things, if not in others. He told us that there were bushels and bushels of berries on the vines, and that we would have no difficulty in filling the coffee-pot by the time he should get a full load on, and that then we might ride home on the top, which pleased us very much; but as we hurried toward the meadowside next the woods, where the blackberry-vines were, he called after us, saying we must be very careful, for he expected likely enough there were a hundred snakes there—thus making us as uncomfortable as possible. It was always the way with Peter, if he made us happy in one way, he made us unhappy in another. At first we were afraid, and kept along the edges of the "patch," as we called it. There were not so many berries as Peter had said, but there were a good many, and we picked industriously, and at last had partly filled the pot, and were about to start toward home, for our fingers were full of little thorns that made them ache, and our faces were scratched badly, when Peter, who had taken one load of hay into the barn and was come for another, leaving his team, came to assist us. In a few minutes he had trodden paths for us in deep among the briers, where the berries were large and ripe, so that we forgot the thorns and the scratches, and picked with new energy and far more success.

We had the coffee-pot filled so that we could not shut the lid down, in a little while, and were making our way out of the briers, talking of what nice pies we should have the next day, when Peter called to us, "Look here!" and, turning toward him, we saw that he was running toward us, with a great black snake dangling from his pitchfork. We were terribly frightened, as may be supposed, and, as we ran, spilled the berries so carefully gathered. He called us to stop, saying the snake was dead. It was long before we could be persuaded to do so; but at length he threw it across the fence, and seemed so heartily sorry for what he had done, that we tried to still the beating of our hearts, and gather up the berries from the ground. He aided us with right good will, and gathered other berries from the vines, until we had quite as many as at first. He then coaxed us to go close to the snake, then hanging limberly over the fence. We were afraid to go very near, though it was dead, and not quite dead either, for its slim, bluish tail moved, though its small head was mashed flat, and its white belly spotted with blood. Then Peter took it in his hands, and put it around his neck, to show us that he was not afraid, and that it could not hurt us. Afterward he lifted us up to the top of the load of hay, and told us, if we would not tell about his scaring us, he would take us to town the next morning, and that we might sell our berries for money enough to buy us each a new dress, perhaps. Of course, we were delighted, and promised Peter that we would not tell, but that he must ask if we might go. He knew that it had not been right to frighten us, and though we assured him we would not say anything about it, he kept repeating over and over, "Now you won't—now you mustn't say a word about it—if you do, I will not take you to town."

There was no need of his fear; we could not have been hired for a thousand dollars to tell it, for that would have been a small thing compared to going to market with Peter, and buying dresses with the money we had earned ourselves. We were little girls, I don't know precisely how old, but somewhere about ten years, I should think, and Rosalie twelve; I had been to town once, and she never. In her fancy, she pictured it like places we read of in Fairy-land; and, indeed, it was a scene of wonderful beauty, even to me. I supposed that the people who lived there were a great deal happier than we, having almost everything they wanted. Once my mother had taken me there with her, and bought me some cakes, and showed me the outside of the Museum, and a great big building, with a fine yard, and trees about it, where she said children lived whose fathers and mothers were dead. I thought they must be happy, whether they had anybody to love them or not; I have learned better since.

Peter was very eloquent in our behalf, and I need not say that we pleaded our own cases very earnestly. Peter would take good care of us, we knew; and, besides, we could take care of ourselves; and we were sure we wanted to see something, some time in our lives; then we could sell our berries, and get something, and we could see the town, and go to Aunt Wilton's; and we finished every sentence with, "Come, mother, let us go!" Peter said we would be just as safe as we would be in our beds; that he would engage to bring us home well and hearty; that it would afford us more pleasure, maybe, than it would to go to London, when we were big—which was very true. So, at last, quite against her judgment I think, she said, if we would promise to be right good girls, we might go, but that Peter must not set out until daylight.

Perhaps there were never two happier children in the world than we were that night; we were helping mother, and helping Peter, and helping everybody—now gathering plantain leaves to lay over the basket of butter that was to be done up in white cloths and hung down in the well until morning; now assisting Peter to put the tar on the wheels of the little market wagon; now combing our hair, though we were yet to sleep a night, and knew it would be of no use; and now examining our nice shoes and dresses, to see that all was right. Our berries we spread out in two large, flat milk-pans, and set out in the dew, to keep as nice and fresh as possible. Afterward we went with Peter to the orchard, and when he shook down the yellow apples from what we called the early tree, we gathered them in baskets, until we had two or three bushels of them. Nine o'clock had never come so soon, but when the preparations were done, the time passed very slowly, and it seemed to us that the morning would be long in coming. When Peter got the cup of hot water, and the razor,—for he shaved his face every week when he went to market, though he had no beard,—we told him to hurry, as if that would make it time to go any sooner.

We went to bed at last, having all our things hung over chairs, ready to put on in the morning; and, guessing at the amount of money we should get for the berries, and planning what we should do with it, we fell asleep.

"Come, girls, are you going to town?" said our mother, coming close to the bed with a lighted candle in her hand. "Yes!" we said, and were both wide awake and dressing ourselves in a minute. We could hear the rattling of the harness, and the treading of the horses, and knew that Peter was "hitching up," and trembled lest he should go and leave us; but he did not, and we were soon sitting, side by side, on the straw that filled the wagon-bed, with baskets of apples, butter, blackberries and all.

There were no signs of daylight yet, for Peter had started sooner than he said, and a smart sough of wind put the candle out just as our mother said good-by, but not until I had seen how thoughtful and uneasy she looked about us. We passed several market wagons on the way, but none passed us, for Peter was a fast driver, and, indeed, would have been quite ashamed to have anybody's horses surpass his. We had gone down a long hill, over which was a very bad road, with only a narrow strip of the woods cut away, where Peter told us a man had been seen walking without any head, and then we came into a flat open valley, where there was a creek, with a covered bridge over it, before we saw the white daylight sprinkled along the eastern hills. Then the houses began to be closer together, and finer than they were where we lived, and Rosalie and I wished each one we passed was our home. I remember the blue gate-posts before one house, the winding walk that went up to another, and the white porch, full of pots and flowers, that fronted another. Peter told us who lived in those places, and that the owners were very rich, describing their wealth as greater than it really was, I suspect, as if in some way it were an honor to him to know anything of men possessing an extraordinary amount of money.

The sun was not yet risen when we rode into town, crossed two or three canal bridges, passed along a common, and through several streets, into a wide one, where the market was held. The market-house itself was a long low building, roofed over, but open at the sides, and furnished with continuous rows of stalls, for meat and vegetables. On each side of this, and close against the sidewalk, stood the wagons of the country people, from one end of which the horses were eating oats and corn, with their harnesses on, while at the other stood men, women and children, selling eggs, and butter, and apples, and cheese and berries, and home-made yarn and stockings, and many other things, which I need not mention.

Peter soon backed his wagon into a little space between two others, and, unharnessing the horses, gave them their bait of corn and of fresh clover.

Rosalie and I took the leaves from the top of the basket of berries, and, placing them in full view, waited for somebody to buy. We supposed they would all be taken in a minute, and that we could get for them almost any price we chose to ask, for Peter had told us so. But, on the contrary, one after another went past, and scarcely looked at our berries when we said they were fifteen cents a quart. All about us there were berries that looked fresher and nicer than ours, and those who had them, sold them too. At first we cared very little for this, so many things did we see to amuse us; for the street was thronged with people of all colors, and ages, and conditions. At last a fat gentleman, who wore a white waistcoat and a gold chain and spectacles, and who had a negro man behind him carrying a great willow basket, and two square tin pails, with lids, stopped, and, smiling, said, "How do you do, my little friends?" And then he asked us if we had ever been to town before, and said he supposed we intended to buy everybody out! No, we said, we only expected to get new dresses. "Ah!" he replied, "then you mean to put the rest of your money in the bank." We didn't know of any banks but the clay ones at home, and we knew we were not going to bury our money there; so we said, "No, sir!" and that was all. "Well, then," said he, "if you don't want to buy out the town, nor put your money in the bank, why do you ask a thousand dollars for a quart of your berries?" Of course, we told him we did not ask a thousand dollars a quart, but only fifteen cents. "Well, my little girls, I'll tell you what I'll do," and, taking out a purse of red netted silk, through which gold and silver shown temptingly, he selected two ten-cent pieces, and, offering one to each of us, said he would give us so much for all the berries we had. We hesitated, and the black man said, "If massa guv you dat, you better 'cept, case dere de wust berries any whars bout."

"They are just like all country folks," said the man in the white waistcoat, who kept eating our berries all the while he stood by us; "they want to get three times as much as a thing is worth; the berries grow while they are asleep, and they ask as much as if they had worked a year to make them;" and so he went along, seeming vexed, and saying, at the last, "My little ladies, your berries taste too much of the silver I'm afraid."

When he was gone, we said we didn't like him as well as we did the man who had told us where to find the berries, though he wore a tow string, instead of a gold chain, to his watch.

Peter had sold all he had to sell long ago, and had left us to dispose of our berries, while he went to buy sugar, and coffee, and tea, and other things to take home, and when he returned, he was to go with us to buy the new dresses.

The sun broke through the mist that obscured it at first, and shone out hot; the horses switched the flies, and drooped their heads, slavering at the mouth, and turning their ears back as though they were tired and mad; and from the loss of sleep, and having had no breakfast, and the jolting ride, we were tired, and began to be discouraged too. The people had mostly bought their marketing and gone home, and though we only asked ten cents a quart for our berries, nobody offered to buy them.

Almost directly facing the wagon there stood a little frame house, painted white, and having green blinds; and fronting it was a yard, not much larger than the coverlet on our bed at home, and here grew a cedar-tree; and the paved walk, leading from the front door to the gate, topped with green, divided and ran on either side of the tree, which kept it from running straight. It was a brick walk, washed red and clean; but, though it looked so nice, an old lady came out and began sweeping it. We thought what a beautiful place it was, and how well we should like to live there, where we could see all the people that came to market; and that little yard and one cedar-tree seemed to us better than all our fields and thick woods at home.

Particularly, we noticed the lady who was sweeping, so tidy and motherly and kind she looked. She was short and thick, and wore a plain cap of thin muslin over her gray hair, and a dress of drab-colored stuff, and a white neckerchief, crossed and pinned smoothly over her bosom.

When she had brushed the walk quite down to the gate, she shook the dust from the broom and looked into the street for a minute. Presently she went back into the house, and directly came out again with a little tin basin in her hand, as if it might be for our berries; and, sure enough, that it was.

When I told her how much we asked for them, she replied, "Thee asks too much, and unless thee sell as others sell, thee will have to take thy berries home." She then offered us a twenty-five cent piece for all we had, and, seeing the people were mostly gone out of the market, we poured them into her basin and took the money. We were disappointed, at first, for we knew that was not enough to buy even one dress; but after a time we began to think what we could buy, and so we climbed out of the wagon and walked along the street.

We had not gone far when we saw an old woman standing by a table, on which were gingercakes and a keg of beer, and tumblers to drink it from. We thought she must be a very nice person, for she asked all the country people to have some of her cakes and beer, which many of them did. We looked wistfully, I dare say, as we saw the beer foaming up in the tumblers, and the hungry men breaking open the round, yellow cakes. "Come, dears, won't you have some too?" she said, filling two tumblers, and reaching them toward us. "What good folks there are in town!" we thought, and, thanking her, we drank the beer, and were turning away, when all at once she seized us each by the arm, saying, "What do you mean, you little wretches! would you steal my beer?"

We fancied ourselves thrust into a dark jail, and starving to death, for we were almost frightened out of our senses, and, laying on the table all the money we had, we ran back to the market wagon as fast as we could, glad to escape with our lives.

The horses were harnessed, and Peter was waiting for us to go and buy the new dresses; but we could buy no new dresses, nor anything else, for the woman had kept all our money; and so we learned that people may offer us beer, or anything else, and expect to be paid for it after all.

Peter had just taken up the reins to start home, saying, we were little fools to give her all the money, when Aunt Wilton came along, carrying a basket not larger than my two hands. She said we must go home with her, but it seemed to me she didn't want us to go all the time. When she went on, Peter said we must go and get some breakfast, or we would be sick, and if she didn't want us, why, he didn't care.

So, feeling uncomfortable, and the more for what he had said, we went to breakfast with Aunt Wilton. About the visit, and whom we met there, and the end of it, I will tell you in another story.

But you will see, from what I have written, that it would have been better if we had taken our mother's advice, and staid at home.

Innocence → experience
rite of passage - female

2 sisters
the implied danger of Peter
associated w/ snake & danger

market as nation

title - Having Our Way. Irony - these girls
do not get anything except bitter experience

GHOST STORY, NUMBER II

NEARLY A YEAR was gone since the time of our meeting Amos in the sugar-camp, and the narration of his curious story. He was done enacting tricks, done telling stories to frighten and bewilder his listeners; and if there was any truth in him he was come to it, for he was gone to that country whence no traveler returns—gone to the presence of the Searcher of hearts. Let us hope he found that mercy which here he bestowed not upon himself; for surely he was his own worst enemy, dealing always harder by himself than he was dealt by.

One way and another he had been the cause of much ill-feeling and ill-fortune in the neighborhood, and yet, as I have before intimated, he was guiltless of premeditated evil.

If he met a timid school-boy he could not resist the temptation of telling him it was an hour or two later than it really was; that he had just passed the school-house and seen the master cutting a switch big enough to goad an ox, and looking in the very direction the belated boy might be expected; or some similar fabrication he would make to send the child needlessly hurrying and fretting on his way. For such boys as loved bird-nesting, he had always some wonderfully pleasing account; and though his character for story-telling was well known, he had ever some new device to deceive the listener, and make him think he, of all the world, was the one Amos best liked—the person selected by him as the repository of his truth-telling.

I remember once when we were gathering nuts in the woods a little way from the school-house, watching for the rap of the master on the window-shutter, for it was nearly time for the afternoon school to begin, Amos Hill came suddenly among us. He was holding his hands tightly against his forehead when we first saw him, and, approaching, said, "O dear, children, how sick I am." After a little he sat down on the grass and then lay down, drawing himself up as one in pain, and groaning and moaning to himself piteously.

We all crowded around and asked what was the matter, and, pressing his hand now on his head, now on his side, and now striking them together as one in terrible misery, he told us he had nearly killed himself, he believed, by falling from a tall tree a mile and a half away, in which he had climbed to get a nest of red-birds; that an old woman of the neighborhood, whom we all knew, named Ann Stacy, had offered him ten dollars for a pair of red-birds, and that he had been at great pains to find them.

We all knew the tree, for it was the tallest one for miles about, and was known by the name of the high oak, and we knew Miss Ann Stacy was a great lover and collector of birds; and, besides, how could we doubt the truth of a man suffering as Amos was! He professed himself a little easier presently, but said he didn't care for the birds nor for any thing else, if he could only live to get home; and that if any of the boys were a mind to go and carry the birds to Ann Stacy, they were welcome to the price of them; he had laid the nest at the root of the tree, and that there were two birds in it nearly large enough to fly. Feeling in his pocket he seemed not to find his handkerchief, upon which he said, "O, I forgot! I spread it over the nest to keep the birds safe; it was a good handkerchief, but the boy that gets there first may have it."

A number of the boys now looked wistfully at the school-house and whispered one to another, that if it were not so near school-time they would go.

Hearing this, Amos said it was no where near the time for school to begin; that as he passed Squire Smith's saw-mill a few minutes before, the men were just going to dinner, and that we could tell by the shadows it was not near school-time. As he talked he groaned, wishing it was later, so the market people would be returning from town, and some of them take him up and carry him home.

A dozen boys set off at once eager to secure the birds, and racing for the sake of the handkerchief, which Amos had said was a very good one. They were no sooner out of sight than the young man said to us who were left with him, that he felt greatly worse, and believed he was going mad, upon which he began to bite at the grass and the air, and then in a hideous tone warned us to fly from him, as he believed he should eat some of us up in a minute more. Afraid of our lives we ran, one over another, and Amos after us, snapping his teeth together and growling like a mad dog.

In the hollow near the school-house he fell down to die, as we supposed, and with hair wildly tossed and teeth chattering we gained the master's protection just at the right moment. A stern, hard man was our master; and when we told him Amos was dying in the hollow, he said nobody would be the loser, and went on with the lessons as though nothing had chanced. The girls whose brothers had gone for the birds, suffered not a little in view of their protracted absence, and the long, limber switch which lay on the master's desk, and which he eyed occasionally as though it gave him great satisfaction.

I need scarcely say that Amos betook himself to his feet, and went home elated with the uncommonly good joke he had played off, and they—the boys—returned at a late hour—having found neither birds nor handkerchief—trembling and sweating, more from the fear of the rod than any thing else.

I remember once the father of Amos, a good and worthy man, when about making a journey, ordered a new coat to be made at the village tailor's, for the old one had quite served out its time. When the day of departure came, and all else was in readiness, Amos was dispatched in great haste to bring home the new coat; but hour after hour the carriage waited at the door, and not a little impatient the good old man waited too. At last came a boy with a bundle, sent by Amos, as he said. It was enough like the young man to keep his father waiting so, but no further annoyance was suspected, and carefully packing away the parcel supposed to contain the new coat, the old gentleman set out on his journey, and not till the time came when he wished to appear unusually well was the discovery made that the graceless son had appropriated the new coat, and sent home his own old one to his father. But I need not instance more of his tricks, or dwell further on the general worthlessness rather than wickedness that characterized him.

Nearly a year, as I said, had gone since our meeting him in the sugar-camp: it was middle winter—a bright moonlight and pleasant for the time of year. The cows were in their sheds, the chickens on the roost, and we children sitting before a great blazing fire of hickory logs wishing for snow to fall, and that a new sled would make itself and stand right before the door in the morning, with a nice bed full of straw, and having a fine coverlid over all. But the wish was no sooner perfected than we amended it by wishing the sled might turn into a sleigh, painted green or red, and having a great brown buffalo-robe over the seat; and further, that the seat might prove a money box, full of gold as it could be, and that we might go to town and buy new dresses at the cost of a thousand dollars per yard, and that the box might still be just as full, and, in fact, never get any the lower, though we should buy a million of things at equally extravagant charges. Our pleasant fancies were pleasantly interrupted by a loud rapping on the door, and presently by the entrance of Nathan Baxter and his wife, Jenny Baxter—or uncle Nat and aunt Jenny, as they were familiarly called by the young folks of the neighborhood. They were come to pass the evening and take supper at our house, as was, with country people, the custom of the times. They were not formal calls, which the neighbors made upon each other in those days, and in dress for the finest effect without any reference to comfort; nor did a few formal phrases, for the concealment of feeling and not the expression of it, make up the conversation. All was genuine. What had been seen, and felt, and thought, was given in exchange for what had been seen, and, felt, and thought.

What a glad surprise their coming was to us all, and with what a cordial sincerity aunt Jenny smiled and said she had been wanting to come for the last six months, but that for one while she had no dress that was really nice, and then she wanted for a new cap; for that when she got one nice thing she wanted another to wear with it, and that having the cap at last her shoes were given out, and so one thing after another had kept her home, greatly against her will, and that she was come at last without every thing she would have liked to have. All this she said and a great deal more, as she untied her close-fitting, white satin bonnet, and unpinned and folded her drab-colored shawl. Not that aunt Jenny was a Quakeress; she simply wore this plain dress as most becoming to her years and position. A smiling, rosy face she had, and a smooth, white brow, that had never seen a wrinkle of care or sorrow; for she regarded this world as a very good sort of place, and esteemed herself as in a good degree necessary to the general well-being of things; not that her self-esteem was so inordinate; it is probable, however, that Mrs. Jenny Baxter had, at various times and on various occasions, whispered Mrs. Jenny Baxter, that she was the chief pillar of the Church, and the leader of the neighborhood society. I am not sure but this comfortable assurance which Mrs. Baxter had made Mrs. Baxter tended to make her all the pleasanter companion and more useful woman.

That so much responsibility rested upon her, caused her to weigh and consider things before action or utterance, and gave to her manner a kind of pomposity which I am sure was quite unaffected. At any rate she was to me one of the pleasantest visitors we ever had, and the white ribbons of her cap, and the white kerchief, neatly pinned across her bosom, and her smoothly ironed black flannel dress gave me real pleasure. There was an appropriateness in whatever she assumed, whether her garment were of wool or silk, that made some less fortunate people call her proud and stylish.

Plainer, by a good many degrees, was uncle Nathan, and older by a good many years—a little bent man with a wrinkled face and thin white hair he was, and the father of half a dozen children that aunt Jenny was not the mother of; and why so pretty a young woman married an old widower was a matter of some curious speculation when she first came into the neighborhood. I do not pretend to have understood this matter better than other people; but that she was a good and faithful wife to uncle Nathan was certainly true. He grew straighter and stronger, smiled more and sighed less after she became his helpmate, and lived at least a dozen years longer with than he would have done without her.

The fire was replenished, the candle snuffed and another one lighted by way of welcoming and honoring our visitors, and our nearest neighbors, Mr. and Mrs. Claverel, were sent for.

Uncle Nathan keeping his broad-brimmed hat on his head, which, by reason of baldness, was always cold, drew up close to the fire, and, leaning on his stout walking-stick, engaged in conversation about the weather and the facilities the fine moonlight afforded for visiting, the prospects for wheat, the general health of the neighborhood, etc.

Aunt Jenny was warm enough and rather drew away from the fire, as she took from her work-basket some blue and white spotted yarn, and began the knitting of a small stocking for one of the afore-mentioned half dozen children. She had thought at first she would make the yarn red and white, she said, as she had always admired red stockings for children; but on further consideration she had feared the red would fade and look worse in the end than the blue. She had knitted the mate of the one she proposed then to make, she told us, while watching a few nights before with the corpse of Amos Hill. At the mention of this watch uncle Nathan groaned loud and long; we could not understand why at first, for Amos was not one to be much mourned for, certainly not by those in no way connected with him.

"It was the awfulest thing I ever saw," he said, directly. "I always expected the devil would get him, but I did not expect to see him come for him as I did."

"Well, Nathan, the old fellow has got his match, if he has got him," said aunt Jenny, and here came in all the history of the young man's life, each one recounting the tricks and falsehoods they had known him to be guilty of up to the time of his death, which had been sudden and violent. Whether in his last moment any thought had reached itself out toward heaven was unknown, for he had died and made no sign. Mr. and Mrs. Claverel now came in, and the circle about the fire was widened, and after an interval devoted to the interchange of gladness and good wishes, the talk about Amos was taken up again; for in the country a death in the neighborhood darkens, for a time, the sunshine of every household.

"I thought Amos was not long for this world for some time before he died," said uncle Nathan.

"Why so?" asked my father, "he looked healthy enough."

Uncle Nathan, who was a firm believer in dreams, and omens, and ghosts, and the like, replied, that one night during the last summer he had dreamed of seeing Amos ride a white horse through the air, and that standing still to look at him he vanished away. Mr. Claverel, who was in no way given to mysticism, laughed outright at this, but said he himself had

had a token more curious than the dream. A week previous to his death he had met Amos as he was going to market, and the young man had told him where he could dispose of the load of oats he was carrying to town on advantageous terms, and that calling at the place indicated he had found the information correct.

Mrs. Claverel, who wore a mourning-ribbon on her cap, and an apron of black silk, in memory of a blue-eyed little girl who the last fall had gone out to play with her sisters and never come back alive, looked all the more grave for the light words of her husband, and said she doubted not but there were such things as warnings, both in dreams and out of dreams. "You know, Samuel," she added, "about the 'land' you missed last year."

Mr. Claverel looked grave, too, now, adding, "Well, Dolly, I don't know, may be there are such things."

"Had you any premonition previous to the demise of your little one?" asked aunt Jenny, precisely and formally, but not the less kindly.

And Mr. Claverel here explained that in sowing his oats the spring past he had missed a "land," which, to own the truth, had caused him some uneasy sensations, and the more for that his little daughter, Adeline, had said one day, seeing the bare ground in the midst of the green grain, that she believed it was a real true sign some body was going to die.

The field of grain had grown opposite our house, and often and often, by one and another, the land missed in sowing had been remarked, and the superstition attaching to such a mistake dwelt upon, so that we had come to regard it almost as an augury, and the death of little Adeline, shortly after the harvest was gathered, as its fulfillment.

The graveyard where she was buried was not more than a quarter of a mile from Mr. Claverel's house; and when good Mrs. Claverel told how their watch-dog had gone there day after day all the past summer, and howled so loud and so lonesome, and that she had felt it a confirmation of her previous fear, uncle Nathan said the howling of a family dog, without any unusual provocation, was a sign of death which he had never known to fail.

All merriment was effectually subdued by the allusion to little Adeline, for all of us had remarked the howling of the dog and the missed land, and all had known, too, the pretty little girl whose death had been, as her mother believed, thus distinctly foretold. The candles and the fire grew dim without notice being taken of them, and the wind moaned at the windows in keeping with the solemn tone of the conversation.

Uncle Nathan related how the night on which his first wife died he was sitting by her bedside at midnight, when there fell a loud knocking on the door of the parlor, which surprised him not a little, inasmuch as it was not the door at which people were accustomed to seek entrance; and that taking with him the candle he opened the door, but found no one there. "It was the wind likely, or Amos Hill at most, feigning to be a ghost," said my father, who had small faith in those impersonal creatures.

"I wish I could think so," said uncle Nathan, and he went on to tell us that he had not only seen ghosts with his own mortal eyes, but that he had heard their footsteps and other more fearful and unmistakable evidences of their proximity. Here he groaned a believing and lamenting groan, and said he wished we could all have seen what he saw, watching with the corpse of Amos. Of course there was a good deal of anxiety expressed to know what uncle Nathan had seen, upon which, with a manner of the utmost sincerity, he related the following.

"It was about midnight, and I sat half asleep by the fire, and trying to drown, with good thoughts, the wicked talk of the two men who watched with me—comrades of the dead they had been, and are, I believe, more lost than he, if possible—when all thought of sleep was driven away by the noise of loud shuffling and opening my eyes I saw, to my horror and astonishment, that they had turned back the lid of the coffin, leaving the dead man's face exposed, and were actually dealing cards upon it. My blood stood still, and I besought them to leave their dreadful trade and go away; that I would rather a thousand times watch alone than have them with me. They replied by laughter, coarse jests, and such oaths as I will not repeat, asking me tauntingly if I was not afraid. I said yes, I was afraid, and had just opened the Bible when there came such a rattling of chains as caused me to let it fall. The reckless fellows were evidently not much less frightened—they forgot what the trump was; and when the slow dragging of the chain was heard again, they left their playing, and, jumping from the open window, ran as fast as they could. I trembled violently, for I still kept hearing the rattling and dragging of the chain, and it was plain enough that the evil one was come to carry off Amos, body and all. I managed to gather up and burn the cards, and for the rest of the night I stood in the open door ready to run, and I am not ashamed to own it," concluded uncle Nathan, wiping the sweat from his forehead.

Mr. Claverel laughed immoderately at the conclusion of the story, and told uncle Nathan that if he had looked out into the moonlight he would have seen in the field next Mr. Hill's house his old kicking cow, on whose leg he had fastened a heavy chain, to cure her of her bad habit; for that he had no doubt but this was what Mr. Baxter had heard.

"Blame it all," exclaimed the old man, more irritated than pleased, "some folks could explain away the very *airth* if you would listen to them."

"Nattie, Nattie, my dear," said aunt Jenny, in half-reproachful, half-coaxing accents, "there is one ghost even Mr. Claverel can't explain away," and she patted his withered hand with her plump white one.

"What is it? what is it?" we all asked at once, and winding up her yarn, and having smoothed the gray hair of her husband, and said he was not always a coward, she turned the wedding ring on her finger and began: "When I was fifteen or thereabouts, my mother died, leaving me alone in the world, for my father had been dead longer than I could remember. We had no money, and, of course, not many friends. There was no alternative for me. I must go out to service, and it was not long till a situation presented itself, which was to assist in the housework of a country tavern in a lonesome neighborhood, a hundred miles from where I was born. My fellow-worker proved to be an old woman, very superstitious, and of a marvelous experience, if her narrations were to be relied upon. There was no other public house within a dozen miles of us, so that we had a good many travelers to entertain—not unfrequently more than we could accommodate, for to say truth we had but three guest chambers. From the first I had noticed an upper room fastened with a padlock, and supposed it to be a store-room, till passing it one day with my workmate she stooped her ear to the door and listened attentively. I inquired what she expected to hear, but she motioned me to keep silence, and presently glided away on tiptoe. Often we must make beds on the floor and resort to other inconvenient means for the accommodation of our guests, which led me to prosecute my inquiries relative to the disused apartment. Tired of my importunity the landlord one day told me the room was haunted, and that he had wished the fact kept from me, inasmuch as not one girl in twenty would remain in the house after learning it. I laughed at the story; said I was not afraid; and getting possession of the key went in to examine the premises, assuring the landlord that I would air and fit it up for use. The sunshine streamed brightly in as I dusted the furniture, made the bed with clean sheets, filled the pitcher, and placed some flowers on the table to make all cheerful. I found it much the prettiest and pleasantest room in the house, and told the landlord, on leaving it, that I would answer for any harm that should happen the guest who slept there that night.

"Toward sunset travelers began to drop in, and two or more had been assigned to each room, leaving only the haunted chamber, when my good man, Nattie here, rode up to the door and requested supper and lodging. Supper was prepared, at which I presided, receiving from the tired stranger more than the share of civilities which I was accustomed to receive.

"Shortly after the meal was concluded, the traveler desired to be shown to his room, when, moved by compassion, the landlord informed him that he must choose between the floor and a haunted chamber, to which Nathan replied that he preferred the bedroom, haunted or not, and was accordingly shown up.

"'Remember your promise,' said the landlord, 'and if we find the man strangled in his bed in the morning, expect to be arrested for the murder.'

"There was so much concern in his manner that the words weighed upon me; and when our work was concluded and we retired for the night, I asked my assistant how the chamber happened to be haunted. After expressing much alarm for the safety of the guest she said, 'It is ten years ago since that room was shut, and for my life I would not sleep in it, nor be the means of any one else sleeping there.' I felt my hand tremble a little as I unclosed the shutter and looked out to be sure all was quiet. The sky was completely overcast, and the winds blowing up through the leaves of the great wood near by, gave a gloomier effect to the distant thunder.

"'Mercy! mercy! the ghost will come to-night,' continued the old woman, 'and if you don't get pulled out of bed by the hair for opening that room it will be a wonder.'

"The rain began falling now, so we were obliged to close the window; and with the lightning flashing right in our faces and the wind driving the little candle flame about, the woman huddled close against me as I sat on an old chest, and went on with the story. She had been an inmate of the house for about twenty years, and for the first ten the haunted chamber had been the favorite room of all travelers. One night, as black and stormy as that, two travelers had called late and asked for entertainment, which was given them. No register was kept, and no names were given or required. One of them was a young and beautiful woman, the other a man, much older, silent mostly, and seemingly stern. They lodged together in the haunted chamber, the woman going thither supperless and tearful, the man leading the way and offering no support or soothing words to the wife, if so she were. Their manners and dress indicated persons of refinement and used to all luxury, and it was a matter of much regret, said the woman, that we could not give them better accommodation.

"'In the morning,' she went on, 'the strange gentleman left before the house was astir, though the rain was still falling and the roads almost impassable. The lady was not able to rise, and on attending her with breakfast, I found her pale, tearless, and as one struck into stone. She neither ate, nor drank, nor smiled, nor in any way noticed my presence. I combed her long hair, bathed her face, and in all ways did for her all I could, for I could not but think her case a very sad one. Two or three days went by, and she had not yet left her room nor spoken, when, on opening her door, I found her in bonnet and shawl; and on asking her what she proposed, she said, "Walk to the post-office." I told her that was six miles away, and she did not look strong enough to walk across the room, and that if she would wait till the evening, or, at furthest, the next morning, I was sure a boy might be spared to do the errand for her.

"'"Then there is a post-office at the cross roads five or six miles from here?" she said, as though glad to be confirmed in what she had only in part believed till then. For a moment she seemed quite happy, smiled and said she would wait; but that if the messenger could go just then she would be so glad—two hours would be so long to wait. I said I would see, and as I left the chamber turned and asked what name should be inquired for.

"'The white cheek clouded with crimson, and after a moment she said, "Never mind; I will go myself." I tried hard to dissuade her, but could not, and with a quick step and an energy that seemed almost superhuman she went away.

"'It was late at night when she returned, looking more like one who had got up out of the grave than a living woman. When I asked if her quest had been successful, she shook her head mournfully, and seating herself at the window overlooking the road, never got up again. All my entreaties could not prevail on her to lie down; with her eyes straining away to the distance and her lips breathlessly apart, she sat hour after hour and day after day. At last I persuaded her to allow me to go to the office, which I did, inquiring for a letter for Mary H—— Such was her direction. I received none, and shall never forget the look of despair that settled in her face when I told her so. Once, and only once, she groaned as if her heart was breaking—I think it was—and motioning me to leave her I did so; and on going next to the chamber I found her still sitting upright at the window, but dead.

"'When we dressed her,' continued the old woman, 'we found a picture in her bosom, which we recognized as that of the man who had brought her to our house.

"'She was placed in a coffin and the door of her chamber locked; for how or where to bury her could not be decided at once. It was a little after sunset when an old man, who seemed more bowed with grief than years, stopped at the house and requested to be shown to a particular room—indicating the one in which the dead body lay. On being told that it was occupied, he said he knew it; that it was his daughter who had the room; that he saw her sitting at the window, and she beckoned him to come in. We told him that was quite impossible; that the lady was dead and in her coffin; but he persisted in saying he had seen his child alive not half an hour before; that she had beckoned him to come in, and that he must see with his own eyes whether or not she were there. So great was his importunity that the chamber was opened, but only the dead lady, and she in her coffin, was found; but no sooner had the old man seen her than he exclaimed, "My sweet Mary, my child, my child!"

"'That night he carried her away, and we never saw or heard any thing as to who they were or what became of them.'

"The old woman further told me," said Mrs. Baxter, "that many a time since then the lady had been seen sitting at the very window where she watched so long, sometimes gazing intently on a picture, and sometimes with a little child in her arms; and that, as often as any guest had been given the haunted chamber, the ghost of a woman had been seen walking up and down the floor as one in great distress, and sometimes taking possession of the bed and sometimes groaning aloud; that one or two persons had been nearly strangled by her; so the chamber had been finally abandoned; but still steps were often heard there, and the door carefully secured at night would be found wide open in the morning.

"The wind blew furiously," Mrs. Baxter went on, "the rain still fell, and altogether it was as dismal a night as ever I saw, and at the conclusion of the old woman's story I confess to some misgivings as to the safety of the person I had caused to sleep in the haunted room. I went to bed, however, and I suppose eventually fell asleep, with much uneasiness as to our guest weighing on my mind. And now, Mr. Baxter," she said, turning smilingly to him, "you may as well tell the rest."

The old gentleman drew himself up, and looking proudly on his wife took up the thread of the story by saying: "Having been told my room was haunted, I looked about carefully on going into it, closed the windows, and placing some chairs against the door, for I found no key, I retired, leaving the light burning. I was tired and soon fell asleep, but not very soundly, I suppose, for some time in the night a little noise about the door awoke me; it was like some one softly trying the key, and raising myself on my elbow I listened close, and became shortly convinced that some one or something was there, for the door now began to be pushed against the chairs. Presently a hand was thrust through the aperture, the chairs removed, and a figure, clothed in white, came noiselessly into the apartment. The light had burned down, and I could not tell distinctly whether it were ghost or woman, and I confess to some shrinking, as it approached the bed and began feeling across it. I was not long in doubt, for the hand no sooner touched my face than I knew it to be a mortal, and a very pretty one, too, and could not resist the temptation of holding it very closely, and afterward of putting my arm around the ghost's neck and waking it—for it was evidently asleep—with a kiss; you can judge of the surprise of Jenny, for it was she, on finding herself in so novel a situation. What the acquaintance, so curiously begun, led to, you all know; but, notwithstanding this pleasant experience in a haunted chamber, I am no less a believer in ghosts."

This story tended to create cheerfulness, and the remainder of the evening was as merry as the opening had been somber. Even Mrs. Claverel smiled, and in the cheerful conversation that was kept up till midnight took her part, and when the ample supper was spread all had appetites to do it justice. Mrs. Baxter "toed off" her little stocking as she talked, for her work did not suffer on account of the pleasant stories she had to tell, in all of which she had figured prominently.

It was midnight, as I said, before the work was put by and the shawls and bonnets brought forth, and when the party separated it was with kindly feeling stirred up, and hearts strengthened and steadied for the work and the warfare of life. Among my pleasantest memories are those of visitors of winter evenings in the country; and if ghost stories were told, so much the better.

Rural neighbors drop in on each other on a winter evening and tell stories. Amos Hill himself an inveterate story teller (liar) is now dead.
Ghost stories - both turn out to be like jokes - one ghost is a cow, the other ghost leads to the romance between the Baxters at a roadside inn. Yet this story covers the tragic story of an abandoned ♀ who died.

recuperates the — story of The Coquette

OLD CHRISTOPHER

POOR OLD Christopher! On a briery-hill, sloping toward the setting sun and into a dismal wood, far from human habitations, and where only once or twice in the year the traveler turns from the clayey road, winding near, to look curiously and sadly over the broken fence, he is lying, fast asleep.

The precise spot where his grave was made, not one of his children could tell, probably—for he was abandoned by even his own sons and daughters long years before all the friend he had, death, took him to himself.

But though his grave is forgotten of men, the angels know where it is; and the last trumpet will have a call for him.

Of all the pictures of childish memory, none is more vivid than his as I used to see him—oftenest when I went to school; for he was crazy, and much given to wandering habits. I was afraid of him; for many curious stories were afloat of his having been seen, of moonlight nights, fighting with demons, or in pleasant converse with angels. I had never seen him so engaged, to be sure; but often and often I had seen him talk with himself, and, to my childish apprehension, his cocked hat and red hunting-shirt were strong suppositions in favor of his supernatural endowments. He wore buckles on his shoes, too, and sometimes the sword, with which, in his younger years, he had done good service for his country. He was quite harmless, so far as his intercourse with mortals went; but still he was shunned by the children as one who had power to do great harm, if he chose. The school where I went was a mile and a half from my father's house, and in a dreary piece of woods through which I had to go was where it seemed to me I oftenest met old Christopher. The road was very crooked through these woods, winding over and around steep clayey hills; so that, try as I would, I could not see on entering whether I would meet him or not. It was a dismal sort of place, and I don't wonder now that I was afraid to pass it alone. There was a grave-yard at the entrance as I went from home, a spot near which children are apt to tread timidly, and the trees which grew thick on either hand, met, and frequently interlocked their dark boughs overhead. On one side the ground lay low and flat, moist throughout, and with here and there a great shallow pool of black sluggish water; opposite ran a deep hollow, through which a creek, wide and muddy, dragged itself along.

Never a crow called to its mate in this lonesome part of my daily journey, but that it startled me; every mark along the dust I construed into the trail of a snake, and every tree, taller than the rest, I singled as a mark for the lightning. About midway of this forest-road, a narrow path was seen trodden among the leaves, and winding among logs and around patches of underbrush, till it was lost in the thick wood through which no glimmer of light from the clearing beyond could be discerned. This path was my special terror, for it was worn by the feet of old Christopher, and led to his dismal hut, which himself had built in the middle of that dreary wood. He cultivated a small garden, and it was his habit to carry the products about the neighborhood for sale during the summer and fall, so that we were often in the high road together. He walked slowly, feeling his way, as it were, with a rough thorny cane, and bearing a basket of his own rude workmanship on one arm, filled with fruits or vegetables, and far streaming down over his red garment fell his white beard and hair, neither of which had been shorn for many years. I used to speak to him when we met, at first from fear, for I fancied that civility might ward off the imprecations which it was rumored he sometimes called down on the heads of those who offended him. I suspect, however, it was only rudeness that brought upon itself his anathemas; for he uniformly showed his pleasure in my little attempts at politeness—always by a sweet smile—sometimes by offering me an apple or a tomato, or whatever his basket held.

With very light and very fleet steps I walked after having passed him; nor did it lessen my trembling to see, as I often did on looking back, that he was standing still in the dusty weeds of the road-side, gazing intently after me. As I grew older, my courage or my curiosity, or both, grew too; and I would stop sometimes, especially if a team were in sight, and exchange a few words with the crazy man. Whether or not he was a prophet, he enjoyed about the country the reputation of one; and so soon as I dared say anything to him, I inquired whether or not it would rain that day. Turning his clear, deep-blue eyes upon me, he replied, "A prophet has no honor in his own country; nevertheless I will tell you." And having leaned thoughtfully on his staff for a few minutes, he told me there would be rain about the fifth hour of the evening; and lifting up his eyes he continued: "Woe unto you, if you be a daughter of the faithless!"

I told him I believed; and though I perhaps exaggerated somewhat my credulity, I certainly felt a vague impression that to his strange deep eyes the future was more open than to most mortal men. Not a cloud was visible in the sky, but at noon they began to gather; and when at night I walked under the leafy arch of the gloomy road, I heard the rain pattering above me, and my faith was confirmed. Ever after that I designated the old man as father Christopher, a title which gave him the greatest satisfaction.

My schoolmates warned me in vain against tampering with the devil—the imputed necromancy had a charm for me; and in course of time a strange joy mingled with the tremor I felt, when I saw in the distance the red mantle of father Christopher fluttering in the winds; and perhaps I was the more willing to listen, from the fact that he often promised to bestow his prophetic powers upon me when he died. Sometimes if I met him as I was returning from school, and so at leisure, I would sit down on some log by the road-side and listen till the stars came out to his curious talk, half mad and half inspired. Sometimes he saw funerals in the clouds, and more than once I remember that his predictions of death in the neighborhood were verified as he foretold—marriages also, and other occurrences of less importance. It was his delight, however, to wander in thought beyond the limits of this world, and bring back the lights and shadows that he met. The songs of the angels, the chariot of the Lord, the trumpet of Gabriel, death, and the death after death, were the themes of his highest eloquence. Many and many a time he told me that he had the day, or the night past, seen his angel wife, Mary—that he had been with her in Paradise; or that she had come to his bedside in the night time, and given him a flower, or mingled on his pillow her golden locks with his white ones. She was beautiful when she lived in the world, he said, and now that she was an angel, he could not tell that she was more lovely than when long ago she sat by his fireside with their baby on her knees. Often he talked wildly—madly almost—of other things, making fearful combinations of light and darkness, love and hate; but when he talked of Mary, it was with the tenderness and pathos of a bereaved lover, and with consistency that impressed me very deeply. Her hair had the same golden brightness always—her hand the same lily beauty, and her eyes the unfathomable splendor of the blue midnight—her voice was always low and loving; and often he said to me, that no serpent ever crossed his garden for forty days after his beautiful Mary had been to his cabin. One time he took from his bosom a flower, which, he said, she had given him the last midnight, calling him softly out of sleep, and putting her arms about his neck as she did so; but if the flower were the gift of any Mary, it must have been years and years away; for it was withered almost to blackness.

I was grown quite to womanhood without having ever been to his house; though we were grown to be friends, and many times he had asked me to visit him. Gladly would I have done so, but was not permitted to go alone; and if I suggested any inclination to any of my friends, they were quick to say I was scarcely less crazy than old Christopher himself—and so they would tell me of the great black dog that was chained at his cabin door, to devour alive any one who dared go near it; and of the sword that shone against the wall, and with which it was supposed he had some time done a murder, about which he had gone crazy; and of the poison herbs that hung in bunches along his ceiling; and of other mysterious furnishings of his house: at all of which I only laughed, and was accused of a disposition to tamper with things forbidden.

If I made inquiries about his history, I learned only the common and obvious facts: he was old crazy Christopher—supposed to have lost his reason in consequence of too much thought about the future; but nobody really knew or inquired—they regarded him as one of the belongings of the neighborhood, that could provide for its needs—giving him no more sympathy than they gave the worn-out horse turned loose to die. His own children sold from beneath his feet the ground his own hands had earned; for he had come, a widowed man, with three little children to our neighborhood a great while before I could remember—cleared the land, built him a home, planted an orchard, and digged a well; and while he was doing all this, the children he brought grew to maturity, and the once clear intellect of the father went blind, and knew them not; and they—O to the shame of humanity be it written!—forsook him; and to a strange hard man sold him, with the ground he had earned by the sweat of his brow.

It was not regarded as any very wicked transaction that I remember of; and with certain pieces of silver in their hands, the sons and the daughter of the mentally blind and doubly pitiable father took honorable leave of the neighborhood, to buy broader lands and build new roofs over their own heads, leaving the gray hairs of their father to bide the peltings of the storms. And so they did, for he refused to sleep beneath the roof of the oppressor, as he called the new proprietor of his estate; and building a small house of logs in the midst of the woods, retired, and lived thenceforward alone. That he was unconscious of the grievous wrong done him I was never satisfied, and sometimes questioned him as to the extent of his lands, the variety of his fruits, and the like; and the propriety and correctness of his replies persuaded me that, however bewildered, neither memory nor the light of reason was altogether lost.

It was a keen, clear, pitiless winter day, that made the beast shiver and man seek the fire; at the close of which I found myself with a walk of two miles and a half before me—for I had been visiting for a day at my grandfather's house. I might shorten the distance for half a mile, I was told, by crossing the fields and woods; and as any shortening of the distance was desirable under the circumstances, I resolved to follow the directions which my friends had very carefully given for my guidance. I must follow the lane till I came to the woods, where I would find a path, in which I must keep till within sight of a designated barn—then I must cross a meadow toward a certain tree, at which place I would find a run, that for another indefinite distance would be my guide; but at a certain turn where a sycamore-tree had fallen, I must leave it, and strike into the woods, and by keeping a north-westerly course I would soon find myself in the main road—home nearly in sight—and besides the shorter journey, the woods, it was argued, would be a protection to me, as the wind must be a good deal broken by the trees. I shaped out the way very clearly, I thought, in my mind, and with a brisk step and the most perfect assurance in my ability to find my way, set forward. The sun was near the setting—the last rays glittering on the steep frosty gable of my grandfather's house as I looked back where the lane terminated in the woods, and before I emerged from their shadows, all was shadow. Such bitter and biting cold I never saw—the clear sky was like a dome of ice, and the meadow grass cracked beneath my feet as I went, so stiff was it frozen—and every track made by man or beast was crusted with a shell that cracked and rattled together in a mass as I passed along. The black, bare branches of the trees stood still—there was no voice of bird or fall of water, but all was as if everything had been frozen, or was freezing into silence.

I don't know how it was, but I failed to see the barn of which I had been told, and thinking I must have gone far enough in one direction, for the intense cold made every step painful, I resolved to be guided by my own apprehensions, and strike at once into the woods. The sun had already been down some time; there was no moon; and the stars that seemed shrunken by the cold, made only here and there a shiver of light through the darkness. Over fallen logs and around them I went, across ponds of ice, and along flat leafy distances, down into deep hollows and over steep hills, looking and looking to discern the light through the woods. In vain—it grew darker and darker till all light was dark. I could not see any light, nor hear any sound when I stopped to listen—which I did time and again. At length my feet began to feel like clumsy pieces of ice, and sitting on a log I felt of them with my hands; but they too were numb, and I could not tell which was frozen, or whether one or both. I was now seriously alarmed, but gathering up all my energy tried to retrace my steps. I soon learned, however, that I could find no landmarks, and though within a short distance of home, was completely lost, benighted, and probably freezing. I walked one way and another for an hour, perhaps, very fast and with no object except the necessity of motion; for though it was possible, it was no longer probable that I should find my way out of the woods that night. Suddenly, I heard a voice, apparently in angry menace; but little cared I whether angry or not—any sound like humanity was welcome. I listened close, afraid that I had deceived myself, or was losing my senses: but no, it was in verity a human voice, and proceeding toward it I soon became aware that it was the imprecations and denunciations of father Christopher, and I understood that he was fighting with the fiends which he supposed to be about him.

More and more distinctly I could hear his beating of the ground and his curses, and fearful noise I confess it was; but demons just then had less terrors for me than the darkness and the cold, and fast as I might I hurried in the direction of his voice. At length I was very near, and stopping, for I was afraid of the weapon which I felt he was wielding with all his might, though I could not see it. I called—"Father Christopher!" "Make as sweet a voice as you may," he cried, "you shall not deceive me, vile imp of the pit—I will stab you through and through;" and as he spoke he made a desperate rush, hewing the darkness as he came. Screening myself behind a tree, I waited till his overwrath had somewhat abated, and then told him my name—reminding him of the times he had prophesied for me, and assuring him that I was lost in the woods, and would die unless he would take me to his house, and allow me to warm by his fire.

He presently knew me, and begged me to forgive him for what he had said, assuring me that he was not to blame, for that it was the demons who persuaded him that I was of their number; and taking my hand he led me carefully and softly as though I had been his own child. I confess that I trembled a little at first, and especially when he led me around something, assuring me that in that spot he had slain a dragon, and that I must, if possible, avoid treading in the blood. The darkness, he said, would not permit him to see how many bad spirits he had slain, but from their howling and crying he believed it could not have been less than ten thousand. I confirmed him in the belief, for it seemed pleasant to him; and moreover, I feared he might be tempted to renew the fight. I told him I had trodden over great numbers, and that he was no less a soldier than a prophet. I had, in truth, great reverence for him, and in some sort I loved him; for the wrongs he suffered from his children and the world first kindled my pity, then grew to interest, and interest to faith and trust. And who is so blind in mind and heart that they are unconscious of trust reposed in them—of love entertained for them? These are the media through which even idiocy sees more clearly; the wild beast is tamed by love, and the madman made at least peaceable.

He no sooner felt that I was not only not afraid of him, but that I besought his protection—that I had confidence in him—than his broken and ruined manhood seemed to be built up into strength and beauty. He fenced the winds from me as he best could, as we went along, and with the utmost tenderness assured me that I should have every care and attention his house afforded, and that I need not fear being frozen, for that it was quite impossible I should be more than severely chilled. I could now and then see the gleam of his white beard, or the shining of his sword blade as we walked, frozen sticks and leaves crushing beneath our feet, and the still cold smiting our faces like sharp blades of steel.

At last a little light shone through the darkness—nearer and nearer we came, and presently were at the door of father Christopher's house. I forgot the black dog I had heard of, and the poison herbs, all but that I had found shelter and fire, and went in with the old man more gladly than I had ever entered house till then.

He hastened to stir open the great bed of coals that lay in the fireplace, and having thrown on some hickory boughs, a warm red light filled all the little room in a few minutes.

The ample hearth was laid with stones, and beside the fireplace was a rude chair in which Christopher made haste to seat me—the floor was of planks, a bed stood in one corner of the room—a table under the small square window, (the only one in the house,) upon which stood a jug of water and a basket of apples. On a shelf at the head of the bed lay a Bible and a miniature case—the wall had many a chink through which the wind came, reminding us of the intense cold without. I need not linger over the aching and tingling in my fingers—over the strange sensations that possessed me on finding myself alone at midnight in the hut of a crazy man, shut out by woods and darkness from help, if danger there were. My suffering from the cold prevented fear, at first, and as I became sensible of new peril I suppressed its manifestation, and presently felt all the confidence I at first affected.

"They call me crazy," said Christopher, speaking at last, "and you must be afraid to stay with me in this lonesome place," and he took my hand as he spoke and looked close in my eyes as though he would see down through them to my soul. I said, "No, you are a prophet, and why should I fear you—have you not foretold storms and deaths, and done me many favors without once harming me?" He smiled at my words, and as he stooped his face toward me I smoothed away the gray hair which fell over his eyes, and when he lifted himself up I saw that they were dim with tears. "No," he said, laying his withered and trembling hand on my head, "I am a prophet, and a wronged and injured old man, but not crazy—no, no, not crazy." The light of a clear intelligence seemed shining in his face as he spoke, and I felt that he was, indeed, a wronged and injured old man, and to this day I believe that for the time the clouds passed from his intellect. While he sat sad and thoughtful at the fire, I took from the shelf the miniature, rather to divert the attention of my friend from the troubled mood in which he seemed to be settling than from any idle curiosity. It was the picture of a young and beautiful woman. Who could it be, I mused as I gazed upon it—

> "Could any Beatrice see
> A lover in that anchorite?"

and I turned from the picture to the miserable old man in whose eyes the light of a clear memory seemed shining sorrowfully out. He took the miniature from my hand, and having kissed it reverently, placed it in his bosom, and with his eyes fixed in the fire and quite forgetful of me, seemingly, he said:—"She loved me once—I am sure she did—we were so happy in our beautiful home. I remember one summer night when her head lay on my arm and the rose-leaves blew in at the window and fell over her head and face—there was a bird singing near, and we had no light but the moonshine—let me see, we were not many months married then—well—would to God I had no darker memory—if she were dead—but she did not die—only the death which is worse than death—could she leave her baby in the cradle, and steal away in the dark with a human devil? No, no, it could not have been—and yet in my veins there is no traitor blood—it must have been from her the children drew their serpent natures—have they not stung me, each one, and after coiled themselves separately away—O, vile mother, and vile children, curses on you all! If I should wrong her—O what a wrong it were—she may have been spirited away—I have searched the world and could never find her grave. We were walking in the garden when the tempter appeared—we had been happy till then, but from that day it seemed as if there was a great gulf between us. When I came home next she was not waiting for me at the window, and though she smiled faintly when I spoke to her, it was as if her heart were otherwhere. One moonlight summer night I came with a quick anxious step, for something boded me evil; I knew not, felt not what it was, but a voice seemed to say to me, Haste, O haste. When I came within sight of the house I almost ran—there was no light at the window as there had always been till then. I opened the door with a trembling hand, for I heard no voice singing, and no footstep in the house—the moonlight streamed over bed and cradle, and the three children slept alone. With the burning lamp I searched the house, feeling at every step how useless was the search. I called aloud through all the house and in the garden—no voice replied—from that night my home was desolate, and more than that my heart was desolate. Once again I saw her like a golden shadow in the dark—what matters it when and where—I never sought to see her again, but with my children crossed the mountains, and with all the strength that was left in me tried to make a new home. Sometimes there came a little light to me when my children played under the trees I had planted—but the serpent's egg hatches a serpent—they grew to maturity and sold me with my oxen and my land—well!"

I knew not then, and know not now, how much of this soliloquy was to be attributed to a wandering imagination; it impressed me like a fragment of truth; perhaps it was so, perhaps not. At daylight I made my way home; Christopher attending me till my path struck into the main road; gentle and loving he was so long as he stayed with me, but when we had been a few minutes divided and I turned to look for him, I heard his voice sounding angrily through the woods; he was fighting with the demons again.

Many years after this occurrence he continued to live his lonesome and isolated life, and was at length, after a colder night than the one I passed in his house, found dead by the fireless hearth: when or how he had gone no one knew; but when they dressed him for the grave, they found, lying close on his bosom, the picture of a fair-faced woman.

Whether or not she were his Mary I cannot tell; or if indeed it were not all a dream—if it were so, God grant the dream may have been only a prophecy, and that he knows now its bright fulfillment. For is not he our Father "who setteth an end to darkness and who searcheth out all perfection?"

"Father" Christopher, the town madman, protects her one night in the forest. The story of his life. Betrayal by wife and children.

PASSAGES FROM THE MARRIED LIFE OF ELEANOR HOMES

A GOOD MANY years ago I fell in love and was married.

"How did it happen?"

Why, how does it ever happen? "I doubt if the sagest philosopher of them all could explain how the like happened unto him, and therefore it were presumptuous to expect a woman to make luminous so great a mystery."

"You think a woman might understand her own heart, even though a philosopher might fail to?"

"Audacious! Don't you know that women shine faintly at best, and by reflection?"

"Really, I don't know. I never thought about it."

"Many women never do, and pass through life without ever being sufficiently grateful for the blessings they are permitted to enjoy. However, I believe the minds of the sexes are wholly dissimilar, even when of an equal power. Women *know* more, but *acquire* less than men; they do not investigate and analyze, and infer and conclude—their inferences and conclusions are independent of any process of reasoning. Since the beginning of time nature has said of every one of them—

> "This child I to myself will take;
> She shall be mine, and I will make
> A lady of my own."

And if each were permitted to follow her instincts, and rely upon her intuitions, there would not be among us so many miserable bewailings. All women have more or less genius—which, after all, is simply power of suspending the reasoning and reflecting faculties, and suffering the light which, whatever it be, is neither external nor secondary, to flow in. But I proposed to tell a story, and repeat, I fell in love, and was married.

"Did I really love?"

I suppose so; indeed I am quite certain, from intimations now and then received, that it was one phase of that capability which lives under wrinkles and grey hairs, in all the freshness of youth. But it is difficult to define the exact limit of positive love—it shades itself by such fine gradations into pity and passion, friendship and frenzy. The state of feeling I fell into was none of these latter, I am quite sure, and yet I should be loth to affirm it was that condition of self-abnegation which admits of no consideration aside from the happiness of the object beloved; for, if I remember rightly, there came to me at rare intervals some visions of my own personal interests and pleasures. And yet I had no hesitancy in pledging myself to love, honor, and obey, because I had no idea that these pledges conflicted with the widest liberty. Was not he to whom I should make these pledges a most excellent and honorable gentleman, who would have no requirement to prefer at variance with my wishes? To be sure he was. Did he not always prefer my pleasure to his own, or rather have no pleasure but mine? So he was pleased to say, and for my part, I never doubted it.

We took long moonlight walks together—talked sentiment, of course—read poetry, and now and then quarrelled prettily about the shade of a rose, or the pencilling of a tulip, and interspersed our discourse with allusions to our cottage that was to be. Should it be smothered in trees or open to the sun?

"Just as you prefer, my dear."

"Oh, no, darling! it shall all be just as you say."

Could I have a pot of geraniums and a canary bird to brighten my cottage window?

"A thousand of them," if I chose; but my own self would be the grace that graced all other graces—the beautifier of every beauty beside.

What should our recreations be? That was an absurd question, and soon dismissed. The introduction of a foreign element would never be necessary into society so perfect as we two should compose.

So we were married—never having exchanged a single thought concerning the great duties and responsibilities of life—I, for my part, having no slightest conception of the homely cares and ingenious planning; of the fearing and hoping, patience, forbearance, and endurance, that must needs make a part of life's drama, wherever enacted.

The bridal veil was never looked through after the bridal day; consequently the world took another coloring before very long. I must be allowed to say I was not yet twenty, as some extenuation of the follies I should have been ashamed of, even then, and must also relate some little incidents and particulars of my married life that gave ineffaccable colors to my maturer mind and character.

My husband's name was Henry Doughty—Harry, I used to call him, partly because the designation pleased him, and partly because I entertained a special dislike for the name of Doughty. I gave a much better one away for it, however.

My maiden name was Homes—Eleanor Homes—Nellie, they called me among my friends, before I was married; afterward, when the novelty of calling me *Mrs.* Doughty was over, they said *poor* Nell.

We had not been an hour from church—my bridemaids were about me, among them my haughty sister Katharine, who had not very cordially received her new relative. Some one rallied me on my promise to obey, and asked Mr. Doughty how he proposed to enforce my obligation.

"Oh, after this sort," he replied gaily, brandishing the little switch-cane he was playing with about my shoulder. I turned carelessly, and the point of it struck my eye.

"It was your own fault?" was his first exclamation. The pain of the wound was intense, but it was the harsh words that made the tears come. I was frightened when I saw them, for I felt that it was an awful impropriety to cry then and there, and putting by all proffered remedies as though the little accident were quite unworthy of attention, I smiled, nay, even affected to laugh, and said it was solely and entirely my own foolish fault, and moreover, that I always cried on like occasions—not, of course, on account of any suffering, but owing to a nervous susceptibility I could not overcome.

Katharine, meantime, to augment the criminality of the offence, was proffering various medicines; among them, she brought me at this juncture, a towel, wet with I know not what.

"Take it away again," said Mr. Doughty; "nothing I so much dislike as nervous susceptibility—pray don't encourage it."

Katharine would not speak, but she replied by a very significant look, and, to conciliate both, I accepted the towel, but did not apply it to the wounded eye—swollen and red by this time to an unsightly degree; in truth, I was afraid to do so. My sensations were certainly new, as I thus trifled with my afflictions, forcing myself even to make pitiable advances toward my offender, in the hope of winning him to some little display of tenderness, for the sake of appearances wholly, for I was not in the mood to receive them appreciatively just then. I was singularly unfortunate, however, and might have spared myself the humiliation.

I had succeeded, in some sort, in reviving my spirits, for it is hard to dampen the ardor of a young woman on her wedding-day, when my enthusiasm received another check. I was sitting at the window, that I might find some excuse for my occasional abstraction in observation, and also to keep the wounded eye away from the company. Happening once to change my position, my husband said to me: "Keep your face to the window, my dear madam; your ridiculous applications have made your eye really shocking!"

"Why, Harry!" I said—if I had taken time to think, I would not have said anything; but the unkindness was so obvious it induced the involuntary exclamation, and everybody saw that I felt myself injured.

By some sisterly subterfuge, Kate decoyed me into her own room, where my husband did not take occasion to seek me very soon. When he did so, he patted my cheek and said half-playfully, "I have come to scold you, Nell."

My heart beat fast. He had felt my absence, then, and was come with some tender reproach. I began to excuse myself, when he interrupted me with an exclamation of impatience. He was sorry to find me so impetuous and *womanish*—exhibitions of any emotion, but more especially of tender emotion, were in bad taste. I must manage in some way to control my impulses, and also to discriminate—he was always pleased to be called Harry, when we were alone, but in miscellaneous company a little more formality was usual!

"Your name is not so beautiful," I replied, angrily, "that you should want to hear it unnecessarily."

He elevated his eyebrows a little, and smiled one of his peculiar smiles, never too sweet to be scornful.

I hid my face in my sister's pillow, and almost wished I might never lift it up.

Seeing me shaken with suppressed sobs, he bent over me and kissed my forehead, much as we give a child a sugar-plum after having whipped it, and left me with the hope that I would compose myself, and not wrong my beauty by such ill-timed tears!

Excellent advice, but not very well calculated to aid me in its execution. Many times after that I wronged such poor beauty as I brought to him, by my ill-timed tears.

The story of the accident, and of my crying on my wedding-day, went abroad with many exaggerations, and my husband gave me to understand, without any direct reference to anything that had taken place, that I had unnecessarily brought reproach upon him. It had been arranged that we were to live at home a year; my parents—foolish old folks! could not bear the thought of giving me up at once—as if the hope to make all things as they were, were not utterly useless, after I had once given myself up.

The experiment proved a delusion—empty of comfort to all parties concerned; and here let me say, that if two persons, when they are once married, cannot find happiness with each other, no third party can in any wise mend the matter.

I think now if there had been no one to strengthen my obstinacy, and hinder such little conciliations as, unobserved, I might have proffered, our early differences might have been healed over without any permanent alienation.

However well two persons may have known each other before marriage, the new relation develops new characteristics, and necessitates a process of assimilation, difficult under the most genial circumstances.

Of course my family took my part, whether or not I was in the right, and thus sustained I took larger liberties, sometimes, than it was wise to take—trifled and played with all my husband's predilections—called them whimsies, if I noticed them, but for the most part affected an unconsciousness of their existence. For instance, I had a foolish habit of turning through books and papers in a noisy way, which I persevered in rather in consequence of his admonitions than in spite of them.

One night he did not come home at the usual time. I grew impatient, uneasy, and at last, in spite of Kate's sneer, took my station at the window to watch for him: in a minute or two thereafter he came up the walk. I opened the door and my arms at the same time, crying, "How glad I am!"

"What for?" he said, gliding past me in his quiet way.

"Are you not glad?" I inquired, determined not to be put out of humor for once; my best feelings had been really stirred.

"Certainly," he answered, seating himself in the corner opposite to me, and opening the evening paper. "I am glad to get home. I am very tired."

He did not once look at me as he said this, and Kate completed my discomfort by saying—

"Well, I suppose Nell is blessed enough to be permitted to look upon you, even in the distance. She used to have a little spirit, but I believe marriage has crushed even that out of her."

"Humph!" said my husband.

"What do you find interesting in the paper to night?" I said, determined to enforce some attention by way of triumph over Kate. He made a motion which deprecated interruption, and taking a new novel from his pocket, threw it into my lap.

"Milk for babes!" said Kate, sarcastically. I said nothing, and she went on provokingly: "Take your plaything away, child, and don't make a bit of noise with it."

Here was a happy suggestion. I had failed in my effort to be agreeable. I would be disagreeable now to my heart's content. I was at some pains to find an old pair of jagged scissors, and having found them, I seated myself at my husband's elbow, and began to saw open the leaves of my book, with the double purpose of annoying him and convincing Kate that I had some spirit left yet.

Now and then I glanced towards him to see if his brows were not knitting, and the angry spot rising in his cheek, but to my surprise and vexation I saw no manifestation of annoyance—he read on apparently completely absorbed, and wearing a smile on his face—a little too fixed, perhaps, to be quite spontaneous.

So I went on to the last leaf, cutting and ruffling as noisily as I could, but I had only my trouble for my pains—he did not lift his eyes towards me for an instant.

When Kate left us alone, I felt exceedingly uncomfortable—for I had felt my behavior countenanced by her presence. After all, I thought, presently, my husband is perhaps quite unconscious of any effort on my part to annoy him; but whether he were so or not, my best course, I concluded, would be to affect unconsciousness of it myself. Thus resolved, I yawned, naturally, I thought, and, as if impulsively, threw down the book—took the paper from his hand with a wifely privilege, and seated myself on his knee. He suffered me to sit there, but neither smiled nor spoke.

"Why don't you say something to me?" I was reduced to ask at length.

"What shall I say?"

"Why, something sweet, to be sure."

"Well, sugar-candy—is that sweet enough?"

"What a provoking wretch you are!" I cried, flying out of the room in hot haste.

I hoped he would forbid my going, or call me back, but he did neither.

After some tears and a confidential interview with Kate, that made me more angry with her and with myself than with my husband, I returned, and found him quietly lolling in the easy-chair, and eating an apple!

As time went by, Kate's arrogance and insolence towards Mr. Doughty became insupportable—twenty times I quarrelled with her, taking his part stoutly against her accusations. One evening, after one of these accustomed disputations, my husband said to me—

"Nell, we must take a house of our own; I can't live in this atmosphere any longer."

"Why can't you?" I knew why, well enough.

"I don't like your sister Kate."

"Does she poison the atmosphere, my dainty sir?"

"Yes."

Of course I flew into a rage and defended Kate with all my powers. She was my own good sister then, and had done every thing to make the house pleasant which it was possible for her to do—I would like to know who would please him.

"You, my dear," he replied.

The end of the matter was, I refused to go away from my father's house with him; said I would not be deprived of the little comfort I now had in the sympathy of, and association with, my family; he had agreed, I reminded him, before our marriage, to my remaining at home one year at least—his promises might pass for nothing with himself, they would not with me; if he chose to take a house he might do so, but his housekeeping would be done independently of me; if my wishes were never to be consulted by him, I should have to consult them myself—that was all.

I never gave him greater pleasure, he replied provokingly, than when I consulted my own wishes; for his part, he could have none in which I did not heartily concur.

He admitted that he had cordially agreed to my remaining at home a year after marriage, but that late experience had slightly modified his views; he was not infallible, however, and probably erred in judgment—indeed, he was quite sure he did, since I differed from him; he hoped I would pardon his unkind suggestion, and believe him what he really was, the most faithful and devoted of husbands.

Amongst my weaknesses was a passion for emeralds. Mr. Doughty had heard me express my admiration for them many a time. The day following our little rencounter he came home an hour earlier than usual, seated himself on the sofa beside me, and taking two little parcels from his pocket and concealing them beneath his hand, said playfully—

"Which one will you have, Nell?"

"The best one!" I replied, reaching out my hand.

"The better one," he rejoined quickly; "the best of the two is not elegant—at least it was not till you made it so."

I withdrew my hand and averted my face. If he and I had been alone, I might have taken the reproof more kindly; but Kate heard it all, as it seemed to me she always did every thing that was disagreeable. I might have made some angry retort, but a visitor was just then announced—an old classmate of Mr. Doughty's, whom I had never seen.

"He is come specially to pay his respects to you," my husband said as he rose to join him. "You will see him, of course."

"If it is my lord's pleasure," I replied; "bring him to me when it suits you."

Involuntarily he put his hand on my hair, and smoothed it away, glancing over me at the same time from head to foot. The motion and the glance implied a doubt of my observance of external proprieties, and also I felt at the moment, personal dissatisfaction with myself. The interview was embarrassed and restrained; I was self-conscious every moment, and crippled completely by the knowledge, that in my husband's eyes I was appearing very badly.

I misquoted a familiar line from Shakespeare; expressed admiration for a popular author, and when asked which of his works I read with most delight, could not remember the name of anything I had read.

My discomfiture was completed when my husband said apologetically, "I dare say that wiser heads than my little Nellie's have been confused by similar questions—in truth, she is not quite well to-day."

The old classmate related some very amusing blunders of his own, calculated to soothe, but rasping my wounded feelings only into deeper soreness, and presently the conversation fell into the hands of the gentlemen altogether; and I am sure it was felt to be a relief, by all parties, when our guest announced the expiration of the time to which he was *unfortunately* limited. My husband walked down street with him, and during his brief absence I wrought myself into a state of unwomanly ugliness, including dissatisfaction with everything and everybody.

The words "my little Nellie," which my husband had used, rung offensively in my ears. *My* little Nellie, indeed! What implied ownership and what tender disparagement!

When my husband returned he took no notice of my ill-humor, but proceeded to his reading as usual. It was never his habit to read aloud; on this occasion I chose to fancy he had, in his own estimation, selected a work above my appreciation.

"There, Nell, I forgot!" he exclaimed after a few moments of silent reading, and he threw into my lap the little box which I had declined to receive. I did not open it immediately, and when I did so I expressed neither surprise nor pleasure, though it contained what I had so much desired to possess—a pin set with emeralds.

"Very pretty," I said carelessly, "for those who can wear such ornaments; as for myself it would only make my plainness seem the plainer by contrast." And before the eyes of my husband, who had thought to make everything right by its purchase, I transferred it to my sister Kate. From that time forth it glittered in the faces of both of us daily, but we neither of us ever mentioned it.

It was not many days after this occurrence that Mr. Doughty informed me that he was called suddenly, by matters of some importance to him, to a neighboring State. He did not say *us,* but limited the interest entirely to himself—nor did he intimate by word or act that the necessity of absence involved any regret. I inquired how long he proposed to remain away—not when should *I* expect him.

He was not definitely advised—from one to three months. We parted without any awakening of tender emotion. Our letters were brief and formal—containing no hints, on either side, of a vacuum in life which nothing but the presence of the other could supply.

I was informed from time to time that affairs protracted themselves beyond his expectation, but the nature of the affairs I was left in ignorance of. The prospect of staying at home a year added nothing to my happiness. Kate and I agreed no better now that we were alone than before. I secretly blamed her for my unfortunate alienation from my husband: it was not the importunate nature of his business that detained him, I was quite sure. I grew uneasy, and irritable, wished to have him back, not for any need my nature had, that he alone could answer. I wanted him to want to come back—that was all.

Kate accused me of unfilial and unsisterly preference for a vulgar and heartless man, to my own family.

"The dear old Nell was completely merged in the selfish Doughty," she said, "and she might just as well have no sister for all the comfort I was to her."

So we kept apart a good deal, and by keeping apart, soon grew apart pretty thoroughly. In truth our natures had never been cast in the same mould, and it was impossible that they should more than touch at some single point now and then.

At the end of six months a portion of my fret and worry had worked itself into my face. My hair had fallen off and was beginning to have a faded and neglected look. I was careless about dress, and suffered my whole outer and inner person to fall into ruins. By fits I resolved to project my general discontent into some one of the reforms, I hardly knew which, when after a day of unusual irksomeness and personal neglect, my husband unexpectedly returned.

He was in perfect health, and rejoiced in the possession of affluent beard and spirits—he was really quite handsome. I looked at him with wonder, admiration, and some pride—kissed him and said I was very glad; but there was no thrill in my heart—no tremor in my voice—the old fires of anger had left the best part of my nature in ashes, I found. He was sorry to find me looking so badly—I must go with him on his next adventure and get back my beauty again! If I could only see his smiling, blushing cousin Jane, it would shame my melancholy and sallow face into some bloom! And by the way, I must know her—he was sure I would love her just as he did—she had done so much to make his banishment from me delightful—no, not delightful—but bearable. He would defy any one to be very miserable where she was. She kept about her under all circumstances such an atmosphere of cheerfulness and comfort; was so self-sustained and womanly, and yet as capable of receiving pleasure as a child; as an example of a beautiful and child-like trait in her disposition, he told with what almost pious care she preserved every little trinket he ever gave her. She would clap her hands and laugh like a very baby over the least trifle bestowed upon her.

I thought of the emerald pin, and of (as doubtless he did) the contrast my whole character presented to his charming wonder.

"Ah, me!" he concluded, and fell into a fit of musing. I did not interrupt him by any poor attempt at cheerfulness I did not feel.

Before long I succeeded in coaxing upon myself a headache—slighted the advice proposed, and at nightfall had my pillows brought to the sofa, and gave up altogether.

I was almost glad to be sick—it would revive in my husband some of the old tenderness perhaps; but what was my disappointment when he took up his hat to leave the house.

"What, you are not going out to night?" I inquired in surprise.

"Why, yes, my dear, why not?"

"If you ask why not, I suppose there is no reason."

"Is there anything I can do, or shall I send the doctor?"

"No, there is nothing special I need, but I thought you would stay at home to-night—I am unhappy every way."

"I am very sorry, but my engagement to-night is imperative—I promised Jenny I would immediately see some friends of hers, here."

I hid my face in my pillows and cried, and I confess there was some method in my tears—I did not think he would leave me under such circumstances. I was mistaken—he did.

"Have you seen any house that you thought would suit us?" I ventured to ask him before long.

"No, I have not been looking for a house."

He did not follow up my suggestion, and I added, as if I had but to intimate my wishes to have them carried out, though the hollowness of the sham was appalling—"I really wish you would look." He still was silent, and I continued—"Won't you?"

He replied, evidently without the slightest interest in the matter, "Why, yes, when I have time." He paid no further attention to my request, however, and when I reminded him of it again, he said he had forgotten it.

It seemed to me I could not live from one day to another—change would be a relief, at any rate, and my husband's indifference to my wishes made me importunate; but from week to week he put me off with promises and excuses, both of which I felt were alike false.

He could not see any places. "Inquire of your friends." He had, and could not hear of any.

"Why, I saw plenty of houses to let, and was sure I could secure one any day—would he go with me some time?"

"Yes, certainly at his earliest convenience."

I awaited his convenience, but it did not come. In very desperation, I set out myself; but searching without having fixed upon any locality, size of house, or price to be paid, was only a waste of time, I felt, and accordingly I wandered about the streets, looking at the outsides of houses, and now and then inquiring the terms at the door, but declining in all instances to examine the premises, or take the slightest step towards the securing of a house.

"Had you not better consider it a little?" Mr. Doughty said at length, as if I had not been considering it for six months!

He feared I would find it lonesome—he might be from home a good deal, such was the unfortunate nature of his prospects. Where was he going and what for?

He was not going at all that he positively knew of, but his affairs were in such a state that contingencies might arise at any time, that would demand his absence for a few weeks or months.

"A happy state of affairs!" I said with womanish spite; "I suppose one of the contingencies is your charming cousin Jenny!"

He would only reply to my foolish accusation by saying it was quite unworthy of my generous nature—I wronged myself and him, and also the sweetest and most innocent little creature in the world.

For some days nothing was said about the house; but I was a woman, and could not maintain silence on a disagreeable subject, so I renewed it with the importunate demand to know, once for all, whether or not we were ever to keep house. Thus urged, he consented to go with me in search of a house.

The air was biting on the day we set out—the streets slippery with ice, and gusts of sharp snow now and then caused women to walk backward, and bury their faces in their muffs.

We turned into streets and out of streets, just as it happened—Mr. Doughty did not care where he looked—anywhere I chose;—sometimes we passed whole blocks of houses that seemed eligible, without once ringing a bell: he did not suggest looking here or there, made no objection to terms, and suggested no proposals. Now we turned into a by-street and examined some dilapidated tenement, and now sought a fashionable quarter, and went over some grand mansion to be let for six months only, and furnished!—an exorbitant rent demanded, of course.

The whole thing was so evidently a sham, that I at last burst into tears and proposed to go home. Mr. Doughty assented, and with my face swollen and shining with the cold, my hands aching and my feet numb, I arrived there in a condition of outraged and indignant feeling that could go no further.

I comforted myself as I best could, for nobody comforted me, and my husband, monopolizing the easy-chair and a great part of the fire, opened the letters that awaited him.

When he had concluded the reading of the first one—addressed, as I observed, in a woman's hand—he said suddenly, "Come here, Nell, and sit on my knee."

I did so.

"What should you think of taking the house in —— street?"

"I should like it very well."

"I think that would suit us—room for ourselves, and a visitor now and then, perhaps."

I did not sit on his knee any longer; I felt instinctively that the letter he had just read was from the charming cousin, and that the prospect of having her for a guest had changed the aspect of affairs.

The house was taken at once, and Mr. Doughty informed me before long that I had a great happiness in prospect—that of knowing the little cousin I had heard him speak of.

She came almost before we were settled; impossible, thought I, that I should be jealous; the idea of affinity between her and Mr. Doughty was so ridiculous. She was white, short, and fat as a worm in a chestnut, and almost as incapable of thought. The flax-like hair was so thin you could see her head beneath it all the time; her cheeks and chin trembled with fatness; her eyes were of the faintest blue, and cloudy with vague apprehension; her arms hung stiff and round as two rolling pins, and her pink and blue silk dresses were pinned up and fringed out, and greasy: but she was amiable—too simple-hearted and indolent to be otherwise, indeed.

"She is a child, you see," said my husband, "and I bespeak for her childish indulgences; you must not be surprised to find her arms around my neck any time—playful little kitten, that she is."

I was not so much surprised to find her big arms about his neck, as by the fact which gradually broke in upon me, that they had power to detain him from the most important duties.

Towards her he was gentle and indulgent to the tenderest degree—towards me exacting, severe, and unyielding.

If I fretted, he was surprised that I could do so with so patient an example before me; if I forbore complaint, he gave me no praise; I had done nothing more than I ought to do. If I slighted or blamed Jenny, as I was sometimes driven to do, he was surprised and indignant that I, a reasonable woman, should treat a mere child, quite incapable of defense or retaliation, so cruelly.

By turns, I resorted to every device: grave and reserved dignity, playful badinage, affected indifference, rivalry in dress and manner, pouting, positive anger, threats of divorce and separate maintenance—all would not do. I ruined thereby the slender stock of amiability and fair looks I began with, and gained nothing. Now I went home for a few days, and now I affected illness; but I gained nothing, for of all lost things most difficult to be regained, lost affection is the most hopeless.

This state of feeling could not last always; the nerves of sensibility could not be laid bare and left bare without becoming indurated, and by degrees I became incapable of receiving or of giving enjoyment. In our treatment of one another, my husband and I fell into a kind of civility which was the result of indifference. Before folks we said "my dear;" and when we were alone—but we never were alone—we had ceased to have any of those momentous nothings to communicate which require to be done without observation. I had no longer any motive in life—duty was tiresome, and pleasure a mask that smothered me; love was a fable, and religion, I knew not what—nothing that comforted me, for it can only enter the heart that is open to the sweet influences of love.

In a fit of the most abject depression I swallowed poison, and lying down on my sofa awaited death with more interest in the process of its approaches than I had felt for months. The pain and the burning were easier to bear than I had borne many and many a time; gradually the world receded; my eyes closed, and a struggle shook my whole frame—death had indeed got hold of me. A terrible noise filled my ears; my dead and stiffening body seemed to drop away; I sat upright and saw about me all familiar and household things. On the floor beside me lay the picture of Mr. Doughty which I had been holding in my hand when I fell asleep—the noise of its falling had waked me.

"Then it had been only a dream, after all?"

"Why, to be sure; did you not see all along that such things could not have really happened?"

ELIZA ANDERSON

Chapter 1

THE FIRELIGHT was beginning to shine brightly through the one small window that looked towards the street—the one small window of a barely comfortable house that once stood in the suburb of a busy little town—busy in a little way. The one blacksmith was exceedingly busy: the clinking of his hammer was heard far into the night often, and on the beaten and baked ground before his door horses were waiting for new shoes from year's end to year's end. The storekeeper was busy too, for he was showman and salesman, and clerk and all; the schoolmaster was busy with his many children in the day, and his debating schools and spelling schools at night; the tailor was busy of course—and one man among them, who might be seen talking with the blacksmith or the storekeeper, or lounging on the bench in front of the tavern some time during every day, was busiest of all; this man lived in the house where the light was shining at the window, and his name was George Anderson. He was always better dressed, and could talk more smartly than most of his neighbors—it was his boast that he could do anything as well as anybody else, and a little better, and he sometimes exemplified to his audience that his boast was not without truth—he could take the blacksmith's hammer and nail on a horseshoe as readily as the smith himself, and, moreover, he could make the nails and beat out the shoe, if he chose, but it was not often he chose so hard a task—he could wrestle with the bar-keeper and get the better of him, drink whisky with him, and in that too get the better, for George Anderson was never seen to walk crooked or catch at posts, as he went along. Now he would step behind the counter, and relieve the storekeeper for an hour, and whatever trades he assumed were sure to be to the satisfaction of everybody—he was good-natured and welcome everywhere, for he always brought good news. It was quite an event at the school-house to have him come and *give out* the spelling lesson, or hear the big girls parse some intricate sentence from Paradise Lost.

The scholars were not afraid of him, and knew they could catch flies and talk as much as they pleased if he were their teacher, and then they felt sure he knew more than the schoolmaster himself.

The firelight was beginning to shine so bright that you might have seen through the naked window all that was in the room—a bare floor, a bed, some chairs and a table were there—a pot and a kettle steaming over the fire—a litttle girl sitting in a little chair, before it, and a woman leaning on the foot of the bed. The table-cloth was laid, but nothing to eat was on the table.

Presently the schoolmaster was seen going that way, walking leisurely, and with a book beneath his arms—he boards with Mrs. Anderson, and is going home. He entered the house, and in less than a minute was seen to come out without the book, looking hurried and flurried, and to walk towards the more crowded part of the town very fast, stopping once at the door of a small house much resembling Mrs. Anderson's own.

He finds the redoubtable George telling a story in the bar-room to a group of admiring listeners, and touching his arm, whispers something, but the story-telling goes on all the same. The schoolmaster repeats the touch, and whispers more emphatically. "Yes, directly," says George. "Now, this moment!" says the schoolmaster, aloud, and he tries to pull the talker away, but not till the story is finished does he start toward home, and then leisurely and smoking a cigar as he goes. The schoolmaster does not return home, but solemnly makes his way to a common not far from it, and crossing his hands behind him, appears lost in contemplating a flock of geese swimming in a shallow pond and squalling when he comes near. Meantime the mistress of the little house, at the door of which he stopped for a moment, has thrown a shawl about her shoulders and runs without bonnet to Mrs. Anderson's house. Another woman, spectacles in hand, and cap border flying, follows directly, and then another, summoned by some secret and mysterious agent, it would seem, for no messenger has been visible.

The window that looks into the street is temporarily curtained now with a woman's shawl—sparks are seen to fly out of the chimney rapidly, and there is much going out and in and whispering of neighbors about their doors and over their garden fences—and it is not long till one of the women comes away from Mrs. Anderson's, leading the little girl who sat by the fire an hour ago. Her black eyes are wide open as if she were afraid, or in doubt what would become of her, and she looks back towards her home wistfully and often, though the woman seems to talk cheerfully as they go, and lifts her with a playful jump over the rough places. Suddenly they turn aside from the path they are in—they notice the schoolmaster pacing up and down beside the pond, and join him, and after some embarrassed blushes and foolish laughter on his part, they go away together. He leads the little girl by the hand, and her thin, white face looks up to him more confidently than to the strange woman. They turn into a little yard, cross a dark porch and open a side door—a glimpse is revealed of a room full of light and children, and all is dark again.

A very good supper the strange woman prepared, of which the little girl and the schoolmaster partook, and afterward he lifts her on his knee, and with the other children gathered about him, tells stories of bears and pirates and Indians till she at last falls asleep, and then the strange woman opens a little bed and softly covers her, and the schoolmaster is shown to a bed in another part of the house. The morning comes, and she goes to school with the master without having gone home, and the day goes by as other days have gone at school—lessons are badly recited and spelling badly spelled; and the schoolmaster takes her hand and helps her down stairs, and walks on the rough ground, leaving the smooth path for her, and they pass the pond where the geese are swimming, and the strange woman's house, and go in at home, the child still holding the master's hand.

"Well, Lidy," says the woman, who is there preparing the supper, "what do you think happened when you were asleep last night?" Lidy can't guess, and the master says he can't guess, though older eyes than Lidy's would have seen that he suspected shrewdly. "Why," says the strange woman, "the prettiest little brother you ever saw in your life was brought here, for you!" Lidy's black eyes open wide with wonder, anad she holds fast the master's hand, and looks at him inquiringly as if she wished he would tell her whether to be glad or sorry. He puts his arm around her and draws her close to his side, and says something about how happy she will be, but he says it in a misgiving tone, and smooths her hair as if it were a piteous case. The strange woman leaves her bustling for a moment, and whispers at the bedside there is no tea. A pale hand puts by the curtain, and a low voice says something about having told George, three hours past, to go to the tailor who owes her for sewing, get the money and bring home tea and sugar, and some other things, anad she wonders he does not come. The strange woman says she wonders too, but she whispers to the schoolmaster that it is enough like *somebody* to stay away at such a time, and she lifts the tea-kettle from the coals, and lights the candle.

Lidy is told to sit down in her little chair, and make a good, nice lap, which she does as well as she knows how—and the dear little brother, about whom she is still half incredulous, is brought, and in long flannel wrappings laid across her knees. "Now ain't he a pretty baby though!" exclaims the strange woman, "with his itty bitty boo eyes, and his hair des as nice as any of 'em and ebrysing." The latter part of the speech was made to the wonderful baby, whom Lidy was told she must kiss, and which she did kiss as in duty bound. The wonderful baby scowled his forehead, clenched his fists and began to cry. "Jolt your chair a little, sissy," says the strange woman, and then to the wonderful brother, "Do they booze itty boy! Well, 'em sant do no such a sing! no, 'en sant!" Then to the schoolmaster, who is bending over his Latin grammar, she exhibits one of the feet of the remarkable boy, and says she believes in her heart, he could hardly wear the moccasin of her little Mary who is nine months old—then she falls to kissing one of the hands of the wonderful baby, and calls him in her loving fondness, "a great big, good-for-nossen sugar-plum." Then she exhibits one of the wonderful hands, that clenches and claws most unamiably as she does so, and informs the schoolmaster that she believes in her heart, the hands of the wonderful boy are as large, that very minute, as her Tommy's, and he will be two years old the seventeenth day of next month—then she addresses herself to the baby again, and calls his feet "ittle footens," and makes a feint of eating both at once.

And all this while the remarkable boy has been fretting and frowning on the lap of his little sister, who is told she is very much blest in having a little brother, and who supposes she *is* blest, and trots him, and kisses him, and holds him up and lays him down again, but in spite of all her little efforts he frowns and fidgets as if she did not, and could not do half enough for him.

By and by a slow footstep is heard, and a whistle, and directly afterward Mr. Anderson comes in and gives the strange woman a little parcel—briskly she measures the tea, and briskly she fills up the teapot and rattles the cups into the saucers; the baby is smothered in his long flannels and tucked under the coverlet.

"Come, Casper," says Mr. Anderson, "if you had been at work as hard as I have, you would not want to be called twice."

The schoolmaster lays down his grammar and asks Mr. Anderson what he has been doing—the pale hand puts by the curtain again, and a pale face turns eagerly to hear.

"Why, I could not begin to tell," he says, helping himself freely to everything that is on the table, and he proceeds to mention some of the work. He has broken a colt, he says, which nobody else could manage, and made him kindly, both under the saddle and in harness—he has drawn a tooth which the dentist could not draw, he has turned off two flour barrels for the cooper, and driven the stage-coach seven miles and back, besides a dozen other things, none of which was the least profit to his family. The light goes out of the pale face that turned so eagerly towards him, and a low voice says, "Did you see the tailor, George?"

"Why, to be sure," he answers, "I sewed a seam for him as long as from here to the gate and back again." He has not answered her question as she expected, the hand that holds the curtain shakes nervously, and the low voice says,

"Did he—did—did you get the tea, George?"

"Why, to be sure, and most excellent tea it is," and as the strange woman drains the last drop into his sixth cup, he adds, "won't you have a cup, mother?"

He turns partly towards her as he confers upon her the honor of this inquiry, and the low voice trembles as it says, "No" and the pale hand lets the curtain drop. Poor woman! perhaps she saw the bright new waistcoat that George wore, with its double rows of shining buttons, perhaps she saw this and knew the way her hard earnings had gone. The schoolmaster thinks he hears a stifled groan behind the curtain, sets his cup of tea aside, and will not eat any more, and directly returns to his grammar. Mr. Anderson sits in the corner and smokes for half an hour, and then recollecting that some business requires his attention up town, pulls on his gloves, and goes out. The schoolmaster follows shortly, and in a few minutes returns, and gives the strange woman two small parcels, one containing crackers and the other raisins—poor Mrs. Anderson thinks it was George brought them, reproaches herself for having wronged him, smiles and is blest again.

The remarkable baby cries and cries, and while the strange woman washes the dishes and makes the house tidy, little Lidy carries him up and down the room, and across and across the room till her arms ache, and she sits down.

"Bless me! you are not tired of your dear little brother already?" exclaims the strange woman, and Lidy says she is not tired—she is very glad to carry him—only her arms won't hold him any longer.

When the house was set in order, the strange woman took the remarkable boy, and with some talk to his "ittle boo, seepy eyes," managed to quiet him, and tucking him away as before, she went home to attend her own house and little ones.

At ten o'clock Lidy had crossed the floor with her blessed brother in her arms hundreds of times, and in a temporary lull was fallen asleep in her chair. A rough pull at her hair caused her to open her eyes suddenly—the baby was crying again, and her father was come and scolding her angrily. "She had not a bit of feeling," he said, "and did not deserve to have such a beautiful brother—somebody would come and take him away if she did not take better care of him." Directly Lidy was pacing the floor again, and the baby crying with all his might.

"Seems to me you don't try to keep your poor little brother still," says the father, for a moment taking the cigar from his mouth, and then puffing away again. He never thought of relieving the little girl, or even of speaking any words of pity and comfort to her—she was not born to pity or comfort from her father—she had committed the offence of inheriting the light of life some years prior to her brother, and from the moment of his birth she had no consideration except with reference to him. Even her mother, though she loved her, gave the baby the preference—Lidy's petticoats were appropriated for his use, and Lidy could not go to school because her shawl must be turned into a baby blanket. Everybody came to see the baby, and everybody said how much prettier than his sister he was, but that she seemed to be a good little girl, and of course she was very much delighted with her new brother—he would be big enough one of these days to play with her, and then she would have fine times.

Mr. Anderson was congratulated, and proud to be congratulated—he could afford to do almost anything since a fine son was born to him, and in higher good-humor than usual he made barrels for the cooper and nails for the blacksmith—treated all the town to brandy instead of whisky, and to the storekeeper traded a very good new hat for a very bad old one!

And patiently Lidy gave up her petticoats, and patiently she stayed away from school and worked all the day—and while her mother sat up in bed to sew for the tailor again, she climbed into her little chair and washed the dishes—it was all for her pretty little brother, her mother said, and by and by he would be big enough to work for them, and then he would buy a new cap for mother, and new slippers for Lidy, and oh, ever so many things.

Lidy quite forgot the sweeping and the dish washing, in the pictures of the new things her little brother was going to buy for her some time.

Now and then of evenings, when the baby was asleep, the schoolmaster would take Lidy on his knee and teach her to read, and she scarcely fell behind the children that were in school every day, he said. Once when he was praising her, her father said her little brother George would soon get before her when he was big enough to go to school. "George will never have her eyes, though," said the schoolmaster, proudly looking into their black, lustrous depths.

Mr. Anderson said the girl's eyes were well enough, he supposed, for a girl's eyes, but George would never suffer in comparison with her, and from that time the schoolmaster, whose name was Casper Rodwick, was designated as "Old Casper," by the father of the remarkable boy.

Chapter II

YEARS WENT AWAY, and one frosty moonlight night, the same neighbor who led little Lidy away and kept her before, was seen hurrying across the common, again, and the schoolmaster to come forth and go searching about the town—the storekeeper laid down his measure, saying, "Is there any bad news, Mr. Rodwick?" for he knew by the manner of his inquiry for George, that poor Mrs. Anderson was dead.

The husband wore a new hat deeply shrouded with crape at her funeral, and new gloves, and George, who was grown to be a big, saucy boy, wore gloves too, while Eliza wore an ill-fitting bonnet that was not her own, and no gloves at all.

From that time Mr. Anderson did not look, nor seem like himself, people said, and it was believed he was grieving himself to death. They did not know, and he did not know, that he had drawn all his life from his wife—she had bought his food and his clothes, she had held him up and kept him up, and when the crape he wore at her funeral grew dusty and fell to pieces, he fell to pieces with it. He called Lidy to his bedside, one day, and told her that her brother would soon have a fine education—she must be content to suffer some privations till that was accomplished, and then he would repay her handsomely—he was a noble-hearted lad, and wonderfully gifted. Lidy must look to him for advice now, and in all things subserve his wishes.

"Dear, dear father," cried Lidy, "you must not die—I can not live without you," and with all the power that was in her, she strove to make pleasant the sick-room. She placed her geranium pots and myrtles where he could see them, and let the sunshine in at the windows that he might feel how bright the world was without—but his eyes could not see the brightness anywhere, and at length one night Casper was called to write his will—he had nothing to bequeath, and his will was a record of his wishes only. Little more was written than he had spoken to Lidy, and all was to the effect that George was her natural and proper guardian, that he was superior to her in wisdom, and should be so in authority, and that if ever his daughter forgot it, he wished her to read this testimonial of her father's will.

So they were left alone in the world, the two orphans, with no friend but the schoolmaster. Eliza Anderson had all her mother's energy and aptitude. She could not only sew for the tailor, but she could make caps and collars for the ladies of the town, and dresses too, and as she was not ashamed to work she got along with her poverty very well. George inherited all his father's smartness, and more than all his irresolution, but as he grew older he grew better tempered, and whatever he was to others, was seldom unamiable to Lidy. How could he be, indeed, unless he had been a demon?

Often when she sat with her sewing at night, she would tell the schoolmaster what great hopes she had of George, and how ingeniously he could turn his hand to anything. Sometimes he would smile and sometimes he would sigh, but whatever he said it was evident he shared none of her enthusiasm. This rather offended Lidy, for she received any slight to George as a personal insult, and she would sit all the evening after some hopeful allusion to him, silent, often sullen, saying to all the master's little efforts to please her, that she had not a friend in the world, and it was no use ever to hope for sympathy. It was true that from the first the master had not loved George much—first he had taken the petticoats from his little favorite, then her playthings, and then she began to be big enough to work for him, and from that time it was nothing else but work for him, and for the master's part he could see no prospect of anything else.

One night she appeared unusually happy, and to find her own heart company enough. Once or twice she seemed on the point of telling something to the master, but she checked herself, and if she said anything it was evidently not what she at first thought. "Well, Lidy," he said, at length, "what is it?" and at last it came out—about George, of course. He was going to stay away from school and work in the garden the half of every day! and Eliza thought it not unlikely that he would learn more in half the day, after such healthful exercise, than he had done in the whole day. She had spent more money for the hoe, and the spade, and garden seeds, to be sure, than she could well afford, but then it was all going to be such an improvement to George, to say nothing of the great advantage it would be to her?

"Don't you think it will be a good thing for us both?" and she went on to say it was a wonderful idea, and all his own—she had never suggested anything like it to George. Did it not look like beginning to do in earnest? and she concluded, "maybe, after all, you will find you were mistaken about him!"

"And maybe not," said the schoolmaster, coolly—"where is the boy?"

Eliza did not know where he was, and to be avenged upon him for the humiliating confession he obliged her to make, she said she did not know as it was any of his business.

"Of course it is not my business, but I can't bear to see you so imposed upon," and he very gently took her hand as he spoke. She withdrew it blushing; covered her face, and burst into tears. She was not a child, and he was her friend and schoolmaster no more. She was become a woman, and he her interested lover.

He had been gone an hour to the little chamber adjoining his schoolroom, where he had slept since her mother's death, when George came.

Lidy kept her face in the dark that he might not see how red her eyes were, for she could not explain why she had been crying. She hardly knew herself—and in a tone of affected cheerfulness told him of the garden tools she had bought, and produced her package of seeds.

"Call me early," he said, "I am going to work in earnest. I am twelve years old now, and can do as much as a man!"

Lidy promised to call him, and never once thought necessity ought to wake him, as it did her.

She was astir an hour earlier than common the next day—and having called George, set to digging in the garden beds with good-will. She was determined the schoolmaster should find the work begun when he came to breakfast. Two or three times she left her work to call George again, and at last, yawning and complaining, he came. "He thought he would feel more like working after breakfast," he said, "rising so early made his head dizzy," and sitting down on a bank of grass, he buried his forehead in his handkerchief, and with one hand pulled the rake across the loose earth which his sister had been digging. Poor boy, she thought, a cup of coffee will do him good, and away she flew to make it.

"Really, George," said the schoolmaster, when he sat down to breakfast, "you have made a fine beginning—if you keep on this way we shall be proud of you."

Lidy noticed that he said, *we* shall be proud of you, and in her confusion she twice put sugar in his coffee, and forgot to give sugar to

George at all. He sulked and sat back from the table, affecting to believe that his sister had deprived him of sugar in his coffee for the sake of giving the master a double portion. And he concluded with saying, "It's pretty treatment after my getting up at daybreak to work for you."

"You ought to be ashamed of yourself," said the master, provoked by his insolent words and sulky manner beyond silent endurance, "as if you ought not to work for your sister, and moreover it is for yourself you are working." And he added between his teeth, "if I had the management of you, I'd teach you what pretty treatment was!"

"But you haven't the management of him, Mr. Rodwick," said Eliza, moving her chair further from him and nearer to George.

"I am aware of it, Miss Anderson," he replied, "and if you will uphold him in his ugliness after this fashion, I must say I should be sorry to be connected with him in any way!"

A look that was half defiance and half sneer, passed over the face of Lidy, but she said nothing. At this moment the blacksmith stopped at the door, to offer some seeds of an excellent kind of cucumbers to his neighbor, whom in common with all the village he greatly esteemed.

"You look pale, ma'am," he said, as he laid the seeds on the table beside her, "I'm afeard you have been working beyond your strength;" and turning to the master, he explained how he had seen her digging in the garden since daybreak. Her face grew crimson, for she had not only suffered the master to attribute the work to George, but had herself helped to deceive him.

One glance he gave her, which to her appeared made up of pity and contempt, and without one word went away from the house. If her little deception had not been discovered, she could have borne herself very proudly towards the master, but now she was humiliated, not only in his estimation, but her own. She was angry with him, with the blacksmith, with George, and with herself. Yet for a good while she would not give up even to herself, but sat sipping coffee and eating dry bread, as if nothing disturbed her in the least, but all the while the bitter tears kept rising and filling her eyes, for she would not wipe them away. One moment she thought she did not care for what had happened, and that she had a right to work in the garden, and was not obliged to tell the master of it either, as she knew of, and that if he had ever given George credit for anything, she would not have tried to deceive him, and at any rate, what she did was nothing to him; he had no authority over either of them, she was glad of that. But under all this bolstering, which she heaped up under her failing heart, she felt sorry and ashamed, and knew that the master was in the right, that he was a strict disciplinarian, and that in some sort he was entitled to some authority over George, at least. He had lived in the house with them always, had been their teacher, and since their father's death their friend and guardian. George was a bad, idle boy, she knew, and ran away from school when he chose, and she knew too that he required a severe master, and if Mr. Rodwick had softened matters a little she would not have cared; but he was not the man to disguise plain truth—as far as he saw he saw clearly, and made others see clearly too.

But when it was all turned over and over, Eliza was angry with him more than with George, angry, because he knew the truth, and angry because the truth was the truth—in some way, his knowledge of facts made the facts, she thought.

And all the while she was turning things about, and yet not reconciled to herself, nor to the master, nor to George, he sat sullenly away from the table biting his finger-nails, and waiting to be coaxed to eat.

For once there was no coaxing for him, and the breakfast was removed without his having tasted it. Pulling his hat over his eyes, he was about leaving the house, when Eliza drew him back and demanded authoritatively where he was going. "To the tavern, to buy my breakfast."

"No, you shall not," she said, and forcing him to sit down she sat by him and repeated to him the sacrifices she had all her life made for him, "and what, after all, is the result?" she said, "why, the more I do the more I may, and the less you care for me?" and seeing that he was grinning in his hat, she told him that she knew somebody who *could* make him mind, thus owning to his face, like a weak, foolish, loving woman, that she had no power over him.

"Well, Madam Rodwick," he said, coolly, when she had exhausted all epithets of threat and entreaty, and tenderness and reproach, "if you have concluded your sermon I'll go and get my breakfast."

"You will go to work in the garden!" said the sister, "that is what you will do!" and straight way she fell down to entreaty, and with tears counted the money she had paid for spade and hoe and seeds, and how illy she could afford it, and how she had hoped, and how she still hoped that he was going to be a good boy, a help and comfort to her.

"Well, I shan't mind old Casper, anyhow," said the boy, at length; and it was finally settled that he would go to work in the garden, and that she would prepare him a nice, warm breakfast. A few shovels of earth he moved from one place to another, but there was really no work done, and Eliza saw there was none done when she called him to the second breakfast. She was completely discouraged and broken down now, and told George so, and seeing that he heeded nothing, she buried her face in her hands and fell to crying. She did not know as she would ever do anything again, she said, and indeed she felt little courage to go to work. George would not help her, and she was tired of working alone.

"It was too hot now, to work in the garden," he replied, "and too late to go to school," and so he sauntered away, his sister saying, as he went, "She did not know as she cared where he went, nor what became of him."

It was noon before she knew it, and the master came home, and there was no dinner prepared; and the tailor called for some promised work, and Eliza had been crying all day, and it was not ready. He was disappointed, vexed, and said if she could not keep her engagements he would find somebody that would.

The master saw how it all was—that George was the beginning of trouble, and that Eliza herself was not a little to blame, and if he had said anything, he would have said what he thought, but she asked for neither advice nor sympathy; and having told her she need prepare no dinner for him, he returned to the schoolhouse and its duties, and as usual maintained a calm and quiet demeanor, however much he might have been troubled at heart.

When the school was done with, he did not return home at once as was his custom, but opening his grammar, remained at the window as long as he could see, and till after that.

All day George had not been seen nor heard of—and all day Eliza had done nothing but cry and fret; but when night came, and a messenger with it to say he was lying on the ground, a little way out of town, drunken as he could be, she began to see how much less to blame the schoolmaster had been than she had tried to believe.

From her heart she wished he would come, but though suffering most intensely she would not seek him, nor would she allow him to know her wretchedness when he should come, so she resolved. But all her proud resolves would not do. He came at last in the same calm, confident way he always came, and with some common words, meant to show that all was right, and that he felt as usual, opened his book to await his supper, which he saw no indication of.

"Mr. Rodwick," she said, directly, in a voice that trembled in spite of herself.

"Yes, what is it?" he answered, without looking from his book.

It was hard and very humiliating to tell him what it was, but her love for George, and the fear that he might be run over where he lay, overcame the last remnant of her pride, and hiding her face, she sobbed out her sad confession and appeal.

He did not say, "I knew it would be so," nor "You are to blame;" he only said, "Don't cry, Lidy—don't cry," and putting down his book, hurried away. In half an hour he came back, and George with him, staggering and swearing, his clothes soiled and his face dirty—bleeding at one side where he had fallen against the rough ground. He would not be persuaded to have his face washed, and his clothes brushed, nor would he sit down or go to bed, nor do anything else, but swear that in spite of old Casper or his old sister he would go back to the tavern, he had enough good friends there.

Casper had returned to his book, and not till Eliza begged him to interfere, did he speak one word, or seem to notice what was passing, but he no sooner laid his hand on the boy, and spoke a few words in his quiet, determined manner, than he ceased to offer resistance, and was led away to bed without more ado.

When the supper was eaten, Casper would have gone, but Eliza said, "No, I want to talk about George."

"Very well," he said, seating himself, "what have you to say?"

Eliza knew not what to say—she knew that she was troubled and tormented, that George was idle enough and unpromising enough, but that she loved him after all, and could not bear that he should be compelled to right ways by any one but herself. This was the amount of all she could say.

A clear, practical, common sense view of things the schoolmaster took. He loved Eliza, and he said so, he admired all that was good and discreet and womanly in her, and he said so: he did not love George, and he disliked and disapproved of her wavering and compromising course with him. He had no great hopes of him at the best, nevertheless he could bring him under subjection in some way, if Eliza would give him the right to do so.

He told her what his fortunes and prospects were, without exaggeration or depreciation; he numbered his years, every one of them up before her, and her own, which were not half so many, and then he said that all he was, and all he had, and all he could do, which was not much, were hers to accept if she would, but with the understanding that George should be subject to his authority.

Eliza reminded him of her promise to her dead father: how could she break that and be at peace with herself? and, moreover, he admitted that he did not love George, and how could she hope the boy would be made any better by him? The schoolmaster argued that if she were willing to trust herself with him, it was natural that she should be willing to trust the management of her brother: and as for the sacred promise she laid so much stress on, it was a bad promise exacted by a bad father, and better broken than kept. And now, he concluded, with the calmness of a third party summing up evidence, "You have all the facts before you—look at them and decide as your conscience dictates."

The facts were unpleasant ones, some of them, and Eliza did not like to look them in the face—she did not like to say definitely what she would do nor when she would do it. When George was older and provided for, or capable of providing for himself, their lives should be joined and flow through all fortune in a sentimental sunshine. All of which to the schoolmaster was nothing but moonshine. With it he was not contented—he wished to see the ground he stood upon, whatever it was, and finally, when they separated, it had been agreed that whenever George should be provided for they should be married; and that during school hours he should be under the master's control, and at other times Eliza's will should be his law.

Neither was satisfied with this arrangement, for both foresaw it would result badly, in the beginning.

Chapter III

THE BREAKFAST was a pleasant one. George had been working in the garden for two hours, he said, and should have half the seeds in the ground before dinner.

Eliza was greatly elated, and saw the fulfillment of her best hopes speedily coming. She could not praise him enough, and she could not help thinking the schoolmaster a little ungenerous in accepting what seemed to her a wonderful performance, as a matter of course.

"Don't you think, Casper," she said, at last, determined to force some praise from him, "that George is a pretty good boy, after all?"

She had better not have asked it. He had simply done his duty, Casper said, but the motive seemed to him questionable. It was partly the result of shame, and partly an effort to buy off punishment. As soon as George betrayed indications of any thorough reformation, he should be glad to acknowledge it.

Pretty industriously for half a day George kept at work, and with the assistance of Eliza, part of the seeds were got into the ground, and when at noon he related his achievement to Casper, she made no mention of the hand she had lent.

"Now you are to go to school," she said, when the dinner was past; but George replied that he was too tired, and could not learn if he did. With much coaxing and many promises, he was induced to set out at last: but one excuse for loitering offered itself after another, and finally at the pond he stopped, and having pelted the geese for an hour, he stretched himself in the shavings before the cooper's shop, and slept away another hour; another was passed in shaving hoop-poles and piling staves, and then the school was dismissed, and joining the other boys the truant went home.

With a good deal of coaxing, and hiring, and scolding, and some wholesome fear of the master, the garden was at last planted; but Eliza, though she tried to conceal it, had done most of the work, and all the while George had only gone to school when he chose.

One day he told his sister he knew a little boy who had made dollars the last year by selling eggs, and if she would buy a hen and a dozen chickens, oh he would be the best boy in the world, and do everything she desired. He knew where he could get them if he only had two dollars.

Of course Eliza gave the money. She would work a little later every night and soon earn it, and of course she told Casper about it, and insisted that he should see in it great speculative ability on the part of George, but he could only see that she had thrown away her money, and said so, which displeased her, of course, and there was an interval of estrangement.

The seeds were soon mostly picked out of the garden beds, and the beds scratched level with the paths, and then the mother hen came daily home from travelling through the weeds, or from some neighbor's garden with a broken legged chicken, or with a diminished number, till finally she drowned herself in trying to rescue the last one from a pail of milk, and so ended the garden and the chicken speculation.

George now professed himself inclined to return to school. He believed he would be a teacher after all—Eliza concluded his strongest bent was towards learning, and he went to school.

But his zeal soon abated—he liked work better—the cooper would pay him four shillings per day; and packing his books he went to work with the cooper. Eliza was telling the master how well he was doing, when he came in with one hand bandaged and bleeding—he had cut off two fingers!

In the course of a few months the wound was healed, but he should never be able to work, and one day, about the middle of the afternoon, found him in school. He soon told his sister—"old Casper" could not teach him anything. Perhaps it would be the very making of him to send him to the academy three miles away. George would walk the distance, the exercise would be beneficial, and she must manage some way, she hardly knew how, to pay for it. His old hat would not do to wear to the academy, he must have a new one—his old coat would not do, the tailor would furnish one, and Eliza would sew for it. At last arrangements were concluded, and he went to the academy. He soon discovered the walk to be too long, it so overcame him that he could not study. He knew of a horse he could hire to ride for a trifle, and the horse was hired and George rode to school, and Eliza worked later into the night and earlier in the morning. She had never been so hopeful—he would be able to teach in the academy after a while, and all her troubles past. If he had the time for books, he said, that was consumed in riding to and from school, and then if he could have a room and study as the other boys did, of evenings, he should get on twice as well. So the horse was given up. It took almost as much to pay for riding as to hire board, Eliza said, and George was provided with board and lodging at the academy, and patiently she toiled on.

The days were the happiest now she had ever seen. Casper was all kindness when the boy was out of his sight; they would be so happy, and her toils would all be over before long—she was telling him so, and he listening in half credulous delight, for what lover has not some faith in his mistress, when George, books and bundles and all, strode into the house, and a great chilly, black shadow came in with him.

He did not like the boys at the academy, nor the teachers, nor anything. He could not eat at his boarding-house—he was sick with all, and believed he was going to die: and Eliza believed he was sick, and feared he would die; but the master neither believed the one nor feared the other, and so the old estrangement came again.

When the youth professed himself well he went to work with the tailor, but did not like it, and so was home for awhile; then he went with the blacksmith, but that was too hard; then he was home for awhile, helping her, Eliza said; then he went into the store, grew tired and was home for awhile, helping Eliza again.

She was discouraged now, and a good deal in debt. She was growing old faster than years made her grow old; the rose died in her cheek, and her eyes lost their lustre—even the master did not praise them any more, and this made her sadder than all.

Suddenly George formed the resolution of going to school again. He believed "old Casper" was a pretty good teacher, after all.

Eliza began to think she would allow Casper the right to control him now, by becoming his wife, but he did not urge the marriage any more. She was almost resolved to approach the matter herself. George should be kept at school whether he would or not—she would tell Casper so that night. She arose with the resolution and looked towards the school-house, and there came George, running crookedly home, his eyes blind with tears, and holding up the crippled hand as if it had been mutilated anew.

"The master had struck his poor hand with a rule," he said, "and all for laughing because he saw him kiss Sophie Swain, and not because he did anything wrong."

There was a quick revulsion of sympathies and resolves on the part of Eliza. Sophie Swain was a pretty girl of sixteen, the daughter of the richest man in town. She saw plainly enough now why Casper said nothing about marriage, and she thought it was too bad that he should take to abusing her poor brother as well as herself on account of his charmer. As long as she lived, George should not be maltreated in that way, that he shouldn't.

All this and more, Eliza resolved she would say, and all this and more she did say in tones of no measured mildness. Of course she did not care how often the master kissed Sophie Swain, nor how soon he married her, if he wanted to. She was sure she would not stand in his way if she could, and she knew very well that she could not; he had ceased to feel even the commonest interest in her. But one thing she would and could do—she would prevent him from beating poor George to death.

When she had exhausted all epithets of reproach and denunciation, and was still from sheer prostration, the master replied in his perfectly quiet and self-possessed way, which to Eliza was especially provoking, that it was true as George said. He had kissed Sophie Swain, that he could not be blind to her beauty, and she seemed not averse to his acknowledgment of it. He had made no love to her, and did not propose to if Eliza would grant him the happiness of continuing his suit, or rather if she would be reasonable and terminate it in marriage, this he professed himself willing, nay, anxious to conclude at once. Not only his heart but his judgment, he said, sanctioned the proposal he had made her.

"It was true he had struck George," he said, "but not injuriously, and Eliza should have sense enough to know it. And besides, the youth merited twice as much as he had received. It was the first time he ever used the liberty herself bestowed on him, and he insisted that then and there their relations should be definitely settled."

In all he said he neither elevated nor lowered his voice in the least. If he saw Eliza's tears, he did not seem to see them, nor did he once touch her hand, nor move one inch towards her, but having concluded what he had to say awaited her answer, snapping the blade of his pen-knife backward and forward, and not even lifting his eyes towards her.

This conduct was certainly badly calculated to make a passionate woman reasonable.

Checking her tears in very anger, she told him he was a strange lover. He replied that he had a strange mistress, and besides she must remember he was not a passionate boy. Eliza begged his pardon. She had, for the moment, forgotten that only his judgment sanctioned his proposal to her, and that his heart was averse to it—interested, doubtless, in a much younger and handsomer woman.

"If you will make gratuitous interpretations, you must make them," said the master, his lip curling slightly; "but I have no replies for them."

Eliza insisted that she had interpreted his words legitimately, and that for her part she saw no reason why he should drag his judgment in at all. To which he replied most provokingly, that he feared his judgment had been dragged forward less than it should have been!

There were some more words, as angry and unreasonable as they could be on one side, and most severely reasonable and concise on the other. When they parted, it was with the declaration, on the part of Eliza, that Mr. Rodwick was free to use his judgment as he liked, for the future, it was nothing to her. And when he asked if he might not hope for leniency, she said, "No!"

Chapter IV

YEARS AGO all this happened, and what either party, or both have suffered, only themselves know. The same house, shabbier than it used to be, with the one uncurtained window towards the street, is standing yet. Sometimes in the evening twilight you will see there a plain, pale woman, with grey hair, sewing by the last light. She does not smile, nor look as if she had smiled for many years, or ever would again. Often three bright, laughing children go in at the gate with parcels of sewing, and they climb over her chair and kiss her, and wonder why she is not gay and laughing like their mother; and when they go away, they are sure to leave more money than she has earned, behind them; they are Casper's children, and the woman is Eliza Anderson.

Sometimes you will see there a ragged, wretched man, lame in the right leg, and with one arm off at the elbow—his face has in it a look of habitual suffering, of baffled and purposeless suffering, as if all the world was set against him, and he could not help it; and that is George.

Sometimes in the night, when all is dark and still, a white-haired man leans over the broken gate, forgetting the white wall of his own garden, and all the roses that are in it, and the pretty children that are smiling in their dreaming: and even the wife, gone to sleep too, in the calm, not to say indifferent confidence, that he will take care of himself, and come home when he gets ready. He leans there a long while thinking, not of what is, but of what might have been, and wondering whether eternity will make whole the broken blessings of time. That is Casper, to be sure—who else should it be?

The life story of Eliza A. from the time her baby brother is born until old age. She sides w/ her brother against her suitor, Casper the schoolmaster. Everyone makes mistakes and all end unhappy.

AN OLD MAID'S STORY

I WAS SITTING one summer afternoon in the shadow of a grapevine and cherry tree—for the one running through the top of the other cast a shadow on the short, thick grass beneath, through which scarcely a sunbeam found way. I was sitting there with an open book on my knee, but I was not reading; on the contrary, two or three thicknesses of the cloth which I had been sewing at intervals lay on the open page, and on this rested my idle hands. I was not working, nor thinking of work. On the side of the hill, behind me, the mowers were wading through billows of red clover—they were not whistling nor singing that I remember of—they had no grape-vines nor cherry-tree limbs between their bent backs and the sun beams that fell straight and hot upon them—and yet, perhaps, they were happier than I with all my cool shadows, for we have to pay to the uttermost farthing for the enjoyments of this life. The water was nearly dried up in the run that went crookedly across the hollow, and the sober noise it made I could not hear. The grey, dry dust was an inch deep along the road, which was consequently almost as still as the meadows. Now and then a team went by, taking a little cloud with it; and now and then a young woman trotted along on the old mare, which at home did nothing but switch flies, and was evidently averse to any other employment. Two or three young women I remember to have seen go along with bundles on their saddle-horns, and a little cloud of dust, similar to that in which they moved, half a mile, perhaps, behind them, in which trotted the colt, after its mother. I had seen, without especially noticing them, and yet it was an unusual thing that two or three young women should ride along on the same afternoon.

Immediately above my head, and fronting me, there was a porch, level with the second floor of the house, and on this porch a young, rosy-cheeked girl was spinning wool. She was running up and down as gaily as if it were gold and not common wool she held in her hand, and her face was beaming as though the rumble of her wheel were pleasantest music. Her thoughts ran little further than the thread she spun, good simple girl, and, therefore never became so tangled as to vex and puzzle her; and so it was easy to spin and smile, and smile and spin, all day. Once in a while the high well-sweep came down and down, and then went up and up—the iron hoops of the bucket rattled against the curb—some mower drank his fill, and with a deep breath of satisfaction went away, never wondering how or why half the clover along his path drew so bright a red from the black ground, and the other so sweet a white; and it was well he did not wonder, for had he done so ever so much all would have ended in the fact that there was red and white clover, and that the same ground produced both.

A little shower of dust blew over me and settled in the green grass and the white dying roses about me, and Surly, our dapple-nosed house-dog, dashed by me and gave noisy welcome to the visitor then about unlatching the gate. I hastened to conceal my book under the rosebush at hand, and to shake the dust from my work preparatory to using my needle, for to be found reading or idle would have been considered alike disgraceful in the estimation of our neighbors. When the visitor appeared, I recognized Miss Emeline Barker, and at the same time became aware that she was bent on holiday pleasure. She had been riding on horseback, but her white dress showed scarcely a wrinkle, so well had she managed it—a sash of pink ribbon depended from the waist, and the short sleeves were looped up with roses—her straw hat was trimmed with flowers and ribbon, and her boots were smoothly laced with tape instead of leather strings. But more than her dress, her face betrayed the joyous nature of the errand she was bent on. "Somebody is going to be married," was my first thought, "and Emeline has come to invite me to the wedding," and I was confirmed in this when she declined the seat I offered, with the assurance that she had not time to stay a moment. Expectation was on tiptoe, and when I said "how do they all at home?" I had no doubt she would tell me that Mary Ann, who was her elder sister, was to be married; but she answered simply that all were very well, and went on to tell about the harvest, the heat of the day, and other commonplaces, just as if she wore her every-day calico dress and not a white muslin one, looped up at the sleeves with roses.

Directly she bid me good bye without having said anything extraordinary at all, and then, as if suddenly recollecting it, she exclaimed, "Oh! I want to see Jane a moment." I pointed to the porch where Jane Whitehead was spinning, and with my heart drawing strangely into itself took the banished book from its place of concealment, quite careless of what Emeline Barker might think of me.

I felt dissatisfied and unhappy. I knew not why; the shadow of an unseen sorrow had fallen over me, and I could not escape it—in truth, I did not try. If I had taken a few steps I should have found the sunshine, but I did not, and the vague discomfort took a more definite shape.

I lifted the book to conceal my face, which it seemed to me must reflect my unhappy mind, but I did not read any more than before. Another book was opened which seemed to me the Book of Fate, and to be illustrated with one picture—that of an unloved old maid. We might be made wiser sometimes, perhaps, if it were permitted us to see ourselves as others see us, but we should rarely be made more comfortable.

There were whispers and laughter, and laughter and whispers, on the porch, but the rumble of the wheel so drowned the voices that for some time I heard not one word; but the first that reached me confirmed my feeling—myself was the subject of conversation.

"I should have thought they would have asked her," said Jane, half piteously, and turning her wheel slowly as she spoke, but not spinning any more. After a moment she continued, "suppose, Em, you take it upon yourself to invite her."

"Fie!" exclaimed Emeline, "if I were an old maid, I should not expect to be invited to young parties. Let old folks go with old folks, I say; and I am sure we would not be mad if all the old maids in the county should make a frolic and leave us out, would we, Jenny?"

"Why no," replied Jane; "but then this seems like another case, and I can't help liking Miss"——

"So do I like her well enough in her way," said Emeline, "but I would not like her at a party of young folks. She must be as old as the hills, and the dear knows she has no beauty to recommend her."

"Oh, she is not so very old—past getting married to be sure, or being cared for in that way, but she could help sew, you know, and be amused by our fun in the evening. Suppose we ask her to go with us?"

"I tell you she would be in the way," persisted Emeline, "and I suppose if Mrs. Nichols had cared to have her she would have invited her."

"Perhaps she forgot it," insisted Jenny.

"No, she didn't," replied Emeline. "Didn't I hear her talking all about who she wanted and who she did not, and who she felt obliged to ask; and she said if she asked Miss —— there were two or three others a good deal older and less desirable that would think themselves entitled to invitations, and she must stop somewhere, and on the whole might better not begin."

"Well, then, you tell her," pleaded Jane, evidently receiving, and sorry to receive, the stubborn facts.

When I became aware that I was the "old maid," so compassionated and dreaded, I was as one stunned by some dreadful blow. I felt it due to myself to remove from where I sat, but I had no strength to go; I seemed not to be myself. I saw myself by the new light whereby other people saw me. I began to count up my years. I was twenty-five the May past, but my life had been entirely confined to the old homestead, and no special, peculiarly interesting, or peculiarly sorrowful events had broken its monotony, so that I found it hard to realize the truth. I was young in knowledge—young in experience, and one year had been drawn into another without the visible separation of even a New Year's dinner. I had never thought of dividing myself from the younger people of the neighborhood, and till now I had never suspected that they desired to divide themselves from me. Directly Jenny slipped the bands, set by her wheel, and whispering and laughing the two girls came down and essayed to make some explanation which should not be wholly false, and yet soften the truth. Emeline was to remain a little while and assist Jenny, after which the two were to go together to Mrs. Nichols' to help with some sewing she was busy about.

So the old mare was led into the door-yard, Emeline hung her gay hat on a low limb of the cherry-tree, and tying on one of Jenny's aprons the happy pair set busily to work.

My task was much harder than theirs, for I must keep close the misery that was in my heart, and not suffer one single pang to break the expression of quietude in my face. The hat swinging gaily in the wind—the laughter of the girls, smothered away from my participation, seemed like injuries to my insulted sorrow. I could have lifted myself above hatred. Against a false accusation I could have proudly defended myself, but my crime was simply that of being an old maid, whom nobody cared to see, and against that there was nothing I could interpose. For the first time in my life I felt a sort of solemn satisfaction in the white and dying roses, and in the yellow leaves that fell from the cherry-tree over my head and into my lap.

Sometimes, when the girls came near me, they would lift up their voices as if in continuance of a conversation previously going forward, but I understood very well that these clear-toned episodes were put in for the occasion.

When the heart is light the hands are nimble, and the work was soon done, and Jenny ready to make her toilet—a task for which a country girl, at the time and place I write of, would have been ashamed to require more than ten minutes. The shadow of the cherry-tree was stretching far to the east when the old mare, quite used to "carry double," was led to the fenceside, and Emeline and Jane mounted and rode away.

I put my hands before my face when they were gone, but I did not cry. It was a hard, withered feeling in my heart, that tears could not wash away. In all the world I could see no green and dewy ground. There was nothing I could do—nothing I could undo. There was no one I blamed, no special act for which I blamed myself, unless it were for having been born. The sun went down under a black bank of clouds, and the winds came up and began to tell the leaves about a coming storm.

Pattering fast through the dust a little boy passed the gate, climbed into the meadow, and was soon across the hollow, and over the hill. The men were very active now, pitching the mown hay into heaps, turning their heads now and then towards the blackening west, and talking earnestly and loud. The boy drew close to them and seemed to speak, for all the workmen stood silent, and the rake dropped from the hand of the foremost and his head sunk down almost to his bosom. Presently one of the men took up the rake, another brought the coat and hat of the foremost laborer, who had been working bareheaded, and assisted him to put them on, for he seemed as one half dead, and quite unable to help himself—then the little boy took his hand and led him away, and I noticed that he walked with staggering steps, and often passed his hand across his eyes as he went. The men left in the field resumed work directly, but though a deep silence fell with the first shadows I could not hear a word, so lowly they spoke to one another. Till long after dark they kept rolling and tumbling the hay into heaps, but at last I heard them gathering water pails and pitchers together, and soon after they crossed the meadow towards the house—not noiselessly, as they came generally, but speaking few words and the few in low and kindly tones. The black bank of clouds had widened up nearly half the sky, and a blinding flash of lightning showed me their faces as they drew near the well and paused—not so much because they wished to drink, as because they felt reluctant to separate and go their different ways. While one of the men lowered the bucket, another approached me, and wiping his sunburnt face with his red silk handkerchief, said—"One of our hands has had bad news this evening."

I felt what it was before he went on to say, "his youngest child died about five o'clock, and will be buried to-morrow morning, I suppose."

Poor, poor father—no wonder the rake had fallen from his hands, and that he had suffered himself to be led away like a little child. What anguish must be the mother's, thought I, when the sterner and stouter-hearted father so bows himself down, and forgets that there is anything in the world but the cold white clay that is to be buried to-morrow.

I forgot Mrs. Nichols and the gay people she had about her; forgot that I had been forgotten, and remembered only our common humanity and our common need.

The sky was black overhead and the lightning every few minutes illuminated the grey dust before me, that was beginning to be dotted with drops of rain, falling at intervals, as I hurried through the darkness to the humble home where last year a babe had been born, and where the last day it had died. Two or three living children were left, and yet it seemed as if all were gone, the room was so still and gloomy. The little mouth had never spoken, and the little hands had never worked for food or for clothing, yet how poor the parents felt, having the precious burden laid from off their bosoms.

Close by the window, where the morning-glories grew thick, dressed in white and as if quietly asleep, lay the little one, waking not when the flowers dropped on its face, nor when the mother called it by all the sweetest names that a mother's fondness can shape.

"You must not grieve—the baby is better off than we," said a tall woman, dressed in black, and she led the poor mother from the white bed where it lay. After some further words of admonition and reproof, she proceeded to light the candles and to arrange the table preparatory, as I supposed, for morning service.

The rain came plashing on the vines at the window, and the mother's grief burst out afresh as she thought of the grave it would fall upon in the morning. A step came softly along the rainy grass, and a face whose calm benignity seemed to dispel the darkness, drew my eyes from the sleeping baby to itself. But the voice—there was in it such sweetness and refinement—such a mingling of love and piety, that I was blessed, as I had never been blessed, in being permitted to listen to it.

I recognized the visitor for the village clergyman who had lately come among us, and whom I had only seen once, when he gave baptism to the little one that was now returned to dust.

I recognized not only the form and features, but I also recognized, or thought I did, a spiritual kindred—the desolation that had divided me from the world an hour past was gone—heaven came down near to me, so near that earth was filled with the reflection of its glory and happiness.

All the night we were together. There were few words spoken. There was nothing to do but to listen to the rain and the beating of my heart. There was nothing to see but the baby on its white bed, the dimly-burning candle and the calm soul-full eyes of the clergyman—now bent on the sacred page before him, now on the leaves that trembled in the rain, and now, as something told me, for I scarcely dared look up, upon myself.

I wished there were something I might do for him, but I could think of nothing except to offer the rocking-chair which had been given me on my coming, and which was all the luxury the poor man's house afforded. In my over-anxiety to serve, I forgot this most obvious service I could render, and when it occurred to me at last my unfortunate forgetfulness so much embarrassed me that I knew not how to speak or stir. If there had been any noise—if any one had been present but our two selves—if he would speak to me—but as it was, I could not for a long while find courage for that proffer of my simple courtesy. There he sat silent, as far from me as he could well be, and as more time went by, looking at me more and more earnestly, I thought. At last the steadfast gaze became so painful that I felt that any change would be relief, and mastering my embarrassment as I best could, I offered the rocking-chair to the clergyman, whose name was Wardwell, with the energetic haste with which one touches the lion he would tame.

"No, my child," he said, very calmly, "you have most need of it."

I know not what I said, but in some vehement way, which I afterwards feared expressed all I was most anxious to conceal, made my refusal.

He smiled and accepted the chair, I thought in pity of my confusion, and rather to place me at ease, than for the sake of his own comfort.

He asked me directly whether I had ever been far from the village—a natural question enough, and asked doubtless for the sake of relieving the tedium of silence—but I saw in it only the inference of my rusticity and want of knowledge, and replied with a proud humility that I was native to the village—had scarcely been out of sight of it, and had no knowledge beyond the common knowledge of its common people.

With a changed expression—I could not tell whether of pain or annoyance—Mr. Wardwell moved his position slightly nearer me, but the habitual smile returned presently, and he rocked quietly to and fro, saying only, "well, well."

There was nothing in the tone or the manner to give force to the words. They might indicate that it was as well to live in the village as any other place. They might indicate that he had no interest in the inquiry—and none in the answer—or it might be that they expressed the fixedness of a foregone conclusion. I chose to receive the last interpretation, and leaned my head on the hard sill of the open window to conceal the tears with which, in spite of myself, my eyes were slowly filling.

All the time the clergyman had remained silent I had longed with a sincere and childish simplicity to be noticed or spoken to, and now if I could have unsaid the few words he had directly addressed to me a tormenting weight would have been lifted from my bosom.

The wet leaves shook almost in my face, and now and then some cold drops plashed on my head; but I would not manifest any inconvenience. I felt as if Mr. Wardwell were responsible for my discomfort, and I would be a patient martyr to whatever he might inflict.

"My child, you are courting danger," he said, at last; "the chill air of these rainy midnights is not to be tampered with by one of your susceptible organization."

Ah, thought I to myself, he is trying to pour oil on the wound he has made, but doubtless he thinks no amount of chill rain could injure me, for all of his soft speaking. So I affected to sleep, for I was ashamed to manifest the rudeness I felt, though my position was becoming seriously uncomfortable, to say nothing of its imprudence. My heart trembled, audibly, I feared, when Mr. Wardwell approached, and stooping over me, longer I thought than need were, softly let down the window. I would have thanked him, but to do so would have been to betray my ill-nature, which I was now repentant, and ashamed of. He passed his hand over my wet hair, and afterwards brought the cushion of the rocking-chair and placed it stealthily beneath my head. Soothed from my sorrow, and unused to watching, I was presently fast asleep. I dreamed I was at home, and that some one was walking across and across my chamber, and so close to my bedside that I felt a distinct fear. So strong was the impression I could not rid myself of it, even when, fully conscious, I unclosed my eyes and saw the still baby before me, and the clergyman apparently dozing in his chair. Was it he who had been walking so near me, in forgetfulness of me and simply to relieve the monotony of the time? Yes, said probability, even before my eyes fell upon a handkerchief of white cambric, lying almost at my feet, and which I was quite sure was not there when I took my seat at the window.

I took it up, partly from curiosity, partly for the want of other occupation, examined the flowers in the border, and read and re-read the initial letters, worked in black in one corner—C.D.W. I fancied the letters had been wrought by a female hand, and with a feeling strangely akin to jealousy, and which I should have blushed to own, tossed the handkerchief on the table and took my own from my pocket, more aware of its coarseness and plainness than I had ever been till then. It was as white as snow, neatly folded, and smelling of rose-leaves; but for all that I felt keenly how badly it contrasted with that of the clergyman.

I wished he would wake, if he were indeed asleep—move ever so slightly, look up, or speak one word, no matter what; but for all my wishing he sat there just the same—his eyes closed, and his placid face turned more to the wall than to me.

From the roost near by, and from across the neighboring hills, sounded the lusty crowing—it might be midnight or daybreak; I could not tell which, for the night had been to me unlike any other night. I arose softly, and taking the candle which burned dimly now, held it before the white face of the skeleton of a clock, to tell the hour, but the clock had been forgotten and was "run down."

I crossed the room on tiptoe and reseated myself without noise, but had scarcely done so when Mr. Wardwell, evidently aware of my movements and wishes, took from his vest an elegant watch and named the time, which was but half an hour after midnight. I sighed, for I felt as if the morning would never come.

"The time is heavy to you, my dear child," he replied, as if in answer to my sigh, and replacing the cushion, he offered me the easy-chair, blaming himself for having deprived me of it so selfishly and so long—and professing to be quite refreshed by the sleep which I suspected he had not taken.

I tried to decline, for in my heart I wished him to have the best chair, but when he took my hand with what I felt to be rather gallantry than paternal solicitude, I could no longer refuse, and in affectation of a quietude I did not feel, took up the hymn-book which lay at hand, and bent my eyes on the words I did not read.

"Will you read the poem that interests you?" asked Mr. Wardwell, coming near, and turning his bright, blessed face full upon me.

I trembled, for it seemed to me that my heart was open before my companion, and even if it were not I knew my cheek was playing the tell-tale, but in some way I stammered an answer to the most obvious sense of the words, and replied that it was the hymn-book I held.

"I know it," replied my pleasing tormentor; "but it is a *poem* you are reading for all that."

I said there were some hymns which were almost most ennobling and beautiful poetry, and I went on to instance a few which I regarded as such. He seemed not to hear my words, but said, rather as if musing aloud than speaking to me,—

"Yes, yes, my dear child,"—(he said *dear* child now, and not child as at first)—"at your time of life there are many sweet poems for the heart to read, which it does read without the aid of books."

He looked on me as he spoke with a sort of sorrowful compassion, I thought, and yet there was something tenderer and deeper than compassion, which I could not define.

He was greatly my senior, but it was not a filial thing that caused me to say, I was past the time when frivolous fancy most readily turns evanescent things to poetry, and I mentioned myself as twenty-six the May coming, and not twenty-five the May past, as most women would have done.

"To me that seems very young!" replied my companion, solemnly, "I am"—he hesitated, and went on hurriedly and confusedly I thought, "I am much older than you are."

He went away from me as he spoke, and passed his hand along his deeply-lined forehead and whitening hair, as if in contemplation of them.

I could not bear the solemn gladness that came like a soft shadow over the dewier glow that had lighted his face awhile past, and hastened to say, though I had never thought of it before, that the best experience and the truest poetry of life should come to us in the full ripeness of years. He shook his head doubtfully, smiled the old benignant smile, as he replied:

"It is quite natural, my dear child, that you should think so."

I had no courage to say more, especially as his thoughts seemed to return to their more habitual channels; but oh, how much I wished he could feel this life as richly worth living as I did.

He raised the sash, and leaned his head close to the wet vines, though he had reproved me for doing the same thing, and before I could find courage to remind him of it, or to say anything, he was fast asleep.

I recalled every word I had spoken, and conscious of an awakening interest that I had never before experienced for man or woman, I thought I had betrayed it, and the betrayal had produced the sleepy indifference, which, in spite of myself, mortified me to the quick. I read the hymn-book till I was weary of hymns; and afterwards thought till I was weary of thinking, then read again, and at last, to keep the place which I had no interest in keeping, I placed my handkerchief between the leaves of the book, and so turning my face as to see just that part of the wall which Mr. Wardwell had looked at an hour previously, I forgot him and myself and all things.

It was not the noise of the rain that woke me—nor the crowing of the morning cocks, nor the sun's yellow light that struggled through the room, nor yet the mother calling in her renewed anguish to the baby that smiled not for all her calling, nor lifted its little hands to the bosom that bent above it in such loving and terrible despair—it seemed to me it was none of these, but a torturous premonition of solitude and desolation.

Mr. Wardwell was gone, and the night was gone—but there was a pleasant voice in my ear, and a serene smile, kindling now and then in transient enthusiasm, whichever way I turned.

O night of solemn joy, O humble room, made sacred by the presence of death—O dream, whose sweet beginning promised so beautiful a close, how often have I gone back to you, and hewed out cisterns that I knew must break!

Surely in the mysterious providences that wrap themselves around us and which to our weak apprehensions seem so dark and so hard, there are true and good meanings, if we could but find them out.

Help us to be patient, oh, our Father, and give us the trusting hearts of little children, and the faith that mounts higher and brighter than the fire.

In the southern suburb of the village, and in sight of my own chamber window, is a low, gloomy stone church, which stood there before I was born, and which had scarcely changed any within my remembrance. All the long summer afternoons I used to sit at this window, looking up often from my sewing or my book, and always in one direction—that of the dark little church. I could see the oak trees that grew in different parts of the churchyard, and made deep shadows over the green mounds below, and it pleased me not a little to think Mr. Wardwell might be looking on them at the same moment with myself, for the parsonage, or "preacher's house," as it was called, stood in the same inclosure with the church building.

I could not see the parsonage itself, but I could see the smoke drifting from its chimneys, and know when a fire was being made, and could guess at the probable work that was going on indoors—whether dinner or tea, or whether it were the day for scrubbing or for baking, for I took the liveliest interest in such faint and far-away observations of Mr. Wardwell's household affairs, as I was able to make. Sometimes I would see a white fluttering among the trees, and know it had been washing day at the preacher's house, and then I would imagine the discomfort that had reigned in the kitchen all day, and the scouring of the ash floor, and the brightening of the hearth, that came afterward. I never made my seat under the grape-covered cherry tree, after the day that solemnized my destiny with the appellation of "old maid," and the evening that saw our first hand led away.

The night that followed had opened a new page in my life—a page where I saw my future reflected in colors brighter than my spring flowers, that were all dead now. I did not regret them. Often came Emeline and talked and laughed with Jenny as she spun on the porch, and I praised the pink and blue dresses she wore, and the roses that trimmed her hat, and said I was too old for pink dresses and roses, without a sigh on my lips, or a pang in my heart. I lived in a world of my own now; on Sunday eve we went to church together, and yet not to the same church—we sat in the same pew, but the face of the preacher turned not to the faces of my companions as it sometimes turned to mine, and for me there were meanings in his words which they could not see nor feel.

When he spoke of the great hereafter, when our souls that had crossed their mates, perhaps, and perhaps left them behind or gone unconsciously before them—dissatisfied and longing and faltering all the time, and of the deep of joy they would enter into, on recognizing fully and freely the other self, which, in this world, had been so poorly and vaguely comprehended, if at all—what delicious tremor, half fear and half fervor, thrilled all my being, and made me feel that the dust of time and the barriers of circumstance—the dreary pain of a life separated from all others—death itself—all were nothing but shadows passing between me and the eternal sunshine of love. I could afford to wait—I could afford to be patient under my burdens and to go straight forward through all hard fates and fortunes, assured that I should know and be known at last, love and be loved in the fullness of a blessedness, which, even here, mixed with bitterness as it is, is the sweetest of all. What was it to me that my hair was black, and my step firm, while his hair to whom I listened so reverentially was white, and his step slow, if not feeble. What was it that he had more wisdom, and more experience than I, and what was it that he never said, "you are faintly recognized, and I see a germ close-folded, which in the mysterious process of God's providence may unfold a great white flower." We had but crossed each other in the long journey, and I was satisfied, for I felt that in our traversing up the ages, we should meet again.

How sweet the singing of the evening and the morning service used to be. Our voices met and mingled then, and in the same breath and to the same tune we praised the Lord, for his mercy, which endureth forever.

One afternoon Emeline and Jenny teased me to join them on the porch—they pitied me, perhaps, shut up in the dim old chamber, as we often pity those who are most to be envied, and finding they would not leave me to my own thoughts, I allowed myself to be drawn from my favorite position.

Emeline was cutting some handkerchiefs from a piece of linen, and she asked me for one of mine as a measure. I opened a drawer where my nicest things were, sprinkled over with dried rose-leaves, and took up a white apron with a ruffled border, which I had worn the most memorable night of my life, and folded away just as I wore it—I took it up, thinking of the night, drew a handkerchief from the pocket and laid it across the lap of Emeline.

What laughter and clapping of hands and accusations of blushes followed, and true enough, the blushes made red confusion in my face when Emeline held up, not my own coarse, plain handkerchief, but a fine one with a deep purple border, and marked with the initial letters of Mr. Wardwell's name.

In vain I denied all knowledge of how I came by it; they were merrily incredulous, and asserted that if I knew nothing of the handkerchief I of course cared nothing for it—they would keep it and return it to the owner, who had no doubt dropped it by accident—just as I had taken it up.

I said it must be so, and spoke of the watch we had kept together, which gave the utmost probability to their suggestion, and which involved me in a serious dilemma. In the early twilight, they said we would walk together to the preacher's house—return him the lost handkerchief, and in return for our good office receive some of the red pears that grew at his door.

I could not bear that Mr. Wardwell should be mentioned in the same sentence with red pears—just as I would have mentioned any other person, and yet for the world I would not have had them see him as I saw him. I could not bear the thought of parting with my treasure which I had unconsciously possessed so long; I would speedily have folded it just as I found it and as he had folded it, and replacing it in the pocket of my apron, have kept it forever shut in the drawer among the rose-leaves.

But how to evade the plan of my young friends without betraying my own secret I could not discover. Having forced myself to comply, for they insisted that they would so without me if not with me, I tried to reconcile myself by the light of judgment and the cold probabilities of the case. Between dreaming and waking I must have taken up the handkerchief instead of my own. But convinced against my will, I was of the same opinion still. I remembered very distinctly placing the handkerchief on the table before me, and of seeing it there when I placed my own between the leaves of my hymn-book—and I remembered too, right well, that Mr. Wardwell was gone when I awoke—how then could the accident have occurred? And yet, if not by accident, how came I by the handkerchief? I could not tell, but one thing I was forced to do, to give it back. If it must be done, it should not be the hand of Emeline or of Jenny that did it, but my own. When it was time to go I folded my treasure neatly, and hid it under my shawl and next my heart. It was autumn now and there were no flowers but the few deep red ones that were left on the rose of Sharon that grew by my window. I gathered a green spray that held two bright ones, and hiding my heart as carefully as I did my treasure, I seemed to listen to what my young friends said as we went along.

A little way from the door, in a rustic seat, beneath the boughs of an apple-tree Mr. Wardwell sat reading—as he looked up, the expression of a young and happy heart passed across his face, and gave way to a more sober and paternal one. He laid the book he had been reading in the rustic chair and came forward to meet and welcome us. He called me dear child again and laid his hand upon my head with a solemn and tender pressure, that seemed to me at once a promise and a benediction.

I said why we were come, and in my confusion offered the handkerchief with the hand that held the flowers. He smiled sadly as we sometimes do when we are misunderstood, and pointing my friends to the pears that were lying red on the ground, he took the handkerchief, the flowers and the hand that held them in both his own, and for a moment pressed them close to his bosom. When my hand was restored to me the handkerchief was in it, but not the flowers.

"I want the roses," he said, "and will buy them with the handkerchief, for we must pay for our pleasures whether we will or no."

I knew not how to understand him, and was yet holding my treasure timidly forth, when, seeing my friends approach, he put my hand softly back, and I hastened to conceal it as before—next my heart. The youthful expression, that dewy-rose-look of summer and sunshine, came out in his face again—my heart had spoken to his heart, and we felt that we were assuredly bound to the same haven.

The aprons of my young friends were full of red pears, and their faces beaming with pleasure, and I, whom they compassionated as an old maid, hid my sacred joy deep in my bosom, and turned aside that their frivolous and frolicsome mirth might not mar it. Involuntarily I turned towards the rustic chair, and with an interest which I felt in everything belonging to Mr. Wardwell, opened the book he had left there. It was the well-remembered hymn-book, and my handkerchief was keeping the place of the hymn I had read so often on the most memorable of the nights of my life. How happy I was, and what dreams I dreamed after that. The blessed handkerchief is shut up with rose-leaves in my drawer, but the giver I never spoke with but once again.

It was years after I had learned that my treasure was not an accident, and when Jenny and Emeline were each the happy mother of more than one pretty baby—still liking me a little, and pitying me a great deal because I was an old maid, when one snowy night, the old woman, who kept house at the parsonage, came for me. I must make haste, she said, for good Mr. Wardwell had been that day seized with a fit, and seemed to be slowly dying. It was true, as she said, he seemed but to wait for me. The Bible and hymn-book were by his bedside; the plain linen handkerchief was between the leaves of the latter, and placing his hand on it, he whispered—

"Put this over my face when I am dead and the flowers"—

He could not say more, but I understood him and softly placing my hand on the heart where the life-tide was ebbing, I bent my face down close and kissed the cheek that was already moistening with death-dew. All the face brightened with that sweet, sweet expression that was manhood and angelhood at once—then came the terrible shadow, and the eyes that had known me, knew me no more—the lips gave up their color, but the habitual smile fixed itself in more than mortal beauty. As I unfolded the handkerchief two roses fell from it, which we buried with him.

His grave is at the south of the old church, and a rose-tree, grown from the slip of the one at my window, blooms at his head. Nothing now would tempt me away from the hills I was born among—from the old grey church, and the grave near which I hope to be buried.

"Come see my treasure;" and Abbie Morrison (for that was the story-teller's name) unlocked the drawer, where, folded among rose leaves, almost scentless now, was the handkerchief with dark border, and marked with the initials, C.D.W.

To her neighbors Abbie Morrison is only an old maid in whose praise there is not much to be said. If any one is sick she is sent for, but in seasons of joy nobody has a thought of her. What does she know of pleasure? they say, or what does she care for anything but singing in the church and cutting the weeds from the graveyard?

The children love her sweet voice, and stop on the way to school if she chances to sing in the garden, and, as she gives them flowers, wonder why their sisters call her old and ugly. It may be that angels wonder too.

The story of Abbie told in 1st person. from the day she first realizes that she is considered an old maid til her old age. On that day, a baby dies and she and the bachelor preacher sit watch together and develop a bond — like love but never expressed. They exchange handkerchiefs and when he dies she kisses himm and buries him with her roses and handkerchief.
Lots of meditation on maturity and trans-cending lonliness.

THE GREAT DOCTOR

A Story in Two Parts

Part I

"*HELLO! HELLO!* which way now, Mrs. Walker? It'll rain afore you git there, if you've got fur to go. Hadn't you better stop an' come in till this thunder-shower passes over?"

"Well, no, I reckon not, Mr. Bowen. I'm in a good deal of a hurry. I've been sent for over to John's." And rubbing one finger up and down the horn of her saddle, for she was on horseback, Mrs. Walker added, "Johnny's sick, Mr. Bowen, an' purty bad, I'm afeard." Then she tucked up her skirts, and, gathering up the rein, that had dropped on the neck of her horse, she inquired in a more cheerful tone, "How's all the folks,—Miss Bowen, an' Jinney, an' all?"

By this time the thunder began to growl, and the wind to whirl clouds of dust along the road.

"You'd better hitch your critter under the wood-shed, an' come in a bit. My woman'll be glad to see you, an' Jinney too,—there she is now, at the winder. I'll warrant nobody goes along the big road without her seein' 'em." Mr. Bowen had left the broad kitchen-porch from which he had hallooed to the old woman and was now walking down the gravelled path, that, between its borders of four-o'clocks and other common flowers, led from the front door to the front gate. "We're all purty well, I'm obleeged to you," he said, as, reaching the gate, he leaned over it, and turned his cold gray eyes upon the neat legs of the horse, rather than the anxious face of the rider.

"I'm glad to hear you're well," Mrs. Walker said; "it a'most seems to me that, if I had Johnny the way he was last week, I wouldn't complain about anything. We think too much of our little hardships, Mr. Bowen,—a good deal too much!" And Mrs. Walker looked at the clouds, perhaps in the hope that their blackness would frighten the tears away from her eyes. John was her own boy,—forty years old, to be sure, but still a boy to her,—and he was very sick.

"Well, I don't know," Mr. Bowen said, opening the mouth of the horse and looking in it; "we all have our troubles, an' if it ain't one thing it's another. Now, if John wasn't sick, I s'pose you'd be frettin' about somethin' else; you mustn't think you're particularly sot apart in your afflictions, any how. This rain that's getherin' is goin' to spile a couple of acres of grass for me, don't you see?"

Mrs. Walker was hurt. Her neighbor had not given her the sympathy she expected; he had not said anything about John one way nor another; had not inquired whether there was anything he could do, nor what the doctor said, nor asked any of those questions that express a kindly solicitude.

"I am sorry about your hay," she answered, "but I must be going."

"Don't want to hurry you; but if you will go, the sooner the better. That thunder-cloud is certain to bust in a few minutes." And Mr. Bowen turned toward the house.

"Wait a minute, Mrs. Walker," called a young voice, full of kindness; "here's my umberell. It'll save your bonnet, any how; and it's a real purty one. But didn't I hear you say somebody was sick over to your son's house?"

"Yes, darlin'," answered the old woman as she took the umbrella; "it's Johnny himself; he's right bad, they say. I just got word about an hour ago, and left everything, and started off. They think he's got the smallpox."

Jenny Bowen, the young girl who had brought the umbrella, looked terribly frightened. "*They* won't let me go over, you know," she said, nodding her head toward the house, "not if it's really small-pox!" And then, with the hope at which the young are so quick to catch, she added, "May be it isn't small-pox. I haven't heard of a case anywhere about. I don't believe it is." And then she told Mrs. Walker not to fret about home. "I will go," she said, "and milk the cow, and look after things. Don't think one thought about it." And then she asked if the rest of them at John Walker's were well.

"If it's Hobert you want to know about," the grandmother said, smiling faintly, "he's well; but, darlin', you'd better not think about him; they'll be ag'in it, in there!" and she nodded toward the house as Jenny had done before her.

The face of the young girl flushed,—not with confusion, but with self-asserting and defiant brightness that seemed to say, "Let them do their worst." The thunder rattled sharper and nearer, bursting right upon the flash of the lightning, and then came the rain. But it proved not one of those bright, brief dashes that leave the world sparkling, but settled toward sunset into a slow, dull drizzle.

Jenny had her milking, and all the other evening chores, done betimes, and with an alertness and cheerfulness in excess of her usual manner, that might have indicated an unusual favor to be asked. She had made her evening toilet; that is, she had combed her hair, tied on a pair of calf-skin shoes, and a blue checked apron, newly washed and ironed; when she said, looking toward a faint light in the west, and as though the thought had just occurred to her, "It's going to break away, I see. Don't you think, mother, I had better just run over to Mrs. Walker's, and milk her cow for her?"

"Go to Miss Walker's!" repeated the mother, as though she were as much outraged as astonished. She was seated in the door, patching, by the waning light, an old pair of mud-spattered trousers, her own dress being very old-fashioned, coarse, and scanty,—so scant, in fact, as to reveal the angles of her form with ungraceful definiteness, especially the knees, that were almost suggestive of a skeleton, and now, as she put herself in position, as it were, stood up with inordinate prominence. Her hands were big in the joints, ragged in the nails, and marred all over with the cuts, burns, and scratches of indiscriminate and incessant toil. But her face was, perhaps, the most sadly divested of all womanly charm. It had, in the first place, the deep yellow, lifeless appearance of an old bruise, and was expressive of pain, irritation, and fanatical anxiety.

"Go to Miss Walker's!" she said again, seeing that Jenny was taking down from its peg in the kitchen-wall a woollen cloak that had been hers since she was a little girl, and her mother's before her.

"Yes, mother. You know John Walker is very sick, and Mrs. Walker has been sent for over there. She's very down-hearted about him. He's dangerous, they think; and I thought may be I'd come round that way as I come home, and ask how he was. Don't you think I'd better?"

"I think you had better stay at home and tend to your own business. You'll spile your clothes, and do no good that I can see by traipsin' out in such a storm."

"Why, you would think it was bad for one of our cows to go without milking," Jenny said, "and I suppose Mrs. Walker's cow is a good deal like ours, and she is giving a pailful of milk now."

"How do you know so much about Miss Walker's cow? If you paid more attention to things at home, and less to other folks, you'd be more dutiful."

"That's true, mother, but would I be any better?"

"Not in your own eyes, child; but you're so much wiser than your father and me, that words are throwed away on you."

"I promised Mrs. Walker that I would milk for her to-night," Jenny said, hesitating, and dropping her eyes.

"O yes, you've always got some excuse! What did you make a promise for, that you knowed your father wouldn't approve of? Take your things right off now, and peel the potaters, and sift the meal for mush in the morning; an' if Miss Walker's cow must be milked, what's to hender that Hobe, the great lazy strapper, shouldn't go and milk her?"

"You forget how much he has to do at home now; and one pair of hands can't do everything, even if they are Hobert Walker's!"

Jenny had spoken with much spirit and some bitterness; and the bright defiant flush, before noticed, came into her face, as she untied the cloak and proceeded to sift the meal and peel the potatoes for breakfast. She did her work quietly, but with a determination in every movement that indicated a will not easily overruled.

It was nearly dark, and the rain still persistently falling, when she turned the potato-peelings into the pig-trough that stood only a few yards from the door, and, returning, put the cloak about her shoulders, tied it deliberately, turned the hood over her head, and, without another word, walked straight out into the rain.

"Well, I must say! Well, I *must* say!" cried the mother, in exasperated astonishment. "What on airth is that girl a-comin' to?" And, resting her elbows on her knees, she leaned her yellow face on her hands, and gathered out of her hard, embittered heart such consolation as she could.

Jenny, meantime, tucked up her petticoats, and, having left a field or two between her and the homestead, tripped lightly along, debating with herself whether or not she should carry out her will to the full, and return by the way of Mr. John Walker's,—a question she need hardly have raised, if unexpected events had not interfered with her predeterminations. At Mrs. Walker's gate she stopped and pulled half a dozen roses from the bush that was almost lying on the ground with its burden,—they seemed, somehow, brighter than the roses at home,—and, with them swinging in her hand, had well nigh gained the door, before she perceived that it was standing open. She hesitated an instant,—perhaps some crazy wanderer or drunken person might have entered the house,—when brisk steps, coming up the path that led from the milking-yard, arrested her attention, and, looking that way, she recognized through the darkness young Hobert Walker, with the full pail in his hand.

"O Jenny," he said, setting down the pail, "we are in such trouble at home! The doctor says father is better, but I don't think so, and I ain't satisfied with what is being done for him. Besides, I had such a strange dream,—I thought I met you, Jenny, alone, in the night, and you had six red roses in your hand,—let me see how many have you." He had come close to her, and he now took the roses and counted them. There were six, sure enough. "Humph!" he said, and went on. "Six red roses, I thought; and while I looked at them they turned white as snow; and then it seemed to me it was a shroud you had in your hand, and not roses at all; and you, seeing how I was frightened, said to me, 'What if it should turn out to be my wedding-dress?' And while we talked, your father came between us, and led you away by a great chain that he put round your neck. But you think all this foolish, I see." And, as if he feared the apprehension he had confessed involved some surrender of manhood, he cast down his eyes, and awaited her reply in confusion. She had too much tact to have noticed this at any time; but in view of the serious circumstances in which he then stood, she could not for the life of her have turned any feeling of his into a jest, however unwarranted she might have felt it to be.

"My grandmother was a great believer in dreams," she said, sympathetically; "but she always thought they went by contraries; and, if she was right, why, yours bodes ever so much good. But come, Hobert, let us go into the house: it's raining harder."

"How stupid of me, Jenny, not to remember that you were being drowned, almost! You must try to excuse me: I am really hardly myself to-night."

"Excuse you, Hobert! As if you could ever do anything I should not think was just right!" And she laughed the little musical laugh that had been ringing in his ears so long, and skipped before him into the house.

He followed her with better heart; and, as she strained and put away the milk, and swept the hearth, and set the house in order, he pleased himself with fancies of a home of which she would be always the charming mistress.

And who, that saw the sweet domestic cheer she diffused through the house with her harmless little gossip about this and that, and the artfully artless kindnesses to him she mingled with all, could have blamed him? He was given to melancholy and to musing; his cheek was sometimes pale, and his step languid; and he saw, all too often, troublesome phantoms coming to meet him. This disposition in another would have incited the keenest ridicule in the mind of Jenny Bowen, but in Hobert it was well enough; nay, more, it was actually fascinating, and she would not have had him otherwise. These characteristics—for her sake we will not say weaknesses—constantly suggested to her how much she could be to him,—she who was so strong in all ways,—in health, in hope, and in enthusiasm. And for him it was joy enough to look upon her full bright cheek, to see her compact little figure before him; but to touch her dimpled shoulder, to feel one tress of her hair against his face, was ecstasy; and her voice,—the tenderest trill of the wood-dove was not half so delicious! But who shall define the mystery of love? They were lovers; and when we have said that, is there anything more to be said? Their love had not, however, up to the time of which we write, found utterance in words. Hobert was the son of a poor man, and Jenny was prospectively rich, and the faces of her parents were set as flints against the poor young man. But Jenny had said in her heart more than once that she would marry him; and if the old folks had known this, they might as well have held their peace. Hobert did not dream that she had talked thus to her heart, and, with his constitutional timidity, he feared she would never say anything of the kind. Then, too, his conscientiousness stood in his way. Should he presume to take her to his poor house, even if she would come? No, no, he must not think of it; he must work and wait, and defer hope. This hour so opportune was also most inopportune,—such sorrow at home! He would not speak to-night,—O no, not to-night! And yet he could bear up against everything else, if she only cared for him! Such were his resolves, as she passed to and fro before him, trifling away the time with pretence of adjusting this thing and that; but at last expedients failed, and reaching for her cloak, which hung almost above him as he sat against the wall, she said it was time to go. As frostwork disappears in the sunshine, so his brave resolutions vanished when her arm reached across his shoulder, and the ribbon that tied her beads fluttered against his cheek. With a motion quite involuntary, he snatched her hand, "No, Jenny, not yet,—not quite yet!" he said.

"And why not?" demanded Jenny; for could any woman, however innocent, or rustic, be without her little coquetries? And she added, in a tone that contradicted her words, "I am sure I should not have come if I had known you were coming!"

"I dare say not," replied Hobert, in a voice so sad and so tender withal, as to set the roses Jenny wore in her bosom trembling. "I dare say not, indeed. I would not presume to hope you would go a step out of your way to give me pleasure; only I was feeling so lonesome to-night, I thought may be—no, I didn't think anything; I certainly didn't hope anything. Well, no matter, I am ready to go." And he let go the hand he had been holding, and stood up.

It was Jenny's privilege to pout a little now, and to walk sullenly and silently home,—so torturing herself and her honest-hearted lover; but she was much too generous, much too noble, to do this. She would not for the world have grieved poor Hobert,—not then,—not when his heart was so sick and so weighed down with shadows; and she told him this with a simple earnestness that admitted of no doubt, concluding with, "I only wish, Hobert, I could say or do something to comfort you."

"Then you will stay? Just a moment, Jenny!" And the hand was in his again.

"Dear Jenny,—dear, dear Jenny!" She was sitting on his knee now; and the rain, with its pattering against the window, drowned their heart-beats; and the summer darkness threw over them its sacred veil.

"Shall I tell you, darling, of another dream I have had to-night—since I have been sitting here?" The fair cheek bent itself close to his to listen, and he went on. "I have been dreaming, Jenny, a very sweet dream; and this is what it was. You and I were living here, in this house, with grandmother; and she was your grandmother as well as mine; and I was farmer of the land, and you were mistress of the dairy; and the little room with windows toward the sunrise, and the pretty bureau, and bed with snow-white coverlet and pillows of down,—that was"—perhaps he meant to say "*ours,*" but his courage failed him, and, with a charming awkwardness, he said, "yours, Jenny," and hurried on to speak of the door-yard flowers, and the garden with its beds of thyme and mint, its berry-bushes and hop-vines and beehives,—all of which were brighter and sweeter than were ever hives and bushes in any other garden; and when he had run through the catalogue of rustic delights, he said: "And now, Jenny, I want you to tell me the meaning of my dream; and yet I am afraid you will interpret it as your grandmother used to hers."

Jenny laughed gayly. "That is just what I will do, dear Hobert," she said; "for she used to say that only bad dreams went by contraries, and yours was the prettiest dream I ever heard."

The reply to this sweet interpretation was after the manner of all lovers since the world began. And so, forgetting the stern old folks at home,—forgetting everything but each other,—they sat for an hour at the very gate of heaven. How often Hobert called her his sweetheart, and his rosebud, and other fond names, we need not stop to enumerate; how often he said that for her sake he could brave the winter storm and the summer heat, that she should never know rough work nor sad days, but that she should be as tenderly protected, as daintily cared for, as any lady of them all,—how often he said all these things, we need not enumerate; nor need we say with what unquestioning trust, and deafness to all the suggestions of probability, Jenny believed. Does not love, in fact, always believe what it hopes? Who would do away with the blessed insanity that clothes the marriage day with such enchantment? Who would dare to do it?

No royal mantle could have been adjusted with tenderer and more reverent solicitude than was that night the coarse cloak about the shoulders of Jenny. The walk homeward was all too short; and whether the rain fell, or whether the moon were at her best, perhaps neither of them could have told until they were come within earshot of the Bowen homestead; then both suddenly stood still. Was it the arm of Jenny that trembled so? No, no! we must own the truth,—it was the arm through which hers was drawn. At her chamber window, peering out curiously and anxiously, was the yellow-white face of Mrs. Bowen; and, leaning over the gate, gazing up and down the road, the rain falling on his bent shoulders and gray head, was the father of Jenny,—angry and impatient, past doubt.

"Don't stand looking any longer, for mercy's sake!" called the querulous voice from the house. "You'll get your death of cold, and then what'll become of us all? Saddle your horse this minute, and ride over to John Walker's,—for there's where you'll find Jinny, the gad-about,—and bring her home at the tail of your critter. I'll see who is going to be mistress here!"

"She's had her own head too long already, I'm afeard," replied the old man, turning from the gate, with intent, probably, to execute his wife's order.

Seeing this, and hearing this, Hobert, as we said, stood still and trembled, and could only ask, by a little pressure of the hand he held, what was to be said or done.

Jenny did not hesitate a moment. "I expected this or something worse," she said. "Don't mind, Hobert; so they don't see you, I don't care for the rest. You must not go one step farther; the lightning will betray us, you see. I will say I waited for the rain to slack, and the two storms will clear off about the same time, I dare say. There, good night!"—and she turned her cheek to him; for she was not one of those impossible maidens we read of in books, who don't know they are in love, until after the consent of parents is obtained, and blush themselves to ashes at the thought of a kiss. To love Hobert was to her the most natural and proper thing in the world, and she did not dream there was anything to blush for. It is probable, too, that his constitutional bashfulness and distrust of himself brought out her greater confidence and buoyancy.

"And how and where am I ever to see you again?" he asked, as he detained her, against her better judgment, if not against her will.

"Trust that to me,"—and she hurried away in time to meet and prevent her father from riding forth in search of her.

Of course there were fault-finding and quarrelling, accusations and protestations, hard demands and sullen pouting,—so that the home, at no time so attractive as we like to imagine the home of a young girl who has father and mother to provide for her and protect her, became to her like a prison house. At the close of the first and second days after her meeting with Hobert, when the work was all faithfully done, she ventured to ask leave to go over to John Walker's and inquire how the sick man was; but so cold a refusal met her, that, on the evening of the third day she sat down on the porch-side to while away the hour between working and sleeping, without having renewed her request.

The sun was down, and the first star began to show faintly above a strip of gray-cloud in the west, when a voice, low and tender, called to her, "Come here, my child!" and looking up she saw Grandmother Walker sitting on her horse at the gate. She had in the saddle before her her youngest granddaughter, and on the bare back of the horse, behind her, a little grandson, both their young faces expressive of the sorrow at home. Jenny arose on the instant, betraying in every motion the interest and sympathy she felt, and was just stepping lightly from the porch to the ground, when a strong hand grasped her shoulder and turned her back. It was her father who had overtaken her. "Go into the house!" he said. "If the old woman has got any arrant at all, it's likely it's to your mother and me."

Nor was his heart melted in the least when he learned that his friend and neighbor was no more. He evinced surprise, and made some blunt and coarse inquiries, but that was the amount. "The widder is left purty destitute, I reckon," he said; and then he added, the Lord helped them that helped themselves, and we mustn't fly in the face of Providence. She had her son, strong and able-bodied; and of course he had no thoughts of encumbering himself with a family of his own,—young and poverty-struck as he was.

Mrs. Walker understood the insinuation; but her heart could not hold resentment just then. She must relieve her burdened soul by talking of "poor Johnny," even though it were to deaf ears. She must tell what a good boy he had been,—how kind to her and considerate of her, how manly, how generous, how self-forgetful. And then she must tell how hard he had worked, and how saving he had been in order to give his children a better chance in the world than he had had; and how, if he had lived another year, he would have paid off the mortgage, and been able to hold up his head amongst men.

After all the ploughing and sowing,—after all the preparation for the gathering in of the harvest,—it seemed very hard, she said, that Johnny must be called away, just as the shining ears began to appear. The circumstances of his death, too, seemed to her peculiarly afflictive. "We had all the doctors in the neighborhood," she said, "but none of them understood his case. At first they thought he had small-pox, and doctored him for that; and then they thought it was liver-complaint, and doctored him for that; and then it was bilious fever, and then it was typhus fever; and so it went on, and I really can't believe any of them understood anything about it. Their way seemed to be to do just what he didn't want done. In the first place, he was bled; and then he was blistered; and then he was bled again and blistered again, the fever all the time getting higher and higher; and when he wanted water, they said it would kill him, and gave him hot drinks till it seemed to me they would drive him mad; and sure enough, they did! The last word he ever said, to know what he was saying, was to ask me for a cup of cold water. I only wish I had given it to him; all the doctors in the world wouldn't prevent me now, if I only had him back. The fever seemed to be just devouring him; his tongue was as dry as sand, and his head as hot as fire. 'O mother!' says he, and there was such a look of beseeching in his eyes as I can never forget, 'may be I shall never want you to do anything more for me. Cold water! give me some cold water! If I don't have it, my senses will surely fly out of my head!' 'Yes, Johnny,' says I,—and I went and brought a tin bucketful, right out of the well, and set it on the table in his sight; for I thought it would do him good to see even more than he could drink; and then I brought a cup and dipped it up full. It was all dripping over, and he had raised himself on one elbow, and was leaning toward me, when the young doctor came in, and, stepping between us, took the cup out of my hand. All his strength seemed to go from poor Johnny at that, and he fell back on his pillow and never lifted his head any more. Still he kept begging in a feeble voice for the water. 'Just two or three drops,—just one drop!' he said. I couldn't bear it, and the doctor said I had better go out of the room, and so I did,—and the good Lord forgive me; for when I went back, after half an hour, he was clean crazy. He didn't know me, and he never knowed me any more."

"It's purty hard, Miss Walker," answered Mr. Bowen, "to accuse the doctors with the murder of your son. A purty hard charge, that, I call it! So John's dead! Well, I hope he is better off. Where are you goin' to bury him?"

And then Mrs. Walker said she didn't charge anybody with the murder of poor Johnny,—nobody meant to do him any harm, she knew that; but, after all, she wished she could only have had her own way with him from the first. And so she rode away,—her little bare-legged grandson, behind her, aggravating her distress by telling her that, when he got to be a man, he meant to do nothing all the days of his life but dig wells, and give water to whoever wanted it.

It is not worth while to dwell at length on the humiliations and privations to which Jenny was subjected,—the mention of one or two will indicate the nature of all. In the first place, the white heifer she had always called hers was sold, and the money tied up in a tow bag. Jenny would not want a cow for years to come. The piece of land that had always been known as "Jenny's Corner" was not thus denominated any more, and she was given to understand that it was only to be hers *conditionally*. There were obstacles put in the way of her going to meeting of a Sunday,—first one thing, then another; and, finally, the bureau was locked, and the best dress and brightest ribbon inside the drawers. The new side-saddle she had been promised was refused to her, unless she in turn would make a promise; and the long day's work was made to drag on into the night, lest she might find time to visit some neighbor, and lest that neighbor might be the Widow Walker. But what device of the enemy ever proved successful when matched against the simple sincerity of true love? It came about, in spite of all restraint and prohibition, that Jenny and Hobert met in their own times and ways; and so a year went by.

One night, late in the summer, when the katydids began to sing,

Jenny waited longer than usual under the vine-covered beech that dropped its boughs low to the ground all round her,—now listening for the expected footstep, and now singing, very low, some little song to her heart, such as many a loving and trusting maiden had sung before her. What could keep Hobert? She knew it was not his will that kept him; and though her heart began to be heavy, she harbored therein no thought of reproach. By the movement of the shadow on the grass, she guessed that an hour beyond the one of appointment must have passed, when the far-away footfall set her so lately hushed pulses fluttering with delight. He was coming,—he was coming! And, no matter what had been wrong, all would be right now. She was holding wide the curtaining boughs long before he came near; and when they dropped, and her arms closed, it is not improbable that he was within them. It was the delight of meeting her that kept him still so long, Jenny thought; and she prattled lightly and gayly of this and of that, and, seeing that she won no answer, fell to tenderer tones, and imparted the little vexing secrets of her daily life, and the sweet hopes of her nightly dreams.

They were seated on a grassy knoll, the moonlight creeping tenderly about their feet, and the leaves of the drooping vines touching their heads like hands of pity, or of blessing. The water running over the pebbly bottom of the brook just made the silence sweet, and the evening dews shining on the red globes of the clover made the darkness lovely; but with all these enchantments of sight and sound about him,—nay, more, with the hand of Jenny, his own true-love, Jenny, folded in his,—Hobert was not happy.

"And so you think you love me!" he said at last, speaking so sadly, and clasping the hand he held with so faint a pressure, that Jenny would have been offended if she had not been the dear, trustful little creature she was.

There was, indeed, a slight reproach in her accent as she answered, "*Think* I love you, Hobert? No, I don't think anything about it,—I *know.*"

"And I know I love you, Jenny," he replied. "I love you so well that I am going to leave you without asking you to marry me!"

For one moment Jenny was silent,—for one moment the world seemed unsteady beneath her,—then she stood up, and, taking the hand of her lover between her palms, gazed into his face with one long, earnest, steadfast gaze. "You have asked me already, Hobert," she said, "a thousand times, and I have consented as often. You may go away, but you will not leave me; for 'Whither thou goest I will go, where thou diest will I die, and there will I be buried.'"

He drew her close to his bosom now, and kissed her with most passionate, but still saddest tenderness. "You know not, my darling," he said, "what you would sacrifice." Then he laid before her all her present advantages, all her bright prospects for the future,—her high chamber with its broad eastern windows, to be given up for the low dingy walls of a settler's cabin, her free girlhood for the hard struggles of a settler's wife! Sickness, perhaps,—certainly the lonesome nights and days of a home remote from neighbors, and the dreariness and hardship inseparable from the working out of better fortunes. But all these things, even though they should all come, were light in comparison with losing him!

Perhaps Hobert had desired and expected to hear her say this. At any rate, he did not insist on a reversal of her decision, as, with his arms about her, he proceeded to explain why he had come to her that night with so heavy a heart. The substance of all he related may be recapitulated in a few words. The land could not be paid for, and the homestead must be sold. He would not be selfish and forsake his mother, and his younger brothers and sisters in their time of need. By careful management of the little that could be saved, he might buy in the West a better farm than that which was now to be given up; and there to build a cabin and plant a garden would be easy,—O, so easy!—with the smile of Jenny to light him home when the day's work was done.

In fact, the prospective hardships vanished away at the thought of her for his little housekeeper. It was such easy work for fancy to convert the work-days into holidays, and the thick wilderness into the shining village, where the schoolhouse stood open all the week, and the sweet bells called them to church of a Sunday; easy work for that deceitful elf to make the chimney-corner snug and warm, and to embellish it with his mother in her easy-chair. When they parted that night, each young heart was trembling with the sweetest secret it had ever held; and it was perhaps a fortnight thereafter that the same secret took wing, and flew wildly over the neighborhood.

John Walker's little farm was gone for good and all. The few sheep, and the cows, and the pig, and the fowls, together with the greater part of the household furniture, were scattered over the neighborhood; the smoke was gone from the chimney, and the windows were curtainless; and the grave of John, with a modest but decent headstone, and a rose-bush newly planted beside it, was left to the care of strangers. The last visits had been paid, and the last good-byes and good wishes exchanged; and the widow and her younger children were far on their journey,—Hobert remaining for a day or two to dispose of his smart young horse, as it was understood, and then follow on.

At this juncture, Mr. Bowen one morning opened the stair-door, as was his custom, soon after daybreak, and called harshly out, "Jinny! Jinny! its high time you was up!"

Five minutes having elapsed, and the young girl not having yet appeared, the call was repeated more harshly than before. "Come, Jinny, come! or I'll know what's the reason!"

She did not come; and five minutes more having passed, he mounted the stairs with a quick, resolute step, to know what was the reason. He came down faster, if possible, then he went up. "Mother, mother!" he cried, rushing toward Mrs. Bowen, who stood at the table sifting meal, his gray hair streaming wildly back, and his cheek blanched with amazement, "Jinny's run away!—run away, as sure as you're a livin' woman. Her piller hasn't been touched last night, and her chamber's deserted!"

And this was the secret that took wing and flew over the neighborhood.

Part II

FIVE OR SIX years of the life of our hero we must now pass over in silence, saying of them, simply, that Fancy had not cheated much in her promises concerning them. The first rude cabin had given place to a white-washed cottage; the chimney-corner was bright and warm; the easy-chair was in it, and the Widow Walker often sat there with her grandson on her knee, getting much comfort from the reflection that he looked just as her own Johnny did when he was a baby!

The garden smiled at the doorside, and the village had sprung up just as Fancy promised; and Hobert and Jenny walked to church of a Sunday, and after service shook hands with their neighbors,—for everybody delighted to take their strong, willing hands, and look into their honest, cheerful faces,—they were amongst the first settlers of the place, and held an honored position in society. Jenny was grown a little more stout, and her cheek a little more ruddy, than it used to be; but the new country seemed not so well suited to Hobert, and the well-wishing neighbor often said when he met him, "You mustn't be too ambitious, and overdo! Your shoulders ain't so straight as they was when you come here! Be careful in time; nothing like that, Walker, nothing like that." And Hobert laughed at these suggestions, saying he was as strong as the rest of them; and that, though his cheek was pale, and his chest hollow, he was a better man than he seemed.

The summer had been one of the wildest luxuriance ever known in the valley of the Wabash; for it was in that beautiful valley that our friend Hobert had settled. The woods cast their leaves early, and the drifts lay rotting knee-deep in places. Then came the long, hot, soaking rains, with hotter sunshine between. Chills and fever prevailed, and half the people of the neighborhood were shivering and burning at once. It was a healthy region, everybody said, but the weather had been unusually trying; as soon as the frost came, the ague would vanish; the water was the best in the world, to be sure, and the air the purest.

Hobert was ploughing a piece of low ground for wheat, cutting a black snake in two now and then, and his furrow behind him fast filling with water that looked almost as black as the soil. Often he stopped to frighten from the quivering flank of the brown mare before him the voracious horse-flies, colored like the scum of the stagnant pools, and clinging and sucking like leeches. She was his favorite, the pride of his farm,—for had she not, years before, brought Jenny on her faithful shoulder to the new, happy home? Many a fond caress her neck had had from his arm; and the fine bridle with the silver bit, hanging on the wall at home, would not have been afforded for any other creature in the world. Hobert often said he would never sell her as long as he lived; and in the seasons of hard work he favored her more than he did himself. She had been named Fleetfoot, in honor of her successful achievement when her master had intrusted to her carrying the treasure of his life; but that name proving too formal, she was usually called Fleety. She would put down her forehead to the white hands of little Jenny, four years old and upward now, and tread so slow and so carefully when she had her on her back! Even the white dress of Johnny Hobert had swept down her silken side more than once, while his dimpled hands clutched her mane, and his rosy feet paddled against her. He was going to be her master after a while, and take care of her in her old age, when the time of her rest was come; he knew her name as well as he knew his own, and went wild with delight when he saw her taking clover from the tiny hand of his sister or drinking water from the bucket at the well.

"She grows handsomer every year," Hobert often said; "and with a little training I would not be afraid to match her against the speediest racer they can bring." And this remark was always intended as in some sort a compliment to Jenny, and was always so received by her.

On this special day he had stopped oftener in the furrow than common; and as often as he stopped Fleety twisted round her neck, bent her soft eyes upon him, and twitched her little ears as though she would say, "Is not all right, my master?" And then he would walk round to her head, and pass his hand along her throat and through her foretop, calling her by her pet name, and pulling for her handfuls of fresh grass, and while she ate it resting himself against her, and feeling in her nearness almost a sense of human protection. His feet seemed to drag under him, and there was a dull aching in all his limbs; the world appeared to be receding from him, and at times he could hardly tell whether he stood upon solid ground. Then he accused himself of being lazy and good for nothing, and with fictitious energy took up the reins and started the plough.

He looked at the sun again and again. He was not used to leaving off work while the sun shone, and the clear waters of the Wabash held as yet no faintest evening flush. There were yet two good hours of working time before him, when the quick shooting of a pain, like the running of a knife through his heart, caused him to stagger in the furrow. Fleety stopped of her own accord, and looked pityingly back. He sat down beside the plough to gather up his courage a little. A strange sensation that he could not explain had taken possession of him, a feeling as if the hope of his life was cut off. The pain was gone, but the feeling of helpless surrender remained. He opened his shirt and passed his hand along his breast. He could feel nothing,—could see nothing; but he had, for all that, a clearly defined consciousness as of some deadly thing hold of him that he would fain be rid of.

He had chanced to stop his plough under an elm-tree, and, looking up, he perceived that from the fork upward one half of it was dead; mistletoe had sucked the life out of it, and lower and lower to the main body, deeper and deeper to the vital heart of it, the sap was being drawn away. An irresistible impulse impelled him to take the jack-knife from his pocket, and as far as he could reach cut away this alien and deadly growth. The sympathy into which he was come with the dying tree was positively painful to him, and yet he was withheld from moving on by a sort of fascination,—*he* was that tree, and the mistletoe was rooted in his bosom!

The last yellow leaves fluttered down and lodged on his head and shoulders and in his bosom,—he did not lift his hand to brush them away; the blue lizard slid across his bare ankle and silently vanished out of sight, but he did not move a muscle. The brown mare bent her side round like a bow, and stretched her slender neck out more and more, and at last her nose touched his cheek, and then he roused himself and shook the dead leaves from his head and shoulders, and stood up. "Come, Fleety," he said, "we won't leave the plough in the middle of the furrow." She did not move. "Come, come!" he repeated, "it seems like a bad sign to stop here";—and then he put his hand suddenly to his heart, and an involuntary shudder passed over him. Fleety had not unbent her side, and her dumb, beseeching eyes were still upon him. He looked at the sun, low, but still shining out bright, and almost as hot as ever; he looked at his shadow stretching so far over the rough, weedy ground, and it appeared to him strange and fantastic. Then he loosed the traces, and, winding up the long rein, hung it over the harness; the plough dropped aslant, and Fleety turned herself about and walked slowly homeward,—her master following, his head down and his hands locked together behind him.

The chimney was sending up its hospitable smoke, and Jenny was at the well with the teakettle in her hand when he came into the dooryard.

"What in the world is going to happen?" she exclaimed, cheerfully. "I never knew you to leave work before while the sun shone. I am glad you have, for once. But what is the matter?"

He had come nearer now, and she saw that something of light and hope had gone out of his face. And then Hobert made twenty excuses,—

there wasn't anything the matter, he said, but the plough was dull, and the ground wet and heavy, and full of green roots; besides, the flies were bad, and the mare tired.

"But you look so worn out, I am afraid you are sick, yourself!" interposed the good wife; and she went close to him, and pushed the hair, growing thinner now, away from his forehead, and looked anxiously in his face,—so anxiously, so tenderly, that he felt constrained to relieve her fears, even at some expense of the truth.

"Not to look well in your eyes is bad enough," he answered, with forced cheerfulness, "but I feel all right; never better, never better, Jenny!" And stooping to his little daughter, who was holding his knees, he caught her up, and tossed her high in the air, but put her down at once, seeming almost to let her fall out of his hands, and, catching for breath, leaned against the well-curb.

"What is it, Hobert? what is it?" and Jenny had her arm about him, and was drawing him toward the house.

"Nothing, nothing,—a touch of rheumatism, I guess,—no, no! I must take care of the mare first." And as she drank the water from the full bucket he held poised on the curb for her, he thought of the elm-tree in the field he had left, of the mistletoe sucking the life out of it, and of the unfinished furrow. "Never mind, Fleety," he said, as he led her away to the stable, "we'll be up betimes to-morrow, and make amends, won't we?"

"I believe, mother, I'll put on the new teacups!" Jenny said, as she set a chair before the cupboard, and climbed on it so as to reach the upper shelf. She had already spread the best table-cloth.

"Why, what for?" asked the provident mother, looking up from the sock she was knitting.

"O, I don't know; I want to make things look nice, that's all."

But she did know, though the feeling was only half defined. It seemed to her as if Hobert were some visitor coming,—not her husband. A shadowy feeling of insecurity had touched her; the commonness of custom was gone, and she looked from the window often, as the preparation for supper went on, with all the sweetness of solicitude with which she used to watch for his coming from under the grape-vines. Little Jenny was ready with the towel when he came with his face dripping, and the easy-chair was set by the door that looked out on the garden. "I don't want it," the good grandmother said, as he hesitated; "I have been sitting in it all day, and am tired of it!"

And as he sat there with his boy on his knee, and his little girl, who had climbed up behind him, combing his hair with her slender white fingers,—his own fields before him, and his busy wife making music about the house with her cheerful, hopeful talk,—he looked like a man to be envied; and so just then he was.

The next morning he did not fulfil his promise to himself by rising early; he had been restless and feverish all night, and now was chilly. If he lay till breakfast was ready, he would feel better, Jenny said; she could milk, to be sure, and do all the rest of the work, and so he was persuaded. But when the breakfast was ready the chilliness had become a downright chill, so that the blankets that were over him shook like leaves in a strong wind.

Jenny had a little money of her own hidden away in the bottom of the new cream-pitcher. She had saved it, unknown to Hobert, from the sale of eggs and other trifles, and had meant to surprise him by appearing in a new dress some morning when the church-bell rang; but now she turned the silver into her hand and counted it, thinking what nice warm flannel it would buy to make shirts for Hobert. Of course he had them, and Jenny had not made any sacrifice that she knew of,—indeed, that is a word of which love knows not the meaning.

"We will have him up in a day or two," the women said, one to the other, as they busied themselves about the house, or sat at the bedside, doing those things that only the blessed hands of women can do, making those plans that only the loving hearts of women can make. But the day or two went by, and they didn't have Hobert up. Then they said to one another, "We must set to work in earnest; we have really done nothing for him as yet." And they plied their skill of nursing with new hope and new energy. Every morning he told them he was better, but in the afternoon it happened that he didn't feel quite like stirring about; he was still better, but he had a little headache, and was afraid of bringing on a chill.

"To be sure! you need rest and quiet; you have been working too hard, and it's only a wonder you didn't give out sooner!" So the two women said to him; and then they told him he looked better than he did yesterday, and, with much tender little caressing of neck and arms and hands, assured him that his flesh felt as healthy and nice as could be.

Nevertheless, his eyes settled deeper and deeper, and gathered more and more of a leaden color about them; his skin grew yellow, and fell into wrinkles that were almost rigid, and that beseeching, yearning expression, made up of confidence in you, and terror of some nameless thing,—that look, as of a soul calling and crying to you, which follows you when you go farther than common from a sick-pillow,—all that terrible appealing was in his face; and often Jenny paused with her eyes away from him, when she saw that look,—paused, and steadied up her heart, before she could turn back and meet him with a smile.

And friendly neighbors came in of an evening, and told of the sick wife or boy at home; of the mildewed crop, and the lamed horse; of the brackish well, and of the clock bought from the pedler that wouldn't go, and wouldn't strike when it did go;—dwelling, in short, on all the darker incidents and accidents of life, and thus establishing a nearness and equality of relation to the sick man, that somehow soothed and cheered him. At these times he would be propped up in bed, and listen with sad satisfaction, sometimes himself entering with a sort of melancholy animation into the subject.

He would not as yet accept any offers of assistance. The wood-pile was getting low, certainly, and the plough still lying slantwise in the furrow; the corn-crop was to be gathered, and the potatoes to be got out of the ground,—but there was time enough yet! He didn't mean to indulge his laziness much longer,—not he!

And then the neighbor who had offered to serve him would laugh, and answer that he had not been altogether disinterested; he had only proposed to *lend* a helping hand, expecting to need the like himself one day. "Trouble comes to us all, Mr. Walker, and we don't know whose turn it will be next. I want to take out a little insurance,—that's all!"

"Well, another day, if I don't get better!"

And the long hot rains were over at last; the clouds drew themselves off, and the sharp frosts, of a morning, were glistening far and near; the pumpkin-vines lay black along the ground, and the ungathered ears of corn hung black on the stalk.

Hobert was no better. But still the two women told each other they didn't think he was any worse. His disease was only an ague, common to the time of year and to the new country. It had come on so late it was not likely now that he would get the better of it before spring; making some little sacrifices for the present, they must all be patient and wait; and the nursing went on, till every device of nursing was exhausted, and one remedy after another was tried, and one after another utterly failed, and the fond hearts almost gave out. But there was the winter coming on, cold and long, and there was little Hobert, only beginning to stand alone, and prattling Jenny, with the toes coming through her shoes, and her shoulder showing flat and thin above her summer dress. Ah! there could be no giving out; the mother's petticoat must be turned into aprons for the pinched shoulders, and the knit-wool stockings must make amends for the worn-out shoes. So they worked, and work was their greatest blessing. A good many things were done without consulting Hobert at all, and he was led to believe that all went easily and comfortably; the neighbors, from time to time, lent the helping hand, without so much as asking leave; and by these means there were a few potatoes in the cellar, a little corn in the barn, and a load of wood under the snow at the door.

The table was not spread in the sick-room any more, as it had been for a while. They had thought it would amuse Hobert to see the little household ceremonies going on; but now they said it was better to avoid all unnecessary stir. Perhaps they thought it better that he should not see their scantier fare. Still they came into his presence very cheerfully, never hinting of hardship, never breathing the apprehension that began to trouble their hearts.

It was during these long winter evenings, when the neighbors sat by the fire and did what they could to cheer the sick man and the sad women, that the wonderful merits of the great Doctor Killmany began to be frequently discussed. Marvellous stories were told of his almost superhuman skill. He had brought back from the very gate of death scores of men and women who had been given up to die by their physicians,—so it was said; and special instances of cures were related that were certainly calculated to inspire hope and confidence. None of these good people could of their own knowledge attest these wonderful cures; but there were many circumstances that added weight to the force of the general rumor.

Dr. Killmany lived a great way off, and he charged a great price. He would not look at a man for less than a hundred dollars, so report said, and that was much in his favor. He had a very short way with patients,—asked no questions, and never listened to any explanations,—but could tie down a man and take off his leg or arm, as the case might be, in an incredibly short space of time, paying as little heed to the cries and groans as to the buzzing of the flies. If anything further had been needed to establish his fame, it would have been found in the fact that he was very rich, wearing diamonds in his shirt-bosom, driving fine horses, and being, in fact, surrounded with all the luxuries that money can procure. Of course, he was a great doctor. How could it be otherwise? And it was enough to know that a Mr. A had seen a Mr. B who knew a Mr. C whose wife's mother was cured by him!

At first these things were talked of in hearing of the sick man; then there began to be whispers about the fire as to the possibility of persuading him to sell all that he had and go to the great Doctor; for it was now pretty generally felt that the ague was only the accompaniment of a more terrible disease.

Then at last it was suggested, as a wild pleasantry, by some daring visitor, "Suppose, Hobert, we should send you off one of these days, and have you back after a few weeks, sound and vigorous as a young colt! What should you say to that, my boy?"

To the surprise of everybody, Hobert replied that he only wished it were possible.

"Possible! Why, of course it's possible! Where there's a will, you know!" And then it began to be talked of less as an insane dream.

One morning, as Jenny came into the sick man's room, she found him sitting up in bed with his shirt open and his hand on his breast.

"What is it, Hobert?" she said; for there was a look in his eyes that made her tremble.

"I don't know, Jenny; but whatever it is, it will be my death," he answered, and, falling upon her shoulder,—for she had come close to him and had her arm about his neck,—he sobbed like a child.

The little hand was slipped under his, but Jenny said she could feel nothing; and I think she will be forgiven for that falsehood. He was sick, she said, worn out, and it was no wonder that strange fancies should take possession of him. She had neglected him too much; but now, though everything should go to pieces, he should have her first care, and her last care, and all her care; he should not be left alone any more to conjure up horrors; and when he said he was weak and foolish and ashamed of his tears, she pacified him with petting and with praises. He was everything that was right, everything that was strong and manly. A little more patience, and then it would be spring, and the sunshine would make him well. She put the hair away from his forehead, and told him how fair in the face he was grown; and then she shoved his sleeve to his elbow, and told him that his arms were almost as plump as they ever were; and so he was comforted, cheered even, and they talked over the plans and prospects of years to come. At last he fell asleep with a bright smile of hope in his face, and Jenny stooped softly and kissed him, and, stealing away on tiptoe, hid herself from her good old mother and from the eyes of her children, and wept long and bitterly.

And the spring came, and Hobert crept out into the sunshine; but his cheek was pale, and his chest hollow, and there was more than the old listlessness upon him. As a tree that is dying will sometimes put forth sickly leaves and blossoms, and still be dying all the while, so it was with him. His hand was often on his breast, and his look often said, "This will be the death of me." The bees hummed in the flowers about his feet, the birds built their nests in the boughs above his head, and his children played about his knees; but his thoughts were otherwhere,—away beyond the dark river, away in that beautiful country where the inhabitants never say, "I am sick."

It was about midsummer that one Mrs. Brown, well known to Mrs. Walker's family, and to all the people of the neighborhood, as having suffered for many years with some strange malady which none of the doctors understood, sold the remnant of her property, having previously wasted nearly all she had upon physicians, and betook herself to the great Dr. Killmany. What her condition had actually been is not material to my story, nor is it necessary to say anything about the treatment she received at the hands of the great doctor. It is enough to say that it cost her her last dollar,—that she worked her slow way home as best she could, arriving there at last with shoes nearly off her feet and gown torn and faded, but with health considerably improved. That she had sold her last cow, and her feather-bed, and her tea-kettle, and her sheep-shears, and her grandfather's musket, all added wonderfully to the great doctor's reputation.

"You can't go to him if you don't go full-handed," said one to another; and he that heard it, and he that said it, laughed as though it were a good joke.

Some said he could see right through a man: there was no need of words with him! And others, that he could take the brains out of the skull, or the bones out of the ankles, and leave the patient all the better for it. In short, there was nothing too extravagant to be said of him; and as for Mrs. Brown, the person who had seen her became semi-distinguished. She was invited all over the neighborhood, and her conversation was the most delightful of entertainments. Amongst the rest, she visited Mr. Walker; and through her instrumentality, his strong desire to see the great Dr. Killmany was shaped into purpose.

Two of the cows were sold, most of the farming implements, and such articles of household furniture as could be spared; and with all this the money realized was but a hundred and fifty dollars. Then Jenny proposed to sell her side-saddle; and when that was gone, she said Fleety might as well go with it. "If you only come home well, Hobert," she said, "we will soon be able to buy her back again; and if you don't—but you will!"

So Fleetfoot went with the rest; and when for the last time she was led up before the door, and ate grass from the lap of little Jenny, and put her neck down to the caressing hands of young Hobert, it was a sore trial to them all. She seemed half conscious herself, indeed, and exhibited none of her accustomed playfulness with the children, but stood in a drooping attitude, with her eye intent upon her master; and when they would have taken her away, she hung back, and, stretching her neck till it reached his knees, licked his hands with a tenderness that was pitiful to see.

"Don't, Hobert, don't take on about it," Jenny said, putting back the heart that was in her mouth; "we will have her back again, you know!"—and she gave Fleetfoot a little box on the ear that was half approval and half reproach, and so led Hobert back into the house.

And that day was the saddest they had yet seen. And that night, when the sick man was asleep, the two women talked together and cried together, and in the end got such comfort as women get out of great sacrifices and bitter tears.

They counted their little hoard. They had gathered three hundred dollars now, and there required to be yet as much more; and then they made plans as to what yet remained to be done. "We must mortgage the land," Jenny said, "that is all,—don't mind, mother. I don't mind anything, so that we only have Hobert well again." And then they talked of what they would do another year when they should be all together once more, and all well. "Think what Dr. Killmany has done for Mrs. Brown!" they said.

And now came busy days; and in the earnestness of the preparation the sorrow of the coming parting was in some sort dissipated. Hobert's wearing-apparel was all brought out, and turned and overturned, and the most and the best made of everything. The wedding coat and the wedding shirt were almost as good as ever, Jenny said; and when the one had been brushed and pressed, and the other done up, she held them up before them all, and commented upon them with pride and admiration. The fashions had changed a little, to be sure, but what of that? The new fashions were not so nice as the old ones, to her thinking. Hobert would look smart in the old garments, at any rate, and perhaps nobody would notice. She was only desirous that he should make a good impression on the Doctor. And all that could be done to that end was done, many friends contributing, by way of little presents, to the comfort and respectability of the invalid. "Here is a leather pouch," said one, "that I bought of a pedler the other day. I don't want it; but as you are going to travel, may be you can make use of it, Walker; take it, any how."

"I have got a new pair of saddle-bags," said the circuit-rider, "but I believe I like the old ones best. So, Brother Walker, you will oblige me by taking these off my hands. I find extra things more trouble to take care of than they are worth."

It was not proposed that Hobert should travel with a trunk, so the saddle-bags were just what was required.

"Here is a pair of shoes," said another. "Try them on, Walker, and see if you can wear them: they are too small for my clumsy feet!" They had been made by the village shoemaker to Mr. Walker's measure. Of course they fitted him, and of course he had them.

"I'll bet you a new hat," said another, "that I come to see you ag'in, say after to-morrer, fur off as I live."

The day after the morrow he did not come: he was "unaccountably hendered," he said; but when he did come he brought the new hat. He thought he would be as good as his word in one thing if not in another, and redeem his bet at any rate.

"I'll bring my team: I want to go to town anyhow; and we'll all see you off together!" This was the offer of the farmer whose land adjoined Mr. Walker's; and the day of departure was fixed, and the morning of the day saw everything in readiness.

"Hobert looks a'most like a storekeeper or a schoolmaster, don't he, mother?" Jenny said, looking upon him proudly, when he was arrayed in the new hat and the wedding coat.

"Why, you are as spry as a boy!" exclaimed the farmer who was to drive them to town, seeing that Hobert managed to climb into the wagon without assistance. "I don't believe there is any need of Dr. Killmany, after all!" And the neighbors, as one after another they leaned over the side-board of the wagon, and shook hands with Mr. Walker, made some cheerful and light-hearted remark, calculated to convey the impression that the leave-taking was a mere matter of form, and only for a day.

As Jenny looked back at the homestead, and thought of the possibilities, the tears would come; but the owner of the team, determined to carry it bravely through, immediately gathered up the slack reins, and, with a lively crack of his whip, started the horses upon a brisk trot.

"Don't spare the money," Jenny entreated, as she put the pocket-book in Hobert's hand; but she thought in her heart that Dr. Killmany would be touched when he saw her husband, and knew how far he had travelled to see him, and what sacrifices he had made to do so. "He must be good, if he is so great as they say," she argued; "and perhaps Hobert may even bring home enough to buy back Fleety." This was a wild dream. And the last parting words were said, the last promises exacted and given; the silent tears and the lingering looks all were past, and the farmer's wagon, with an empty chair by the side of Jenny's, rattled home again.

It was perhaps a month after this that a pale, sickly-looking man, with a pair of saddle-bags over his arm, went ashore from the steamboat Arrow of Light, just landed at New Orleans, and made his slow way along the wharf, crowded with barrels, boxes, and cotton-bales, and thence to the open streets. The sun was oppressively hot, and the new fur hat became almost intolerable, so that the sick man stopped more than once in the shade of some friendly tree, and, placing the saddle-bags on the ground, wiped the sweat from his forehead, and looked wistfully at the strange faces that passed him by.

"Can you tell me, my friend," he said at last, addressing a slave-woman who was passing by with a great bundle on her head,—"Can you tell me where to find Doctor Killmany, who lives somewhere here?"

The woman put her bundle on the ground, and, resting her hands on her hips, looked pitifully upon the stranger. "No, masser, cante say, not for sure," she answered. "I knows dar's sich a doctor somewhars 'bout, but just whars I cante say, an' he's a poor doctor fur the likes o' you,—don't have noffen to do with him, nohow."

"A poor doctor!" exclaimed the stranger. "Why, I understood he was the greatest doctor in the world; and I've come all the way from the Wabash country to see him."

"Warbash! whar's dat? Norf, reckon; well you jes be gwine back Norf de fus boat, an dat's de bery bes' advice dis yere nigger can guv."

"But what do you know about Dr. Killmany."

"I knows dis yere, masser: he mos'ly sends dem ar' as ar' doctored by him to dar homes in a box!"

Mr. Walker shuddered. "I don't want your advice," he said directly; "I only want to know where Dr. Killmany lives."

"Cante say, masser, not percisely, as to dat ar'; kind o' seems to me he's done gone from hur, clar an' all; but jes over thar's a mighty good doctor; you can see his name afore the door if you'll step this yere way a bit. He doctors all de pour, an' dem dat ar' halt, and dem dat ar' struck with paralasy, jes for de love ob de ark and de covenant; an' he's jes de purtiest man to look at dat you ever sot eyes onto. Go in dar whar ye sees de white bline at de winder an' ax for Dr. Shepard, an' when you's once seen him, I reckon you won't want to find de udder man; but if you does, why he can pint de way. An' de Lord bless you and hab mercy on your soul."

The sick man felt a good deal discouraged by what the old slave had said, and her last words impressed him with feelings of especial discomfort. He knew not which way to turn; and, in fact, found himself growing dizzy and blind, and was only able, with great effort, to stand at all. He must ask his way somewhere, however, and it might as well be there as another place.

Dr. Shepard, who happened to be in his office, answered the inquiry promptly. Dr. Killmany was in quite another part of the city. "You don't look able to walk there, my good friend," he said; "but if you will sit here and wait for an hour, I shall be driving that way, and will take you with pleasure."

Mr. Walker gratefully accepted the proferred chair, as indeed he was almost obliged to do; for within a few minutes the partial blindness had become total darkness, and the whole world seemed, as it were, slipping away from him.

When he came to himself he was lying on a sofa in an inner room, and Dr. Shepard, who had just administered some cordial, was bending over him in the most kindly and sympathetic manner. It seemed not so much what he said, not so much what he did, but as though he carried about him an atmosphere of sweetness and healing that comforted and assured without words and without medicine. He made no pretence and no noise, but his smile was sunshine to the heart, and the touch of his hand imparted strength and courage to the despairing soul. It was as if good spirits went with him, anad his very silence was pleasant company. Mr. Walker was in no haste to be gone. All his anxious cares seemed to fall away, and a peaceful sense of comfort and security came over him; his eyes followed Dr. Shepard as he moved about, and when a door interposed between them he felt lost and homesick. "If this were the man I had come to see, I should be happy." That was his thought all the while. Perhaps—who shall say not?—it was the blessings of the poor, to whom he most generously ministered, which gave to his manner that graciousness and charm which no words can convey, and to his touch that magnetism which is at once life-giving and love-inspiring.

How it was Mr. Walker could not tell, and indeed wiser men than he could not have told, but he presently found himself opening his heart to this new doctor, as he had never opened it to anybody in all his life,—how he had married Jenny, how they had gone to the new country, the birth of the boy and the girl, the slow coming on of disease, the selling of Fleety, and the mortgaging of the farm. Doctor Shepard knew it all, and, more than this, he knew how much money had been accumulated, and how much of it was still left. He had examined the tumor in the breast, and knew that it could end in but one way. He had told Mr. Walker that he could be made more comfortable, and might live for years, perhaps, but that he must not hope to be cured, and that to get home to his family with all possible speed was the best advice he could give him. His words carried with them the weight of conviction, and the sick man was almost persuaded; but the thought of what would be said at home if he should come back without having seen the great Dr. Killmany urged him to try one last experiment.

"What do you suppose he will charge me to look at this?" he inquired of Dr. Shepard, laying his hand on his breast.

"Half you have, my friend."

"And if he cuts it out?"

"The other half."

"O, dear me!"—and the sick man fell back upon the sofa, and for a good while thought to himself. Then came one of those wild suggestions of a vain hope. "Perhaps this man is the imposter, and not the other!" it said. "And what do I owe you for all you have done for me to-day?" he inquired.

"Why, nothing, my good friend. I have done nothing for you; and my advice has certainly been disinterested. I don't want pay for that."

"And suppose you should operate?"

And then the doctor told him that he could not do that on any terms,—that no surgeon under the sun could perform a successful operation,—that all his hope was in quiet and care. "I will keep you here a few days," he said, "and build you up all I can, and when the Arrow of Light goes back again, I will see you aboard, and bespeak the kind attentions of the captain for you on the journey." That was not much like an impostor, and in his heart the sick man knew it was the right course to take,—the only course; and then he thought of Mrs. Brown and her wonderful cure, and of the great hopes they were entertaining at home, and he became silent, and again thought to himself.

Three days he remained with Dr. Shepard, undecided, and resting and improving a little all the while. On the morning of the fourth day he said, placing his hand on his breast, "If I were only rid of this, I believe I should get quite well again." He could not give up the great Dr. Killmany. "I do not intend to put myself in his hands,—indeed, I am almost resolved that I will not do so," he said to Dr. Shepard; "but I will just call at his office, so that I can tell my folks I have seen him."

"I must not say more to discourage you," replied Dr. Shepard; "perhaps I have already said too much,—certainly I have said much more than it is my habit to say, more than in any ordinary circumstances I would permit myself to say; but in your case I have felt constrained to acquit myself to my conscience";—and he turned away with a shadow of the tenderest and saddest gloom upon his face.

"Are you, sir, going to Dr. Killmany?" asked an old man, who had been sitting by, eying Mr. Walker with deep concern; and on receiving an affirmative nod, he went on with zeal, if not with discretion: "Then, sir, you might as well knock your own brains out! I regard him, sir, as worse than a highway robber,—a good deal worse! The robber will sometimes spare your life, if he can as well as not, but Dr. Killmany has no more regard for human life than you have for that of a fly. He has a skilful hand to be sure, but his heart is as hard as flint. In short, sir, he is utterly without conscience, without humanity, without principle. Gain is his first object, his last object, his sole object; and if he ever did any good, it was simply incidental. Don't put yourself in his hands, whatever you do,—certainly not without first making your will!" And the old man, with a flushed and angry countenance, went away.

Presently the sick man, relapsing into silent thought, drowsed into sleep, and a strange dream came to him. He seemed at home, sitting under the tree with the mistletoe in its boughs; he was tired and hungry, and there came to him a raven with food in its mouth, and the shadow of its wings was pleasant. He thought, at first, the food was for him; but the bird, perching on his shoulder, devoured the food, and afterward pecked at his breast until it opened a way to his heart, and with that in its claws flew away; and when it was gone, he knew it was not a bird, but that it was Dr. Killmany who had thus taken out his heart. "I will go home," he thought, "and tell Jenny"; and when he arose and put his hand on the neck of Fleety, who had been standing in the furrow close by, she became a shadow, and instantly vanished out of sight. He then strove to walk, and, lo! the strength was gone out of his limbs, and, as he sank down, the roots of the mistletoe struck in his bosom, ran through and through him, and fastened themselves in the earth beneath, and he became as one dead, only with the consciousness of being dead.

When he awoke, he related the dream, having given it, as it appeared, a melancholy interpretation, for he expressed himself determined to return home immediately. "I will take passage on the Arrow," he said to Dr. Shepard; and then he counted up the number of days that must go by before he could have his own green fields beneath his eyes, and his little ones climbing about his knees.

"I wish I had never left my home," he said; "I wish I had never heard of Dr. Killmany!" and then he returned to his dream and repeated portions of it; and then he said, seeming to be thinking aloud, "My good old mother! my dear, poor Jenny!"

"The sick man's brain is liable to strange fancies," says Dr. Shepard; "you must not think too seriously of it, but your resolve is very wise." He then said he would see the captain of the Arrow, as he had promised, and went away with a smile on his face, and a great weight lifted off his heart.

A few minutes after this, Hobert Walker was again in the street, the heavy fur hat on his head, and the well-filled saddle-bags across his arm.

Perhaps sickness is in some sort insanity. At any rate, he no sooner found himself alone than the desire to see the great Dr. Killmany came upon him with all the force of insanity; his intention probably being to go and return within an hour, and keep his little secret to himself. Perhaps, too, he wished to have it to say at home that he had seen the great man for himself, and decided against him of his own knowledge.

Dr. Killmany was found without much difficulty; but his rooms were crowded with patients, and there was no possibility of access to him for hours.

"It cannot be that so many are deceived," thought Hobert. "I will wait with the rest." Then came the encouraging hope, "What if I should go home cured, after all!" He felt almost as if Dr. Shepard had defrauded him out of two or three days, and talked eagerly with one and another, as patient after patient came forth from consultation with Dr. Killmany, all aglow with hope and animation. It was near sunset when his turn came. He had waited five hours, but it was come at last; and with his heart in his mouth, and his knees shaking under him, he stood face to face with the arbitrator of his destiny. There was no smile on the face of the man, no sweetness in his voice as he said, looking at Hobert from under scowling brows, "What brings *you* sir? Tell it, and be brief: time with me is money."

Then Hobert, catching at a chair to sustain himself, for he was not asked to sit, explained his condition as well as fright and awkwardness would permit him to do; going back to the commencement of his disease, and entering unnecessarily into many particulars, as well as making superfluous mention of wife and mother. "It isn't with your wife and mother that I have to deal," interposed Dr. Killmany;—"dear to you, I dare say, but nothing to me, sir,—nothing at all. I have no time to devote to your relatives. Open your shirt, sir! there, that'll do! A mere trifle, sir, but it is well you have come in time."

"Do you mean to say you can cure me?" inquired Hobert, all his heart a-flutter with the excitement of hope.

"Exactly so. I can remove that difficulty of yours in five minutes, and have you on your feet again,—operation neglected, death certain within a year, perhaps sooner. Done with you sir. You now have your choice, make way!"

Hobert went staggering out of the room, feeling as if the raven of his dream already had its beak in his heart, when a pert official reached out his hand with the demand, "Consultation fee, if you please, sir."

"How much?" asked Hobert, leaning against the wall, and searching for his pocket-book.

"Fifty dollars, sir,"—and the official spoke as though that were a trifle scarcely worth mentioning. The hands of the sick man trembled, and his eyes grew blind as he sought to count up the sum; and as his entire treasure was formed out of the smallest notes, the process was a slow one, and before it was accomplished it seemed to him that not only Fleety was turning to a shadow, but the whole world as well.

Somehow, he hardly knew how, he found himself in the fresh air, and the official still at his elbow. "You are not going to leave us this way?" he said. "You will only have thrown your money away." And he pocketed the sum Hobert had just put in his hand.

"Better that than more," Hobert answered, and was turning sadly away.

"Allow me to detain you, sir, one moment, only just one moment!" And the official, or rather decoy, whispered in his ear tales of such wonderful cures as almost dissuaded him from his purpose.

"But I am resolved to go home on the Arrow," he said, making a last stand, "and I must have something to leave my poor Jenny."

And then the offiicial told him that he could go home aboard the Arrow, if he chose, and go a well man, or the same as a well man; and what could he bring to his wife so acceptable as himself, safe and sound! And then he told other tales of sick men who had been carried to Dr. Killmany on their beds, and within a few hours walked away on their feet, blessing his name, and publishing his fame far and wide.

Hobert began to waver, nor is it strange; for what will not a man give for his life? The world had not loosened its hold upon him much as yet; the grass under his feet and the sunshine over his head were pleasant things to him, and his love for his good little wife was still invested with all the old romance; and to die and go he knew not where, there was a terror about that which his faith was not strong enough to dissipate. The decoy watched and waited. He contrasted the husband returning home with haggard cheek and listless step and the shadow of dark doom all about him, having a few hundred dollars in his pocket, with a husband empty-handed, but with bright cheeks, and cheerful spirits, and with strong legs under him! Then Hobert repeated the story he had told to Dr. Shepard,—all about the little treasure with which he had set out, how hardly it had been gathered together, what had been already fruitlessly expended, and just how much remained,—he told it all as he had told it in the first instance, but with what different effect!

Dr. Killmany never touched any case for a sum like that! Indeed, his services were in such requisition, it was almost impossible to obtain them on any terms; but he, the decoy, for reasons which he did not state, would exert to the utmost his own personal influence in Hobert's favor. "I cannot promise you a favorable answer," he said; "there is just a possibility, and that is all. A man like Dr. Killmany, sir, can't be haggling about dollars and cents!" And then he intimated that such things might be well enough for Dr. Shepard and his sort of practice.

There was some further talk, and the time ran by, and it was night. Against his will almost, Hobert had been persuaded. He was to sleep in the Doctor's office that night, and his case was to be the first attended to in the morning. "You can rest very well on the floor, I suppose," the decoy had said, "taking your saddle-bags for a pillow. The whole thing will be over in half an hour, and I myself will see you aboard the Arrow before ten o'clock, and so you need take no more thought for yourself."

That night, when at last Hobert made a pillow of his saddle-bags and coiled himself together, he felt as if a circle of fire were narrowing around him, and yet utter inability to escape.

"You need take no more thought for yourself." These words kept ringing in his ears like a knell, and the mistletoe striking through his bosom, and the beak of the raven in his heart,—these were the sensations with which, long after midnight, he drowsed into sleep.

When he awoke, there was a rough hand on his shoulder and a harsh voice in his ear. The room was light with the light of morning, but dark with the shadow of coming doom. There came upon him a strange and great calmness when he found himself in the operating-room. There were all the frightful preparations,—the water, the sponges, the cloths and bandages, the Doctor with his case of instruments before him, and looking more like a murderer than a surgeon. Almost his heart misgave him as he looked around, and remembered Jenny and the little ones at home; but the carriage that was to take him aboard the Arrow already waited at the door, and the sight of it reassured him.

"You will hardly know where you are till you find yourself safe in your berth," said Dr. Killmany; "and to avoid any delay after the operations, from which you will necessarily be somewhat weak, you had perhaps better pay me now." And these were the most civil words he had yet spoken.

So Hobert paid into his hand the last dollar he had.

"Now, sir," he said; and Hobert laid himself down on the table. A minute, and of what befell him after that he was quite unconscious. It was as the doctor had told him; he knew not where he was until he found himself in his berth aboard the Arrow. "Where am I?" was his first inquiry, feeling a sense of strangeness,—feeling, indeed, as though he were a stranger to himself.

"You are going home, my poor friend,—going home a little sooner than you expected,—that is all."

Then the sick man opened his eyes; for he had recognized the tender voice, and saw Dr. Shepard bending over him, and he knew where he was, and what had happened; for he was shivering from head to foot. The sleeve of his right arm was red and wet, and there was a dull, slow aching in his bosom. "Ay, Doctor," he answered, pressing faintly the hand that held his, "I am going home,—home to a better country. 'T is all like a shadow about me now, and I am cold,—so cold!" He never came out of that chill, and these were the last words he ever spoke.

"That man has been just the same as murdered, I take it!" exclaimed the captain of the Arrow, meeting Dr. Shepard as he turned away from the bedside.

"I must not say that," replied the Doctor; "but if I had performed the operation, under the circumstances, I should think myself his murderer."

"And if you had taken his money, you would perhaps think yourself a thief, too! At any rate, I should think you one," was the answer of the captain. And he then related to Dr. Shepard how the man, in an almost dying condition, had been brought aboard the Arrow by one of Dr. Killmany's menials, hustled into bed, and so left to his fate; and he concluded by saying, "And what are we to do now, Doctor?"

What the Doctor's reply was need not be reported at length. Suffice it to say, that the departure of the Arrow was deferred for an hour, and when she sailed the state-room in which Hobert had breathed his last was occupied by a lively little lady and two gayly-dressed children, and on the wall from which the fur hat and the saddle-bags had been removed fluttered a variety of rainbow-hued scarfs and ribbons, and in the window where the shadow had been a golden-winged bird was singing in the sunshine.

Some two or three weeks went by, and the farmer who had driven to town when Hobert was about to set out on his long journey, starting so smartly, and making so light of the farewells, drove thither again, and this time his wagon-bed was empty, except for the deep cushion of straw. He drove slowly and with downcast looks; and as he returned, a dozen men met him at the entrance of the village, and at sober pace followed to the meeting-house, the door of which stood wide.

A little low talk as they all gathered round, and then four of them lifted from the wagon the long box it contained, and bore it on their shoulders reverently and tenderly within the open gate, through the wide door, along the solemn aisle and close beneath the pulpit, where they placed it very softly, and then stood back with uncovered heads, while a troop of little girls, who waited, with aprons full of flowers, drew near and emptied them on the ground, so that nothing was to be seen but a great heap of flowers; and beneath them was the body of HOBERT WALKER.

Begins w/ the death of John Walker and the poverty of the Walker family

Jenny Bowen is well off and in love w/ Hobert Walker. She runs off w/ him. It is a romance story about class gulf bridged by love and a move west - new opportunities. Fleetfoot, the horse who took them west = Jenny, the wife.

Then, Hobert gets a tumor and is unable to work. All is sold so he can go visit the miracle doctor, Dr. Killmany, in New Orleans. Dr. Shepard, the good doctor, gives him correct advice, but Hobert gets the bad operation and dies. His casket is delivered home. (No mention of Jenny et al and their now ruined prospects.)

Oddly divided story: the sick Hobert part seems to point to fraud and the evils of money and the city. Yet, John Walker's illness was also misdiagnosed and treated - the accusation of doctor = murderer is in both parts.